TRAUMA
AND
THE
12 STEPS:

DAILY
MEDITATIONS
AND
REFLECTIONS

TRAUMA AND THE 12 STEPS:

DAILY MEDITATIONS AND REFLECTIONS

Jamie Marich, Ph.D., LPCC-S
& **Stephen Dansiger**, Psy.D., LMFT

CREATIVE MINDFULNESS MEDIA
PUBLISHING HOME OF THE INSTITUTE FOR CREATIVE MINDFULNESS

Creative Mindfulness Media, the publishing home of The Institute for Creative Mindfulness, is committed to publishing exceptional materials addressing topics in the areas of trauma recovery, addiction recovery, and the use of embodied expressive arts approaches to create healing and wellness.

For more information, visit *www.instituteforcreativemindfulness.com*

Publisher: Creative Mindfulness Media
P.O. Box 8732
Warren, OH 44484
Editor: Dan Mager
Production Director: Mary Riley
Additional Assistance: Erin Kelly

25 24 23 22 21 20   1 2 3 4 5
Library of Congress Cataloging-in-Publication Data

ISBN: 978-1-7337030-3-1

Quotes by Rumi used by permission (Coleman Barks)

Publisher's Note:
This book contains general information about trauma, addiction, recovery, and wellness. The information is not medical advice. This book is not an alternative to medical advice from your doctor or other professional healthcare provider. Our books represent the experiences and opinions of their authors only. Every effort has been made to ensure that events, institutions, and statistics presented in our books are accurate and up-to-date. To protect their privacy, the names of some of the people, places, and institutions in this book may have been changed.

Cover and interior design by Berge Design.

DEDICATION

Dedicated with gratitude to our recovery sponsors
and guides throughout our collective years
trudging the road of happy destiny...

CONTENTS

INTRODUCTION

Jamie's Reflections

Using a daily recovery reader is a practice, and this practice saved my life. When I made a commitment to finally get sober in the summer of 2002, my sponsor Janet suggested that I pray first thing every morning. I had no problem with God at that point and connecting with a Higher Power to ask for help in staying sober was not the issue.

"Janet," I protested, "I am not a morning person! I'm lucky if I can get up, roll out of bed, go to the bathroom, and get to work."

"Oh, you use the bathroom," she said, "Interesting. Why don't you put your Twenty-Four Hour book on the toilet seat? That way if you're going to use the toilet, you will need to pick it up. And while you're doing your business, read the page for the day. It will remind you to pray."

She was right.

I heard somewhere in my studies that if you can do something for 21-30 days in a row it becomes a habit. Do it for 45-60 days and it becomes a lifestyle.

Eighteen years later I am still sober and I cannot begin my day without praying and reading something spiritual or inspirational.

My heart is bursting with gratitude to birth this specific recovery meditation book into existence in concert with one of my dearest friends and professional collaborators. The classic *Twenty-Four Hours a Day* from Hazelden that is well-known to many people in 12-step fellowships, the book that Janet gave me, got the ball rolling. The practice of reading, meditating, and praying the suggestions in that book each day taught me the importance of daily practice. In the years that have passed, I've worked through other daily readers of all kinds—some very general, others more spiritual and inspirational, and other very recovery specific. For many years I've wanted to offer the teachings and ideas of my well-known book *Trauma and the Twelve Steps: A Complete Guide to Recovery Enhancement* (first published in 2012) in the format of a daily reader.

And here we are!

Daily readers or meditation books (use whatever terminology fits best for you) offer us the opportunity to build consistent practice.

Recovery and healing are only possible through the consistent discipline of daily practice.

I long ago learned that if I do nothing to work on myself for six days in a row and then spend only one day on retreat—going to a meeting, attending church, taking a yoga class, or meditating for hours—my internal health will suffer. What happens if a plant that needs a good amount of water to thrive only gets watered once a week? It will likely wilt and die, or at very least, require a lot of specialty care to be revived. The same is true with the practices we need to stay sober, well, or healthy—five minutes of consistent practice each day will serve you better than practicing an hour once a week or all day once a month.

Wellness and recovery practices can take a variety of shapes and forms. Daily practices can include silent meditation, moving meditations like dance or yoga, writing, journaling, making visual art, playing or listening to music, going to meetings, and conversing with others on a path of recovery or wellness.

Steve's Reflections

I have received many gifts in my life. Now over thirty years into my sober journey, I find myself looking at them individually and collectively. Individually, I see them lined up over time, one by one, affecting me in myriad ways. Collectively, I see who I am today, not just informed by all these gifts, but made whole . . . as if the gifts have become one. Of all the gifts I have been given, the meditation and prayer practice of my early 12-step work continues as a daily non-negotiable act, and the collective wisdom that I've gained from these practices probably defines me more than anything else.

So this opportunity to collaborate with my friend, colleague and collaborator on these meditations is a gift of value beyond words. My work with Jamie began because I found and read the original *Trauma and the Twelve Steps* in 2012 and knew that there was a kindred soul in the Midwest who had been thinking about the same things personally and professionally. She had already taken a whole host of actions toward bringing trauma healing into the 12-step experience. Now that we have taken several steps on this path together, we take this opportunity to provide a meditation book experience not available to us when we first entered recovery. The *Twenty-Four Hours a Day* book and the men's meditation book

Touchstones were indispensable to me at the beginning of my path. Our hope is that this book will offer trauma-informed spiritual healing and sustenance for the 21st century person in recovery.

Like Jamie, my first sponsor told me about prayer and meditation, but only after I asked him if there was some alternative program he was working.

"Whaddya talking about?" Randy said. "I pray every day."

My bubble burst, and he alerted me to the Third and Seventh Step prayers, along with the Twenty-Four Hour book. I have never stopped. My primary meditation practice may be silent seated mindfulness meditation, but daily morning readings still help to launch my day. Our hope is that this book can be a catalyst, a guide, a foundation for your days.

How to Use This Reader

Engaging in a daily reading may already be a part of your everyday practice, or this practice may be completely new to you. We have prepared a reading each day—for you. Please avoid the temptation to read ahead and devour the entire book in one sitting, or read it like you would a standard book. The teachings in the reader are designed to be absorbed in small portions on a day-by-day basis. Although we recommend reading the page for the day in the morning to help you set a positive intention for the day, you are free to choose when you do the page for each day.

Daily consistency is most important. You can read in the morning one day and before you go to sleep on another day if that's how your day transpires. If you should miss or skip a day, that doesn't mean you have failed the process. Be kind to yourself. Just pick up on the day when you remember to return to the book again. Don't stress about missing pages—you can always come back to them another year or on a day where you feel you may need some extra help.

Because this reader corresponds with the revised and expanded edition of *Trauma and the 12 Steps: An Inclusive Guide to Enhancing Recovery*, the reflections are made in a voice that is fundamentally pro-12 step. However, as in the main book, we recognize that a purist study of the 12-steps, especially as taught by many rigid followers, is not optimally trauma responsive. We endeavor to blend a spirit of respect for the wisdom of 12-step programs and our knowledge as trauma specialists to this daily approach to recovery and practice. As a result, we've chosen to organize the twelve months of the book to correspond with the core recovery principles often associated with each step. You can consult the following page for an overview before you begin your daily practice and study.

We bring our collective love for both the 12-step path and other contemplative practices to each page. We are both meditation teachers in varied traditions and we are both expressive artists, blending a variety of practices into our daily wellness routines. It's our deep intention to share the fruits of what we have gained individually and collectively over the years with you!

How you approach each page is also completely up to you, although if you have a sponsor or therapist of any kind, you may consider consulting with them about how using this book may best serve you. Of course, you have a right to just read the page. This is a great start. At very least we suggest that you read the page, which generally starts with a quote from one of our teachers or influences, or a snippet from one of our own previously published teachings.

Spend at least a minute or two in silent reflection, or following some of the suggestions for practice. Some days these invitations are more specific than others. If you have more time available, especially if you are attempting to deepen your meditation practice, spend more time in reflection after the reading. You may elect to sit silently for a length of time that feels appropriate to your practice today, connecting with a suggested prayer or intention that we offer for each page. The word you use is largely up to you, depending on where you are spirituality today. You can set an intention without believing in a Higher Power of any kind. Think of intention as the seed you are planting for the day.

If you are engaged in other expressive arts practices as part of your recovery, using one or several of these practices to respond to the reading is also an option. You may decide to do the reading in the morning to start your day and then deepen your connection to the reading with one of these other practices later in the day. The fusions and possibilities are endless. Healthy recovery requires a combination of consistency and structure along with creativity and adaptability. Consider embracing an approach to this daily reader in the same spirit. Let the daily readings offer you a structure, and then decide how it may be of value to expand your connection to the reading through other practices on a day-by-day basis.

THE ORIGINAL TWELVE STEPS OF ALCOHOLICS ANONYMOUS

1. *We admitted we were powerless over alcohol*—that our lives had become unmanageable.*

2. *Came to believe that a Power greater than ourselves could restore us to sanity.*

3. *Made a decision to turn our will and our lives over to the care of God as we understood Him.***

4. *Made a searching and fearless moral inventory of ourselves.*

5. *Admitted to God, to ourselves, and to another human being the exact nature of our wrongs.*

6. *Were entirely ready to have God remove all these defects of character.*

7. *Humbly asked Him to remove our shortcomings.*

8. *Made a list of all persons we had harmed, and became willing to make amends to them all.*

9. *Made direct amends to such people wherever possible, except when to do so would injure them or others.*

10. *Continued to take personal inventory and when we were wrong promptly admitted it.*

11. *Sought through prayer and meditation to improve our conscious contact with God as we understood Him, praying only for knowledge of His will for us and the power to carry that out.*

12. *Having had a spiritual awakening as the result of these steps, we tried to carry this message to alcoholics and to practice these principles in all our affairs.*

*Feel free to replace this word with whatever feels appropriate to your recovery journey. We are flexible and invite you to be as well!

**Make any adjustments you need to make for gender. We embrace an inclusive approach to how you use pronouns and identifiers around Higher Power. "She," "them," or any other proper name is welcome.

The Twelve Steps are reprinted with permission of Alcoholics Anonymous World Services, Inc. ("AAWS") Permission to reprint the Twelve Steps does not mean that AAWS has reviewed or approved the contents of this publication, or that AAWS necessarily agrees with the views expressed herein. AA is a program of recovery from alcoholism only—use of the Twelve Steps in connection with programs and activities which are patterned after A.A., but which address other problems, or in any other non-A.A. context, does not imply otherwise.

To visit a collection of online videos prepared by Jamie and her team that can support you in this work and its invitations, please visit:

www.traumamdesimple.com

JANUARY 1

"Give me a word . . . "

In the 5th century when the earliest Christian monks, often referred to as desert mothers and desert fathers, traveled about, it was a common practice for them to approach a wise elder with the request: *give me a word*. This practice existed when the oral tradition was still the primary way to pass along knowledge. The elder would give the seeker the word and the seeker would meditate on the word for a period of time. In modern times, the *one word practice* has become very popular as a way to set intention and direction for the new year. Particularly if we have difficult formulating an exact intention, focusing on one word can help us keep it simple.

Some people choose their one word as a representation of what they'd like to bring more of into their life during any given year. Many classic words and constructs from recovery can apply here— acceptance, gratitude, serenity, etc. However, you can be as creative as possible in selecting your word. Or maybe you can let the word select you? Perhaps a word seems to be popping up a lot for you lately, maybe at meetings or in your daily life. Or you can draw on the wisdom of the ancients and how they practiced. If you are not sure of a solid *one word* for you to use as intention for the year, consider asking your sponsor, helping professional, or other teacher for a word that they may want to gift to you!

Invitation: Spend 3-5 minutes in a practice of your choice—sitting meditation, walking meditation, or any expressive practice can all work for this purpose. You may even decide to engage in a combination of the practices. If you already have a *one word* intention for the new year, spend some time reflecting on it with these practices and notice what happens in your body. If a word has not yet revealed itself to you, notice what the time in suggested reflection may bring you.

Prayer or Intention: May the one word that I receive or choose empower me and guide the way, today and on the path ahead.

JANUARY 2

Sankalpa: the Sanskrit word for "intention"
Literally translated: *San* = one with;
Kalpa = time + the subconscious mind

Intention is about planting seeds, not forcing outcomes. Setting an intention can be a much kinder and ultimately more powerful practice than setting resolutions, as many cultures can pressure us into at the beginning of a year. When we set a resolution and fall short, we are much more likely to beat ourselves up about not fulfilling that commitment. Resolutions also have a "black or white" quality—they don't take into account that life can happen, causing us to grow in a different direction.

Planting a seed still requires serious commitment. Knowing what you want to grow is important. For instance, you wouldn't plant seeds for cucumbers if you wanted to grow squash. Seeds need water, air, soil, and sunlight in order to grow. Nothing will happen if you leave the seeds in the packet. You may choose to open the packet, although these other elements are required to bring about growth. The same applies to the intentions we set for our wellness and recovery. You can't force them to grow as all growth takes time. You can, however, tend to them and notice what will happen. You may be surprised by the results. And even if you take a wrong turn in caring for the growing plants, you may learn important lessons about the type of care that may be required when trying again.

Invitation: Spend 3-5 minutes sitting with the word *intention*. This may be challenging if you've only approached the start of a new year with resolutions or goals previously. How might the word *intention* feel different to you as you contemplate it. After noticing the word for a while, what feels like an organic intention may emerge that you would like to set for the year ahead. Knowing that, simply start with today.

Prayer or Intention: Help me to plant the seed of my intention today. Show me how I will need to tend this seed in order for it to grow.

JANUARY 3

"Always we begin again." ~St. Benedict of Nursia

Many faith traditions as well as approaches to meditation work with this idea of beginning again. One way to describe mindfulness is as the process of beginning again—of returning to focus, even when our attention seems to wander and drift. In recovery, beginning again can mean coming back home to yourself and to the things you know will work to get you well. The practice of beginning again is especially important if we have relapsed or have otherwise experienced a rough patch in our recovery journey. If you find that you're judging yourself too harshly for veering off course, please know that you are in good company. Anybody on a path of growth and wellness has needed to practice beginning again and will likely need to continue cultivating this skill on the road ahead.

The new year is a particularly good time to look at this concept of beginning again. Although we can sometimes put too much pressure on concepts like New Year's resolutions, consider how approaching the new year as a chance to begin again—however that might look for you—that offers you a unique opportunity.

Invitation: Take 3-5 minutes to engage in a seated mindfulness practice, setting a timer if possible. Sit in a position of attention and awareness although try not to obsess on the particulars of your posture. You can close your eyes or leave them open; whatever feels safer while also allowing you to fully focus. Make a deliberate intention to stay focused on your breath. If you notice that your attention wanders away from the breath, simply say (to yourself or aloud) the anchor phrase, "Always we begin again." Use this phrase as an invitation back to your breath.

Prayer or Intention: Help me to know that no matter how far off a path I have stumbled, I can always begin again.

JANUARY 4

"Eat some scrambled eggs and call me back."
~Jim, one of Steve's first sponsors

The connections we make at the beginning of our recovery are so important. From these new relationships in the program I can learn about how to stay sober for today, and I can also learn the basics of self-care. Sometimes I need to be listened to, to try and process my thoughts with another alcoholic. But sometimes we need to take care of the simple things first, to take care of the needs of our bodies. Ignoring those needs or simply not being able to see them often represents a big part of the concept of "unmanageability."

In recovery we learn how to take care of our basic needs so that we can then reach out to others. Jim was not being mean during those phone calls, not at all. Nor was he abandoning me. He was nurturing me, encouraging me to feed my body, and then he would be there when I was ready to connect and work toward psychological health.

Invitation: Spend 3-5 minutes in a practice of your choice (e.g., sitting meditation, walking meditation, or an expressive practice). If you can, notice what you need for your body in this moment. If you need food or drink see if you might take them in mindfully, a little more slowly than usual.

Prayer or Intention: Today let me notice my self-care, and let me notice the support I have from others toward my self-care.

JANUARY 5

"People often say that motivation doesn't last. Well neither does
bathing—that's why we recommend it daily."
~Zig Ziglar

Motivation is really just a fancy word for *push* or *drive*. It's the force that
allows you to work on the intentions and maybe even the goals that
you set for yourself. Sometimes what motivates us is a combination of
internal (e.g., my desire to be a better person) and external (e.g., my
family, keeping my job) forces. As it relates to recovery, any form of
motivation that keeps you moving and helps you to practice recovery
with daily consistency is useful. Even if that means, to intone Zig
Ziglar's wisdom, taking a bath or a shower as a deliberate spiritual or
recovery practice each day!

For many of us, practicing literal movement is the most direct
way that we can stay motivated. This can come in the form of taking
a walk, practicing yoga, dancing, or engaging in any other type of
exercise. This reminds us that motivation is, after all, about what keeps
us moving forward. Not too long ago I saw a hilarious joke on the
Internet where the therapist asks, "What motivates you to get out of
bed in the morning?" The patient responds, "My bladder mostly." See,
the body does not lie. Learn that vital lesson and make your body an
ally in your recovery.

Invitation: Spend 3-5 minutes in a practice of your choice (e.g.,
sitting meditation, walking meditation, or an expressive practice) and
contemplate the idea of motivation. What motivates you in recovery
today? You may even consider making a column with two sides, doing
an inventory on both your internal and external sources of motivation.
What can this mini-inventory teach you about motivation today?

Prayer or Intention: Today I recognize that motivation for recovery
and healing comes in a variety of forms. To keep accessing it, I need
to practice daily.

JANUARY 6

"The fact is that most alcoholics, for reasons yet obscure, have lost the power of choice in drink. Our so-called will power becomes practically nonexistent." ~*Alcoholics Anonymous*, p. 24

Why are we powerless? Why has life become unmanageable? Is it because of some terrible flaw we have? No, implicit in Step 1 is that trauma responses, including anything that has brought us into 12-step recovery, have been enacted and ingrained through maladaptive storage of memories. Indeed, we can become powerless over our limbic brain and our reptile brain. Yet, these parts of us are there to help us survive.

It is in admitting that we cannot think our way out of these responses that we begin to heal. We can heal these parts of us so that our thinking brain can start to have a say, start to make decisions on our behalf. The steps that follow Step 1 all help us in this journey. The First Step allows for the beginning of self-forgiveness and a place to start.

Invitation: For your practice, choose whatever type of practice feels most settling to you and your body today. Notice where you experience a sense of lack of power, but also sense where you might already have power. Spend 5 minutes noticing the potential for powerlessness to become infused with healthy power.

Prayer or Intention: Today allow me to be in the First Step. Let me know that powerlessness and unmanageability are not all my fault, and that I can heal into power.

JANUARY 7

"We're all addicts in a sense. We're all attached, if not addicted, to
our possessions, careers, relationships, identities—to name a few."
~Darren Littlejohn, *The 12-Step Buddhist*

I continue to identify as an alcoholic and an addict because *it keeps me
in touch with reality.* The reality is that alcohol and drugs won every time.
I believe that if I chose to put them back into my body, the chance of
them engulfing me again is quite high. Sure, I now have an enhanced
understanding about the traumatic and biochemical origins of my
addiction. Yet the reality is, drugs and alcohol made a dangerous
impression on my body, mind, and spirit.

I choose to identify as an alcoholic and addict, to keep me in
touch with the reality of where using these substances took me. Being
reminded of this reality has special purpose for me because I drank,
used, and engaged in other dangerous activities to *escape* reality. One
of the primary objectives of my recovery and wellness today—just as
it was on day one sober—is to learn how to more effectively live in the
reality of this waking state. Learning to embrace, instead of reject the
reality that each day brings, is an empowering experience for me in
recovery. And it results from first admitting that I am powerless over the
drugs, alcohol, and other objects of addition. Making this admission
does not require me to say that I am weak, flawed, or lacking power
as a person.

Invitation: Practice sitting, walking, or journaling (written word or
visuals) for the next 3-5 minutes on what it means to you to admit
powerlessness over your addictions, compulsions, or attachments. Are
there any struggles that come up around making this admission? While
you are never required to utter the words "I am an alcoholic, I am an
addict, I am a co-dependent," etc. to begin recovery (as there are many
paths to getting well), consider what you might learn about yourself
and the process by reflecting on any areas of struggle.

Prayer or Intention: Help me to accept the reality of the present
moment and what I have learned about myself in the process of
recovery. In practicing this daily, may I learn to live more effectively in
my life as it is.

JANUARY 8

"You must crawl into your wounds to discover where your fears are,
because once the bleeding starts, the cleaning can begin."
~Tori Amos

Going to the source of our hurt and our pain can feel daunting. The wound metaphor can be helpful throughout our process of healing. The trials of living have made us familiar with how physical injuries need to be cared for in order to heal. So why wouldn't we apply this same logic to healing our traumas, when trauma (from the Greek language) simply means *wound*?

Instead of approaching the road ahead as trauma recovery, what if you could view it as wound healing? Sometimes the word trauma is a sticking point for us, and other times the sheer idea of doing trauma work is what overwhelms. In returning to the source of what trauma means—notice if you receive new insight into the healing that you need.

Invitation: Spend 3-5 minutes in a practice of your choice (e.g., sitting meditation, walking meditation, or an expressive practice) and bring to mind a time when you had to recover from a physical injury. Even something as simple as a cut or a scrape will suffice for this meditation. What did you need to do (or not do, since rest may have been an imperative) to heal? How can you apply the wound metaphor to healing your emotional wounds? Care is required here too.

Prayer or Intention: May I take active steps, which may include rest, to heal the wounds that keep me stuck today.

JANUARY 9

"Turn your wounds into wisdom." ~Oprah Winfrey

Many people we meet in our work have been wounded in the rooms of 12-step meetings or by people professing to walk a 12-step path. Both of us can describe horrible things we have experienced in meetings and from other recovering folks too. None of us are immune to going through such things in recovery contexts. Our hearts break to think that you may have experienced further triggering, or even trauma or abuse at the hands of people who profess to be helping you in recovery. While our fundamental position is that the steps can still be very valuable when people in recovery are also healing their trauma, the reality is that the Twelve Steps are used and professed by a lot of people who are imperfect and wounded themselves.

Having gone through such experiences may be a deal breaker for you in giving 12-step recovery another try. This is certainly your right, as we do believe there are many ways to get and stay sober. But before throwing the baby completely out with the bathwater, consider that a new tide is turning and many of us are calling out long-standing problems involving how the steps and 12-step recovery are sometimes misused and abused. Consider that not all meetings, not all treatment centers, and not all people are created equally within the larger scope of a 12-step program. You may be able to find a different experience if you are willing to seek it out.

Invitation: Spend 3-5 minutes in a reflective practice of your choice (e.g., sitting meditation, walking meditation, or an expressive practice) and notice if a previous experience in the rooms of 12-step recovery, at a treatment center, or with an unhealthy person professing to work a 12-step program is a deal breaker for you in moving forward with your recovery. Based on this experience of what didn't work, what can you learn about what you need in your recovery going forward? Are you willing to try some different meetings, reach out to new people, and investigate whether or not there is another way?

Prayer or Intention: I recognize and honor that I have been hurt by others before in recovery. Today, may I turn these wounds into wisdom as I forge ahead.

JANUARY 10

"If you have never reached rock bottom, you have never attended the school of greatness." ~Matshona Dhliwayo

Many a recovering person has uttered words to the effect of, "I didn't arrive here on wings of glory," to describe their entry into 12-step recovery. Encountering the First Step and the daunting prospect of eleven steps to follow usually does not inspire feelings of greatness. And perhaps this sentiment might not seem like it fits the beginning of the recovery road. However, it is never too early to cultivate the understanding that we are on a path back to our true nature, a true nature that was derailed by trauma and adverse life events.

In order to work a program, one doesn't need to hit rock bottom in any particular way or to any particular depth. We just need to find that moment, thought, or feeling that lets us know that the time has come to set a new foundation. We will discover the meaning of greatness is simply the process of allowing ourselves heal.

Invitation: Spend 3-5 minutes in a practice of your choice (e.g., sitting meditation, walking meditation, or an expressive practice). Meditate upon the event, thought, or feeling that brought you into recovery. Notice that you are in a new moment. Notice if there is any shift in your thinking, feeling, or body sensations.

Prayer or Intention: As I set my sights on the recovery path, allow me to allow myself to heal.

JANUARY 11

"Untreated post-traumatic stress disorder (PTSD) is
a risk factor to relapse." ~Dusty Miller and Laurie Guidry

Getting sober can feel wonderful initially. However, it requires that we give up our most reliable skills in numbing or changing the feelings brought up by trauma—drinking, drugging, or other reinforcing behaviors. The feelings and impact of the trauma are still there. So, in the absence of other skills or strategies to manage them, going back to what our bodies know works—at least temporarily—becomes appealing again. For some of us, it literally feels like no other choice exists to deal with the legacy of unhealed trauma, so relapse inevitably results.

True, deep healing from our addictions also requires us to address the impact of unhealed trauma in our bodies and in our lives. This healing requires us to learn new, healthier coping skills to deal with the triggers of day-to-day life and the emotions that they can bring up. To truly prevent relapse long-term, engaging in deep, inside-out healing to transform the impact of trauma in our lives is wise. This requires courage, commitment, and usually a great deal of help.

Invitation: Spend 3-5 minutes in a reflective practice of your choice (e.g., sitting meditation, walking meditation, or an expressive practice) and think about previous attempts you've made to get sober or healthy. Even if chemical or behavioral relapse has not been a part of your recovery experience, you can use a time in your recovery where you felt like you slipped into an emotionally low or unhealed place, maybe leading to some other problems in your life. In your contemplation, consider what role unhealed traumas or wounds may have played in bringing about the relapse or problem? Based on what you learn by asking this question, what can you do differently today and on the path ahead?

Prayer or Intention: Today may I recognize that getting sober or stopping a behavior alone is not enough for long-term wellness. May I accept healing from the inside out.

JANUARY 12

"The long-range result is that the peace of mind you deserve
in the present is held hostage by the terror of your past."
~Lily Burana, *I Love a Man in Uniform* (on PTSD)

Slogans like "one day at a time" and "just for today" are common in the rooms of 12-step recovery. Like many slogans used in 12-step programs, the intention is solid. If you dwell in your past or try to jump too far ahead into the future, it will be difficult to stay sober and heal. Indeed, these slogan are compatible with the core teachings of both mindfulness and yoga: the only place you ever really exist is here and now. Being here now is the key to happiness and a major component in alleviating one's own suffering.

The logic sounds so simple, so why is it so hard for us to put *one day at a time* or *be here now* into practice? Our limbic brain or midbrain—the seat of emotions and learning that filters all incoming information and codes it as dangerous or not dangerous—is the main culprit involved in unhealed trauma. When we are living in a great deal of limbic activation, we tend to see most things in our lives as dangerous or a potential source of pain. And the limbic brain has no clock; it does not operate on a time scale like the neocortex, the place where our wisdom to know the difference lives. As a result, something that happened to you thirty years ago, if left unhealed, can feel like it's still a part of your today—the today that everyone seems to be asking you to live in!

Invitation: *One day at a time*, *just for today*, and *be here now* can all feel maddening when people offer them to us as advice, as the solution. However, they are all solid ideas that we can work towards as goals for recovery. We need to practice staying in today on a regular basis, and the healing that we receive through recovery in the form of meetings, therapy, or other support can help our limbic brain to heal enough to realize the fruits of our practice. What is one thing you can do to *practice* staying in the day, or better yet, even staying in the moment today? Once you identify it, make a commitment to do it as your meditation practice today.

Prayer or Intention: May I receive the help and the healing that I need to more effectively live in each day and in each moment.

JANUARY 13

"Betrayal, addiction and trauma weave a design of continually recycled wounds that create an overarching pattern of compulsive relationships." ~Patrick Carnes

When faced with a new life in recovery, we will hear so much about how we need to work on ourselves and deal with our part in things. This is true to a large extent. We also need to see how powerful addiction and trauma are, and how much they do to our body, mind, emotions, and spirit. And we need to acknowledge that which we had no power over in the form of our survival brain doing what it needed to do, to survive. And we need to see the way that our addictions, however they manifested, betrayed us in the end.

In trauma-informed recovery, there needs to be a balance between seeking out my part in things, and acknowledgement of how much of this is not my fault, and how much of it may have also been driven by the betrayal of others, including those closest to me. This is not *either/ or*, this is *both/and*. Only in this way can we have a balanced First Step and a clear pathway to recovery.

Invitation: Spend 3-5 minutes in a practice of your choice (e.g., sitting meditation, walking meditation, or an expressive practice). Try a brief body scan, regardless of the style of practice. Notice if you can find any body sensations that feel particularly grounding. Lean into that grounding. If you cannot ground, notice that fact with as little judgment as possible.

Prayer or Intention: Today I can acknowledge that there was much I was powerless over before recovery. The steps and my fellows can help to ground me in a new sense of purpose and possibility.

JANUARY 14

"Notice that the stiffest tree is most easily cracked, while the bamboo
or willow survives by bending with the wind." ~Bruce Lee

Rigidity is not trauma-sensitive. How many of us have been wounded
by rigidly strict sponsors, treatment counselors, or other professionals
who insist that their way for us is the *only* way to get sober or well?
Such behavior is often reminiscent of parents or religious figures who
raised us, many of whom were the causes of our traumatic experience.
Yet we've seen time and time again that people can be so desperate
to get sober, they will listen to rigid voices of recovery because they
are so familiar. And sometimes we believe that the strictest voices are
somehow inherently right.

There is nothing wrong with believing strongly in a recovery
path like the Twelve Steps—both of us certainly do. However, when
leaders remain closed to the arieties of human experience and become
resistant to adapting, modifying, or being open to other paths, they are
practicing "contempt prior to investigation." If you are in a position
of leadership, please consider this idea. If you are a person in recovery
who has been wounded by such leadership or guidance, consider that
there is another way.

Invitation: Come in to a standing position if this is available to you.
If you are unable to stand for up to a minute, you can modify this
exercise and still benefit from its teaching in a seated position as long
as you can notice the connection of your body to the chair or bed,
or your feet to the floor. Notice what it feels like to stand—to have
foundation. Notice the support of the ground under your feet, and
feel the energetic connection from the base of your feet all the way
up through the crown of your head. Now, allow yourself to sway a
little bit back and forth. If you are willing, extend the arms out like
branches, inspired by Bruce Lee's quote. Pay attention to how you can
be grounded and fluid in your movement at the same time.

Prayer or Intention: Help me to accept the need for flexibility
today and know that I can stay grounded in what I believe as I respond
to the changing winds.

JANUARY 15

"Even if you have a terminal disease you don't have to
sit down and mope. Enjoy life and challenge the illness
that you have." ~Nelson Mandela

The 12-step approach generally accepts that addiction is a disease. This philosophy is not without controversy as there are people who feel that calling addiction a disease rather than a behavioral failing just gives people an excuse. On the other side of the coin, there are some approaches to healing that believe calling addiction a disease is too stigmatizing and too shaming. For us, realizing that we have a disease we can treat is fundamentally empowering—a main reason that we remain proponents of 12-step recovery.

As addictionologist Kevin Macauley, M.D. explains, for something to be a disease medically there has to be an organ, some defect to that organ, and resulting signs and symptoms. Taking addiction through this medical model, the consequences and life impact that we face as a result of our addiction are the symptoms. Our brain, specifically our limbic brain and its difficulty with regulating pleasure and pain (the defect), is the organ at play. The causes of that defect can be numerous, and unhealed trauma and learned patterns can play a part. Genetic factors can also play a role.

In our experience, professionals can spend so much time squabbling over what causes the defect in the brain that we lose sight of the most important truth—treatment and healing are available! That is the good news when it comes to being diagnosed with the disease of addiction. There is something you can do about it.

Invitation: Spend 3-5 minutes in a practice of your choice (e.g., sitting meditation, walking meditation, or an expressive practice) and contemplate the idea of addiction as a disease that is embraced by 12-step approaches. Is this something that you agree with or do you struggle with it? How can the idea of addiction as a *disease and the implication that treatment is possible*, help to motivate you on the path ahead?

Prayer or Intention: The disease of addiction is also accompanied by the treatment of recovery. Today I recognize that recovery is mine to be had.

JANUARY 16

"You can't stop the waves from coming
but you can learn how to surf." ~Jon Kabat-Zinn

The opening quote offers a powerful metaphor to paint a picture of a very ancient teaching. Stress and adversity are inevitable in life. No amount of recovery or wellness will make all of that stop. The key difference is that as people on a path of recovery and wellness, we are better equipped with skills to help us ride the waves of distress and the intense emotion that can accompany it.

As people in recovery, we must learn skills for *distress tolerance*. This is a term used in modern psychology to suggest that life and its many challenges will continue to happen. They even have the potential to swallow us up like a wave. To use the Kabat-Zinn metaphor, the skills we develop like meditation, embodied practices, other coping devices, and recovery tools can help us to surf; or at least, to swim. What skills do I have today that will help me practice distress tolerance in recovery?

Invitation: Spend 3-5 minutes in a practice of your choice (e.g., sitting meditation, walking meditation, or an expressive practice) and bring up the idea of *distress tolerance*. Notice what you notice, and then lead that noticing into a general evaluation of the skills you have for distress tolerance today. You can even consider writing them down in your journal or on the inside cover of your recovery text. If you notice that your list is rather short, what do you need to do today to add to it?

Prayer or Intention: Today I recognize that life will come at me like waves in the ocean. May I be prepared to swim and to surf.

JANUARY 17

"I believe that when we were active alcoholics we drank mostly to kill pain . . . . If I were you, I wouldn't heap devastating blame on myself for this.. . . ." ~Bill Wilson

Especially in his personal letters, Bill Wilson often was ahead of his time. Much like Gabor Maté and others in the trauma and addiction fields, here he tells us that our acting-out behaviors are in fact adaptive responses to our trauma and adverse life events. Unfortunately, there is a cycle that follows the use of a temporary pain killer that leads to more pain rather than the ending of suffering.

He goes on in this letter to say that, instead of self-blame, we should use our relapse experiences to gain insight. Often the only thing we have to do upon relapse is to avoid the shame spiral that it can create. Then we can re-set our intention, and continue on the recovery path.

Invitation: Spend 3-5 minutes in a practice of your choice (e.g., sitting meditation, walking meditation, or an expressive practice). Spend a few moments noticing any discomfort/pain you are in—physically, emotionally, or psychologically. Notice yourself sit through that pain for this period of practice. Notice the successful application of Step 1 inherent in this act.

Prayer or Intention: Today let me live a life as free of self-judgment and self-blame as possible. Let me know that I am simply a human being trying to end my suffering.

JANUARY 18

"The first step toward emerging from suffering is to accept
the reality of it... as a fact of existence which affects each
one of us in our lives." ~S.N. Goenka

The First Step, especially words like *powerless* and *unmanageability*, can be a struggle for many of us attempting to work a recovery program. The reality of our unhealed trauma can make such words feel shaming or negating to our experience, especially if it feels as though trauma took our power away. Unmanageability may feel like an insult, particularly if we are an overachiever or see ourselves as someone who is doing our best to overcome in spite of it all.

Step 1 asks us to take a good hard look at the reality of our present situation—physically, mentally, socially, spiritually, financially. It's possible to have it together in one area of our lives and be completely unmanageable or destroyed in another. Step 1 is not asking you to shame yourself in any way; it is just asking you to do the challenging work of getting honest with yourself and how the issue bringing you to recovery is affecting your life.

Invitation: Spend 3-5 minutes in a practice of your choice (e.g., sitting meditation, walking meditation, or an expressive practice) and consider the invitation to view the First Step as honesty. Go through the different domains of your life mentioned in this meditation and honestly ask yourself where you are negatively impacted, knowing that you do not have to share this inquiry with a single person yet unless you feel ready.

Prayer or Intention: May I be prepared to take an honest look at all areas of my life today.

JANUARY 19

"All kids need is a little help, a little hope,
and somebody who believes in them." ~Magic Johnson

Asking for help is one of the most vital recovery skills promoted in 12-step circles. Yet asking for help is a difficult prospect for many of us, especially if we grew up in a setting where asking for help was labeled as weak. Many of us have also been impacted by culture and politics on this matter where teachings on the importance of *self-sufficiency* may make us feel ashamed if we can't do something by ourselves.

Help is available in a variety of forms as you embark on your recovery journey or seek to deepen it. Help can come in the form of a sponsor or other members of a group or in the form of professional or other resources in the community. Certain friends and family members may also be in a powerful position to help, even in simply lending an ear and validating what you're experiencing. If you notice you have blocks around asking for help due to unhealed wounds, addressing those issues towards the beginning of your recovery journey may save you a great deal of grief later in the process.

Invitation: Spend 3-5 minutes in a practice of your choice (e.g., sitting meditation, walking meditation, or an expressive practice) and bring up the notion of asking for help. Maybe even say the phrase to yourself—*asking for help*—and notice what kind of response comes up in your body. Whether you are new to the recovery process or have been at this for a while, what are some of the roadblocks that may stand in the way of asking for help for you today? What may you need to do to name those and begin to heal them?

Prayer or Intention: Today I begin to acknowledge that asking for help is a vital part of the recovery process. May I work to heal any wounds around asking for help.

JANUARY 20

"Rock bottom became the solid foundation
on which I rebuilt my life." ~J.K. Rowling

When I was young, I asked my father why houses have basements. Mesmerized by *The Wizard of* Oz at that age, he noted how basements and storm cellars can provide shelter. He further explained to me that houses with basements generally provide a stronger foundation for the rest of the structure. Little did I know how much this teaching would stick with me throughout my life, and provide a very powerful metaphor for recovery.

We talk a great deal in recovery circles about hitting a *rock bottom*. I have a lukewarm connection to this phrase because most people I've met on this path have the capacity to keep digging, even when they have hit a bottom. The idea of the basement resonates more for me. Yes, I've gone to the depths, yet these depths form a foundation on which I can build and continue to add stories to the house of my recovery.

Invitation: Spend 3-5 minutes in a practice of your choice (e.g., sitting meditation, walking meditation, or an expressive practice) and visualize a house, a building, or some other structure. Imagine that structure having a basement. What would constitute your *basement* that brought you in to recovery? How would it feel if you could approach that basement, not as a place of shame but rather, as a foundation for your recovery today? If it works for you, perhaps you can continue to visualize building other stories and other rooms in your house or structure, representing what you've built or your intentions for building in your recovery going forward.

Prayer or Intention: Today I respect the *basement* and my low points as the foundation on which I am building my recovery.

JANUARY 21

"Intention organizes the neuromuscular system."
~Ermgard Bartenieff

Intention is a very powerful force. In addition to being the seed that you plant, the very fact of setting it already begins to put your body in motion for change. There is a common recovery saying that goes, *fake it 'til you make it.* I've never really been a fan of this one because today I am a fan of living an authentic life and I don't particularly care for people being fake with me. However, I can get behind the idea of *acting as if . . .* and behaving in a manner that represents what I want to see realized in my life and in my recovery.

Acting as if is a way that we can begin to put our intentions for recovery and wellness in to motion. Doing so can help to change our attitudes, our outlooks, and our commitment to the recovery process. An example of where you can apply this is to pray or send good thoughts for the people or things you resent. As the Big Book of *Alcoholics Anonymous* suggests, even if you don't mean it, go ahead and do it anyway. Some people see this as inauthentic, although I see it as activating intention. Give it a try, your body will feel it and you may be surprised what happens next!

Invitation: For this practice, you are encouraged to take on the posture of the person you would like to grow into through your recovery and wellness. Even if you can only hold that posture or pose for 15-30 seconds, give it a try. If you normally slouch, see what it would feel like to stand tall. If your shoulders are always up by your ears in high alert, notice what it would feel like to loosen them. This practice may be very difficult if you are new to something like this, so go gently with yourself.

Prayer or Intention: Today I recognize the power of the intentions that I've set for myself and my recovery—they are already working to change my life.

JANUARY 22

"Discomfort is a wise teacher." ~Caroline Myss

People's tendency to drink, drug, or engage in other problematic self-reinforcing behaviors is often fueled by the drive to avoid or to shut down discomfort. Part of recovery can include learning to sit, to be, and to breathe with the discomfort and distress of daily living. Have you ever considered listening to what the discomfort is trying to tell you? Especially if the discomfort persists, it's generally a sign that something is wrong and needs to be addressed.

Every experience of discomfort in our lives can be a teacher. We may need to meet it with our breath or any other adaptive practice that helps us to realize that, as another wise 12-step saying suggests, *this too shall pass*. Or we may come to a greater sense of understanding about what needs to be changed in our lives or what healing work needs to be done so that the discomfort does not persist.

Invitation: Spend 3-5 minutes in a practice of your choice (e.g., sitting meditation, walking meditation, or an expressive practice) and notice where you tend to experience consistent discomfort in your life. Is it around a person, place, thing, general situation, or some aspect of your past? Does this discomfort seem to be alerting you to something that needs to change or be addressed in your own journey of healing and recovery?

Prayer or Intention: May I recognize what the persistent discomfort in my life is trying to teach me. May I be willing to learn from it and make necessary adjustments.

JANUARY 23

"Once you label me, you negate me." ~Soren Kierkegaard

"Hi, my name is Jamie and I'm an addict."
"Hi, I'm Steve and I'm an alcoholic."

We can get so used to hearing these styles of introduction in the rooms of 12-step recovery that it can become an unwritten rule that we must introduce ourselves in this manner. While it is certainly the choice of the individual to introduce themselves in this way, it is *never* required. Indeed, since the advocacy born out of the film *The Anonymous People*, many are choosing to introduce themselves as people in long-term recovery. You can go to a meeting and not introduce yourself at all—if the meeting is practicing the third tradition with full spirit, you will be welcome.

The third tradition of Alcoholics Anonymous states that "the only requirement for membership is a desire to stop drinking," with other fellowships using similar wording. This is *all* that is required for you to attend meetings and begin working a program. If other people are forcing you to identify in a certain way or are making you feel unwelcome at meetings, they are in the wrong. You decide how you identify, if at all, and what that will mean for your recovery.

Invitation: Spend 3-5 minutes in a practice of your choice (e.g., sitting meditation, walking meditation, or an expressive practice) and notice how you typically introduce yourself at 12-step meetings. Is this how you would like to be introducing yourself, or does something else feel more appropriate or authentic? There is no right or correct answer here, you are simply being invited to investigate for yourself.

Prayer or Intention: I am empowered to choose how I identify myself on the path of recovery; may the choice be one that helps me rather than hinders me in my recovery.

JANUARY 24

Tramatikos: the Greek word meaning
"wounds that can be healed"

This is the word origin of the English word *trauma*

There is an iconic scene in the British comedy *Monty Python and the Holy Grail* where a fellow named the Black Knight literally gets one arm chopped off in battle. Then he loses another arm . . . and a leg . . . and another leg. All the while declaring that it is just, after all, a flesh wound! While the scene plays for some pretty marvelous comedy, it also offers a pretty powerful metaphor to what we do when we minimize the impact of trauma on our life.

Remember that trauma means wound—this is a core teaching of the *Trauma and the 12 Steps* work. Holistic recovery, which includes trauma recovery, requires us to recognize our wounds and begin the process of healing them. When we negate the impact of trauma on our lives, just as we may have at one point minimized our drinking and our drug use, we are in essence like the fabled Black Knight. Eventually we'll be rolling around on the ground, just a core of a person, bleeding out emotionally, insisting that everything's going to be okay. It's not. Today, am I more willing than I was yesterday to do something about it?

Invitation: Spend 3-5 minutes in a practice of your choice (e.g., sitting meditation, walking meditation, or an expressive practice) and consider where you may be minimizing the impact of unhealed trauma on your life. As a reminder, if the word *trauma* is a tripping point for you, use the word *wound*. What are the wounds about which you may be in denial, or at very least minimizing? How can admitting that they are even there to begin with help us on our healing journey.

Prayer or Intention: Today I recognize my unhealed wounds and how they have impacted my health and recovery.

JANUARY 25

"If you know how to make good use of suffering,
you can produce happiness." ~Thich Nhàt Han

The First Step is about acknowledging our suffering and considering the possibility of building a new life out of that suffering. This step says there has been a great deal of powerlessness and much unmanageability in our lives due to our afflictions. A trauma-informed First Step acknowledges that the survival parts of our brain did what they needed to do to survive all that we have been through.

Once we come into recovery, we can begin, usually slowly, to engage our cognitive brains to make decisions that will increase our agency over our lives rather than create more suffering. We acknowledge the suffering and the feelings of powerlessness and unmanageability that go with it, and we also set a new intention to walk on a path of recovery. Happiness is what we sought through our escape mechanisms. It may seem counterintuitive, but our happiness will in fact be built out of the truth of our suffering. We will walk a path with others, and we will plant new seeds of love and care.

Invitation: Utilizing your current practice whether sitting, lying down, or in motion, allow yourself to acknowledge the suffering you have been through that brought you to recovery. When you feel you are at your edge, breathe in silently, and breath out, "Enough."

Prayer or Intention: Today I am in the First Step. I acknowledge my suffering, and I set my intention to walk the path of recovery. The path that starts from the truth of suffering is that which can lead to happiness.

JANUARY 26

"We are all addicts. Human being are addictive by nature . . .
all societies are addicted to themselves and create deep codependency
on them." ~Richard Rohr, OFM

Modern societies like to use "addicts," i.e., those of us who are addicted to chemicals and experience some dramatic consequences, as a scapegoat. Even an alcoholic family member of mine will blame the "heroin junkies" for the problems in society. Whenever this person says something of that nature, it becomes very clear to me that it's helping them to feel better about themselves. Many of us on the path of recovery feel stuck because of the shame darts we've endured from the attacks of others. How might my life and my recovery feel different if I can learn to take these with a grain of salt?

I've always drawn great comfort from the reality that all of us are in recovery from something and that all of us have been affected by addiction; especially if we can frame addiction as problematic attachment. If society at large began to see that their own problems and issues are different manifestations of this thing we call *addiction*, perhaps we could move past the *us vs. them* mentality that keeps us painfully stuck.

Invitation: Spend 3-5 minutes in a practice of your choice (e.g., sitting meditation, walking meditation, or an expressive practice) and consider the teaching that addiction is simply a manifestation of unhealthy or maladaptive attachment. Taken in this light, would you agree that all of us are addicted to something? How might looking at your problem within the scope of society at large in this manner help you to be a little kinder and compassionate towards yourself on your recovery journey?

Prayer or Intention: Today I recognize that addiction takes many different forms in the modern world. While this truth is not meant to be an excuse for me today, may it help me to relieve myself from the shame that keeps me stuck.

JANUARY 27

"After everything you've been through, no wonder you turned
out to be an addict. What are you going to do about it now?"
~Janet Leff (Jamie's first sponsor)

Janet's guidance, a fixture in the main text of *Trauma and the 12 Steps*,
offers important wisdom to us all about what it means to be trauma-
informed *and* disciplined in our recovery. When we make our recovery
and making sense of our issues all about the trauma, there can be a
tendency to make excuses for ourselves. "I'm doing this because of what
happened to me," or "If you went through what I went through you
would drink too." While these statements contain some truth, letting
them control our narrative means that our trauma is still controlling
us. Action is required to move out of this explanatory mindset into
more of a solution focus.

Janet's guidance is a brilliant blend of validation and challenge.
Both are required for meaningful recovery. We need to validate what
we have experienced in our lives as painful and likely a direct cause
of us turning to drugs, alcohol, or the addictive behaviors that ended
up controlling us. Receiving validation from others, while never a
guarantee, can certainly be helpful in our healing process. Validation
alone will not get us sober or keep us sober and on a meaningful
path of recovery. We must then embrace the challenge to make the
necessary changes and take the steps to heal.

Invitation: Spend 3-5 minutes in a reflective practice of your choice
(e.g., sitting meditation, walking meditation, or an expressive practice)
and contemplate Janet's teaching that opens this meditation. After
spending a few minutes with the teaching, allow yourself to answer
the question—*What am I going to do about it now?* What does your answer
reveal to you today about what needs to be addressed in your recovery?

Prayer or Intention: Help me to validate the pain of my experiences
while also accepting the challenge to do something proactive in order
to heal the wounds that remain.

JANUARY 28

"To thine own self be true." ~William Shakespeare,
and as written on the back of many 12-step coins

Like many other spiritual programs and paths, the Twelve Steps are full of paradoxes. There seems to be much focus on outside powers being accessed in our lives, as well as an ongoing admonition to focus on helping others. Then there is this message of being true to yourself, which some might interpret as having a whiff of selfishness. Nothing could be further from the truth in trauma-sensitive recovery terms.

So many of us see our lives framed as *before* our active addiction and *after*, or maybe as before a big-T trauma and after. In that before and after process, we lose ourselves. We are not able to make contact with our inner truth and inner strength. Working the Twelve Steps is an act of being true to ourselves. Working the Twelve Steps is our honoring our worthiness to be on the path. The First Step opens the door. The powerlessness is our difficulty in being true to ourselves. The unmanageability is that which occurs when we are not able to be true to ourselves. Our first admission and understanding of this truth is where the rubber meets the road on a path of recovery.

Invitation: Spend 3-5 minutes in a practice of your choice (e.g., sitting meditation, walking meditation, or an expressive practice). Focus on "To thine own self be true" as a mantra. Notice any thoughts, feelings, images/visualizations, or body sensations that arise.

Prayer or Intention: Today I will walk the path of the First Step, and know that I am being true to myself during this day, moment to moment.

JANUARY 29

"Act, and God will act." ~Joan of Arc

Trauma recovery and 12-step recovery are in sync regarding many things. One aspect they share is this: The alignment of our actions with whatever we believe to be our Higher Power, Purpose, Self, or Healing is what shapes and propels our journey. Moving into Step 1 is that first action that feeds all the other actions to follow. Some people call it God, many others have other names and other beliefs as to how this energy manifests.

Buddha taught that wisdom and intention are set first, and then we speak and act based on that wisdom and intention. When the actions are aligned with the wisdom and intention of recovery principles, people manifest change and healing. This is the true meaning of our action and the will of something greater being aligned.

Invitation: Spend 3-5 minutes in a practice of your choice (e.g., sitting meditation, walking meditation, or an expressive practice). Breathe in "Wisdom and Intention." Breathe out, "Action."

Prayer or Intention: Today let me build wisdom, set wise intention, and take healing action.

JANUARY 30

"The three unwritten rules of the alcoholic home are *don't talk,
don't trust, don't feel.*" ~recovery slogan

These unwritten rules are familiar to many of us who grew up with
alcoholism, addiction, and other family dysfunction. To talk, to trust,
or to feel would have disrupted the apple cart of the fragile family
system. If we even dared try, we may have been met with punishment
directly (e.g., being hit, yelled at) or indirectly (e.g., having love or
affection withheld). You may know the hell of these rules all too well
and have experienced their impact for years after officially leaving the
house.

These three rules that can get so ingrained during our formative
years counter what we are asked to do in recovery, especially trauma
recovery: talk (or at least have a willingness to "go there" if we can't
get into specifics), trust, and feel. Part of starting the journey towards
a healthy trauma-focused recovery can include recognizing that
everything you've been trained to believe goes against what you are
being asked to do to heal. Of course this connection doesn't get you
off the hook—you still need to meet the challenge of doing the hard
work. Consider that diffusing the impact of these "rules" may be the
best place for you to begin healing.

Invitation: Spend 3-5 minutes in a practice of your choice (e.g.,
sitting meditation, walking meditation, or an expressive practice) and
bring up the saying *don't talk, don't trust, don't feel.* Of the three, which
one seemed to impact you the most growing up? If you are willing, see
if you can allow yourself to send some healing or love and kindness to
yourself at the age where you first seemed to be affected by that rule.
You can think of this young part as still living inside of you, or you can
imagine a timeline and think about sending the healing and love back
to the place of the rule's origin.

Prayer or Intention: Today I recognize that certain rules I learned
in my past may be affecting my present and future; may I be healed
of their impact.

JANUARY 31

"Yoga can be both a trigger and a resource."
~Mark Lilly, founder of *Street Yoga*

You can replace the word *yoga* in this opening quote with just about any healing path: mindfulness, therapy, treatment, breath work, 12-step recovery. Being triggered is part of the human experience, and triggers are subjective. Even the most highly trained, trauma-focused professional who operates with the highest of integrity has the potential to trigger someone; if that someone had an abusive figure in their life who reminded them of said professional. On top of that, everyone is human, even those of us who aim to be trauma-sensitive in all that we do, and we can be prone to slipping up.

Being triggered can be a very important part of our healing journey if we are able to learn from and to work with triggers when they happen. Building a set of skills and a support system you can reply on can be part of this process of working through triggers. Moreover, if you experience being triggered in a meeting or in a therapy session, consider seeking out support before you leave. There is no shame at all in being triggered. The challenge is to recognize and address it before its impact destroys you.

Invitation: Spend 3-5 minutes in a practice of your choice (e.g., sitting meditation, walking meditation, or an expressive practice) and bring to mind an experience you would describe as a both a trigger and a resource. Meetings are generally good for this exercise, although any other healing practice or relational interaction may work. What did this experience teach you about the potential for two things to be true at the same time? What did you learn about working through being triggered, and can you use this learning for the journey ahead?

Prayer or Intention: May I recognize today that two things can be true at the same time—may I receive what I need to navigate any discomfort this causes.

FEBRUARY 1

"You need a little bit of insanity to do great things."
~Henry Rollins

The word *sanity* is a tripping point in the Second Step for many of us. "Well if I need to be *restored to sanity*, you may protest, that must mean I'm insane. I resent that!" True, there are many negative connotations that go along with the word *insane*, mostly because of sensationalized and stigmatizing portrayals of mental health struggles in our culture. So I once again turn to the word origin to put our minds at rest. *Sane* simply comes from the Latin word *sanus* meaning "healthy." So would it feel different if you read the step: "Came to believe that a power greater than ourselves could restore us to health?"

Most of us can admit that we have been very unhealthy or have done unhealthy things as a result of our addiction and/or unhealed trauma. So this word switch up may help you to more fully embrace the Second Step. And know that you're not alone in being *insane* or *unhealthy*. There's a whole fellowship of people on this path that can relate to you. Moreover, many of us can admit that recognizing our initial insanity led to the healthier lives we have today, and that sanity is not an all-or-nothing construct. Even in healthy recovery, we can all show signs of unhealthy patterns from time to time, showing us what we need to work on next.

Invitation: Spend 3-5 minutes in a practice of your choice (e.g., sitting meditation, walking meditation, or an expressive practice) and bring up the word *insanity*. What are you noticing about what this word does to your body? Then bring up the word *unhealthy* and sit with it for a moment. What are you noticing, if anything, that may be different?

Prayer or Intention: Today I come to believe that a power or force greater than myself can restore me to health.

FEBRUARY 2

"Men never do evil so completely and cheerfully as when they do it from religious conviction." ~Blaise Pascal

For many people in recovery, the block to even approach Step 2 exists because of the wounds we experienced through religious or spiritual contexts. This can include previous 12-step experiences. Spiritual abuse is generally defined as whenever God or some spiritual concept is used at the weapon to control or demean people. Often spiritual abusers (e.g., parents, pastoral figures, meditation teachers, sponsors) believe that they are saying such things out of *tough love* or for *our own good*. Yet, what often gets framed as brutal "spiritual" truth is just brutal, and not very spiritual at all.

Identifying where you have wounds to heal is essential to trauma-focused recovery. And noticing where those wounds may have more spiritual implications or origins is a vital part of the process if you wish to work the steps. Spiritual abuse is a real thing that can keep us blocked from developing a relationship with Higher Power as well as developing healthy human connections in general.

Invitation: Spend 3-5 minutes in a practice of your choice (e.g., sitting meditation, walking meditation, or an expressive practice) and notice the definition of *spiritual abuse*: God (or other spiritual concepts) as the weapon. Have you been wounded in this way in your journey? If so, how might some of these wounds that are in need of healing be keeping you stuck.

Prayer or Intention: Today I recognize where spiritual wounding may be present in my life. To the degree that I am able, I set an intention for these wounds to be addressed and healed.

FEBRUARY 3

"Faith in the face of disappointment is only enhanced
by laughter in the face of pain." ~Marc Maron

We are not always able to find the humor in our struggles, but there
are reasons why there is so much laughter in 12-step meetings: the
laughter of identification, the laughter of the transformation of pain
and suffering, the laughter of the absurdity of the world sometimes. To
laugh at our troubles is not necessarily avoidance or denial, in fact, it
can be evidence of the reprocessing of trauma. And similar to shifting
to a faith that works even in the face of the greatest disappointments,
we also can have a perspective shift that allows us to laugh into our
pain, not at our pain or the pain of others.

There is a great deal of compassion in our laughter, and that
comes from our pain. There is also compassion in having the faith to
continue forward on the path. To be honest, I don't know how I would
have come this far in recovery without the laughter. May you find it
often in your recovery.

Invitation: Spend 3-5 minutes in a practice of your choice (e.g.,
sitting meditation, walking meditation, or an expressive practice).
Notice where you have compassion for your disappointments in life.
Notice where you have compassion for your pain. Notice what it is
like to observe this all with a smile on our face. See if any laughter
arises, and even if you committed yourself to silent meditation, let the
laughter flow.

Prayer or Intention: I have faith that I can rise beyond my
disappointments, and I also have the perspective that allows me to
laugh through pain when it seems and feels right.

FEBRUARY 4

"Religion is for those who are afraid of hell. Spirituality
is for those who have been there."~recovery saying

Many people in recovery identify with a particular religion, but many
do not. In their original formulation the Twelve Steps advocate for a
personal conception of what is referred to as a Higher Power. People
in trauma recovery all qualify for an engagement with spirituality, as
we are people who have certainly been to hell and back. Those who
don't necessarily identify as trauma survivors but are recovering from
an addiction can also attest to the hellish nature of life before recovery.
For some of us, religion becomes the expression of that spirituality. For
many others, it is indeed personal, spiritual, and not necessary aligned
with any particular established religion.

One of the most important features of the Second Step of recovery
is that we have a choice in this matter. It may be the first choice we ever
believed we have had. We get to choose what we believe in, what the
spiritual or non-spiritual definition of a power greater than ourselves
is. We also get to choose where it is located, whether inside ourselves,
up above, in the earth, the universe, wherever or whatever. This is a
major doorway out of hell, the definition of a spiritual solution.

Invitation: Spend 3-5 minutes in a practice of your choice (e.g., sitting
meditation, walking meditation, or an expressive practice). Spend this
time focusing on your current conception of a Higher Power. Notice
what sensations, thoughts and feelings arise upon contemplating this.

Prayer or Intention: I know now that I have the option to maintain
spirituality throughout my recovery lifetime, and that being religious
is optional.

FEBRUARY 5

"Where do we even start on the daily walk of restoration and awakening? We start where we are." ~Anne Lamott

In the practice of restorative yoga, participants are guided through very gentle movement, usually with the assistance of a blanket and many props like bolsters or pillows. The objective of this practice is to get people to rest very deeply and as a result, restore themselves. The concept of restoration is a powerful one in recovery, and it is a hallmark of the Second Step. As I contemplate how much I've personally benefitted from the practice of restorative yoga, it's clear to me that both physical and mental rest have been imperative to my recovery.

In considering the Second Step, we rarely stop to consider the role of rest in bringing us back to physical and mental health. Another fun connection we can make with word origin is to contemplate how the word re + store means to be stocked up or filled again and again. Rest is vital for me, as is engaging in other practices that I require to stay sober and healthy. If my well is empty and I am tired, I am not going to be in a healthy place. Restoration is vital to my process.

Invitation: Spend 3-5 minutes in a practice of your choice (e.g., sitting meditation, walking meditation, or an expressive practice) and contemplate the word *restore* (as it appears in the Second Step) as a blend of re + store. How might this help give you new insight to the objective of the Second Step?

Prayer or Intention: Today I am restored to sanity through being filled again and again with rest and other healthy practices that serve my recovery.

FEBRUARY 6

"One looks back with appreciation to the brilliant teachers, but with gratitude to those who touched our human feelings." ~Carl Jung

When Steve was beginning of his second year of sobriety, his sponsor Randy said, "I have some good news and some bad news. The good news is you get your feelings back. The bad news is . . . you get your feelings back." Those new to recovery are often surprised by the power of gratitude, and even more surprised by the arrival of all their feelings.

Many of us travel through life before recovery with possibly two or three emotions, perhaps elation, anger, and/or sadness. Now we find ourselves being moved emotionally by life, by our friends, by our mentors. Getting our feelings back becomes good news when combined with trauma-informed 12-step recovery fueled by gratitude. We don't have to be at the mercy of our feelings any longer. We can be the stewards of our feelings, taking our actions in life with a grateful heart.

Invitation: Spend 3-5 minutes in a practice of your choice (e.g., sitting meditation, walking meditation, or an expressive practice). Choose an object of meditation, perhaps the breath. Notice what emotions are present for you now. Name the emotion(s), and then return to the breath or other object of meditation. Notice if gratitude arises, and if not, if you can notice that with as little judgment as possible.

Prayer or Intention: I proceed into this day with a grateful heart to start. I am grateful for the fullness of my emotions, and the opportunity to live fully in the moment.

FEBRUARY 7

"The cosmos are also within us." ~Carl Sagan

Higher Power and spiritual components of recovery are a struggle for many of us. Even if we do not specifically identify as atheist or agnostic, we may go through a period where we are not feeling connected to the presence of a God/god/goddess, etc. in which we believe. If you are still wanting to seek recovery on a 12-step path and recognize the importance of stepping out of your own ego, consider using the universe as a Higher Power. Or as Carl Sagan might comment, based on the beautiful teaching that opens this meditation, an Inner Power.

We hear many people refer to the natural flow of the universe as something that works well for Step 2. Even as people who believe in a divine presence, we often find ourselves using this language too—"Let's see what the universe reveals." In doing this, we are surrendering to the natural order of things, recognizing that our agenda does not have the power to change it.

Invitation: Spend 3-5 minutes in a practice of your choice (e.g., sitting meditation, walking meditation, or an expressive practice) and reflect on the teaching that *the cosmos are also within us*. Notice if you feel a sense of connection to the larger universe and its creative powers. Consider how this connection may help to serve you in your recovery today and on the path ahead.

Prayer or Intention: May I recognize that I am connected to the magnificence of the universe and that this connection can support me in my healing journey.

FEBRUARY 8

"The only journey is the one within." ~Rainier Maria Rilke

When faced with the notion of "Came To Believe" and the associated notion of a "Higher Power," many people new to the program get flustered or flummoxed. A re-reading of the Second Step however reveals the admonition is to believe in a power "greater" not "higher." Perhaps that power greater than the power we have been running on is to be found within. And that belief will grow not only through prayer and meditation, but also in the actions we take and the willingness to go inside at times for answers and next steps.

In trauma work, we believe that the expert on you is you. Your brain and body know how to heal, your fellow travelers will only help facilitate that process. And that process will occur within you, whether it involves traditional conceptions of God or Higher Power, or your own conception of what represents a power greater than that which you have relied on until now. Twelve Step healing and trauma healing facilitate this possibility.

Invitation: For your practice, choose whatever type of practice feels most settling to you and your body today. See if you can notice any aspect of your experience that feels like healthy solitude. If that is difficult today, see if you can notice the fear or other emotions related to the practice with as little judgment as possible.

Prayer or Intention: Today allow me to be open to the power found within me to heal and grow.

FEBRUARY 9

AFGO: Another F&%!ing Growth Opportunity
~recovery acronym

I guffawed with laughter when I first heard the acronym AFGO used in reference to the recovery process. Clearly my preference is to go the whole way with cursing as it helps me to expel some pent up energy, although I've heard others in the rooms who do not like this language replace the curse work with *fear-filled*. A major theme in this meditation reader and in the *Trauma and the 12 Steps* work is that life will continue to happen—the waves of stress will come, and it's very likely that you will experience further wounding or grief as a result of living. As a person in recovery becoming ever-present to your emotions and experiences, *life* may hit you even harder now that you are aware.

Even though life may come at you in full technicolor in the healing process, you are also equipped with many more skills, insights, and hopefully deeper layers of healing and perspective that can assist. If this still feels overwhelming, can you appreciate what you may be going through right now as a growth opportunity, or more plainly, a f&%!ing growth opportunity? Is there evidence in your life of how stressful times that you've navigated led you to some higher and fuller growth in your process?

Invitation: Today and over the next week, see if you can practice using the acronym AFGO when you are feeling particularly stressed, overwhelmed, or fearful of the future. If the setting is socially appropriate, go the whole say—stomp and shout out "AFGO," or the entire phrase, and see if this helps you with releasing some of the frustration. Notice whatever you notice.

Prayer or Intention: Today I recognize that all of life presents me with opportunities for growth. Viewing the things that trouble me through this lens may restore me to sanity.

FEBRUARY 10

"There is a force more powerful than steam and electricity: the will."
~Fernán Caballero

Many people have a very narrow interpretation of the role of willpower in the working of the Twelve Steps. There is a hyper-focus amongst many on the importance of powerlessness. A more trauma-informed approach looks at the admission of powerlessness to denote an initial realization, and an initial realization only. We realize that up until this point, we have been powerless over our thoughts and behaviors related to our addiction.

What was missing in the original formulation of the steps was the understanding that our trauma responses are a large part of what make us powerless, as the survival brain overpowers any cognitive decisions we might make. In recovery, once we realize this powerlessness, we immediately have access to power, and to our willpower. We can align that willpower now with the task of recovery. We can apply our will to the Twelve Steps and all our other recovery actions. We become powerful the moment we enter recovery.

Invitation: Spend 3-5 minutes in a practice of your choice (e.g., sitting meditation, walking meditation, or an expressive practice). On the in breath, note that "I was powerless." On the out breath, note that "now I have power."

Prayer or Intention: I will understand and access my recovery power today.

FEBRUARY 11

"Acceptance is the answer to all my problems today."
~*Alcoholics Anonymous*, p. 417

This very-well known line in the AA "Big Book" makes a very big claim. Can acceptance really be the answer to *all* of my problems today? As difficult as this line can be for people in recovery, especially those of us with unhealed trauma, to wrap our heads around, there is so much truth in its wisdom. The bulk of our suffering is about fighting what *is*. This is suffering that we can eliminate if we can just surrender any desire or fight that we have to change it.

To make a few points very clear: Acceptance does not mean resignation. You do not have to *like* something or *endorse* something, especially trauma, abuse or injustice, to practice accepting it. When it comes to situations that have passed, acceptance means your acknowledgement that it happened and that there is nothing you can do to change it. This relieves a great burden immediately, freeing us up to decide what to do next. When it comes to dealing with people or situations currently happening in our life, acceptance means acknowledging that other people are who they are and certain situations may be what they are. Then we can act accordingly. Changing other people is futile; you can only change yourself and how you respond. If we are in a situation to actively fight injustice, consider that acceptance means focusing on what *you* can do to make a difference instead of focusing so strongly on the things that are out of your control.

Invitation: Spend 3-5 minutes in a practice of your choice (e.g., sitting meditation, walking meditation, or an expressive practice) and hang out with the phrase *acceptance is the answer to all of my problems today*. This recovery teaching can serve as an excellent anchor phrase for meditation. Notice what you notice as it comes up for you. If your attention starts to wander or feels pulled away, accept that and then kindly direct your attention back to your phrase.

Prayer or Intention: May I be open to the power of acceptance as the answer to all of my problems today.

FEBRUARY 12

"Believe that our destinies aren't chains around our necks,
but wings that give us flight" ~Roshani Chokshi

One of the legacies of trauma is the notion that we are doomed by our stories, by our traumas, by our addictions. For many if not most of us, we may not have been able to see it any other way, as our traumatic responses come up in the present, feeding the responses of the past, exacerbating further the response of the present. It is hard to make the transition from seeing ourselves as doomed to seeing the possibility of taking flight in recovery.

So, we give ourselves the steps, the support of others, a knowledge of the reality of the effect of trauma and adverse life events on our perceptions, and the internal and external resources that build our resilience. This all allows for the transformation from being perpetually knocked down by our stories to walking the recovery path.

Invitation: Spend 3-5 minutes in a practice of your choice (e.g., sitting meditation, walking meditation, or an expressive practice). Notice one or two of the issues that seem like patterns to you. If it is comfortable, visualize yourself shaking them off, and walking forward into your recovery. Walking meditation might be especially good for this exercise.

Prayer or Intention: I am shaking off my story a day at a time, and moving forward on my recovery path. I believe I can do this.

FEBRUARY 13

"Doubt in my tradition is something that is very helpful. Because of doubt, you can thirst more and you will get a higher kind of proof."
~Thich Nhàt Han

You may have run into people in the rooms of recovery fellowships who try to make you feel like your doubts are an impediment to your progress. I've been placated many of times with the *keep it simple* bit when people seem annoyed by my incessant asking of questions. And I ask *a lot* of questions. It's how I learn, how I grow, and yes, how I tease out my doubts.

Never let anybody, in recovery settings or in other venues of life, make you feel *less than* for doubting. Your doubts and the questions that accompany them can be your best friend on the path of recovery and wellness. The key is to have willingness to explore them with an open heart and an open mind.

Invitation: Spend 3-5 minutes in a practice of your choice (e.g., sitting meditation, walking meditation, or an expressive practice) and notice what areas of recovery, spirituality, or other healing lessons may be bringing up doubt in you today. Take a few moments to allow these doubts to form into questions and let the questions guide you on the next phase of your inquiry.

Prayer or Intention: Today I recognize that having doubts does not make me a bad person. I am willing to form my doubts into questions and be open to the answers revealed.

FEBRUARY 14

"Shame occurs when you haven't been able to get away with the
'who' you want people to think you are."
~Carl Whitaker

In recovery circles, we talk quite a bit about the difference between
guilt and shame. You may have even hear the well-worn teaching that
guilt is when you feel bad about the things you've done and shame
is when you feel bad about who you are. Whitaker and many other
writers and thinkers in a variety of fields have written on the perils
of shame. The impact of unhealed trauma often manifests as shame,
and this can keep us horribly stuck at all levels of our being. Shame
happens when we internalize the negative messages that others or the
world would have us believe about ourselves as a result of traumatic
experiences as the truth.

The process of recovery is learning a different truth, a different
reality about who you really are. Those messages never really defined
you, yet it served others and maybe even the culture in which you
were raised to have you believe those awful things like, "I'm not
good enough," "I'm defective," "I'm ugly," or "I cannot be trusted."
Recovery asks us to examine these beliefs, heal the wounds that brought
them to life, and learn that there is another way of being in the world
and seeing ourselves in it. This part of our recovery is absolutely vital
to our long-term, continued healing.

Invitation: Spend 3-5 minutes in a practice of your choice (e.g., sitting
meditation, walking meditation, or an expressive practice) and notice
the subtle differences between guilt and shame. What is an example of
a negative, false message you carry about yourself that keeps you stuck
in a cycle of shame? What would you like to believe about yourself
instead? Even if you can't hold that preferred belief as true today, see
if you can at least speak it out loud, naming it as an intention.

Prayer or Intention: Today I can recognize where shame is keeping
me stuck and notice how I would like to believe differently about myself.

FEBRUARY 15

"Some things just hurt. But what we don't need is the extra
suffering—the sense of isolation, blame or shame."
~Sharon Salzberg

Some things just hurt, and some wounds never fully heal. But we can
bring our suffering from trauma and adverse life events to an adaptive
resolution and become able to live a more adaptive life. Sometimes
well-meaning people in recovery will try to find a way to eliminate
your hurt, or even convince you that your hurting is your fault. This
is a misguided notion of what it means to change our thinking, and it
leaves out the acceptance found in the Second Step of the program. I
was told early on by my sponsor that the first three steps can be boiled
down to Awareness, Acceptance, and Action.

What is new for most people in recovery is the acceptance step,
and once noticed, it then becomes a lifelong learning mission. When I
become able to accept that some things just hurt, then the action I will
take next will be wiser. Instead of knee jerk attempts to fix things or to
dive into the vortex of shame or blame, I might rest if I need rest, eat
if I need to eat, seek co-regulation with others if I need company. The
more I can stay out of the extra layer of suffering, the more I will heal.

Invitation: For 3-5 minutes, do a simple breath meditation noticing
a physical or emotional pain you are holding in this moment. See if
you can breathe into the pain, allowing it to simply be "pain." Notice
throughout the mediation if it tends to stay the same, or if it changes
in subtle ways.

Prayer or Intention: As I go throughout my day, may I accept my
pain and difficulty in order that I might find the wise actions that keep
me on the path of recovery.

FEBRUARY 16

"Why don't you just make the Second Step about alcohol for now?"
~Richard, from the 14th Street Workshop (early 1990s)

At times the steps can seem overwhelming. They are especially so when we think that we will finish them up at lightning speed and be made into spiritual beings completely free of any pain. The Second Step can be very challenging in this regard, since it is pointing us directly toward some kind of spiritual experience, the first assertion of its kind in the steps. For the trauma survivor and for the person in recovery, stepping back and looking at the Second Step through the prism of the primary difficulty that brought us into recovery rather than the whole of our human existence gives us a chance to fully experience the step and its benefits.

I only need, in this moment, to believe that there may be an opportunity for sanity as it pertains to my addiction or other dilemma that brought me into recovery. And that "power greater" than me may come in many forms, some of them unexpected and not even considered godly or spiritual. This is in fact the beginning of a spiritual treasure hunt, and we can conduct it somewhat methodically, seeking the power to deal with our primary problem, so that we might then deal with anything and everything beneath it, above it and within it. That is what sanity can mean for today.

Invitation: Spend 3-5 minutes in a practice of your choice (e.g., sitting meditation, walking meditation, or an expressive practice). Once you are settled as well as possible for today in your body, contemplate the Second Step from this perspective, the perspective of finding the power to deal with the primary problem that brought you into recovery.

Prayer or Intention: Today I can come to believe that I can find the people, places, things and spiritual principles to help me not act out on my old behaviors, just for today.

FEBRUARY 17

"Believing takes practice." ~Madeleine L'Engle

Jack Kornfield speaks of forgiveness as a process rather than an event. The same can be said of belief. There are so many stories in the spiritual literature of people having overwhelming conversion or enlightenment experiences. So many of these stories have untold or little told back stories, before the spectacular spiritual event. William James spoke of the educational variety of spiritual experience.

The educational variety comes not just from sitting and waiting, but rather from practicing. Many see the Second Step as sort of the equivalent of seeing a burning bush or suddenly fully understanding the very nature of existence once and for all. In fact, belief is just as much an active practice as getting up in the morning and doing the start-your-day paces.

Invitation: Spend 3-5 minutes in a practice of your choice (e.g., sitting meditation, walking meditation, or an expressive practice). Meditate on what your current beliefs are related to spirituality. If you are atheist or questioning, simply meditate upon what new belief or beliefs your journey has provided you about life and recovery.

Prayer or Intention: Today I will practice believing. I will notice the ebb and flow of my beliefs.

FEBRUARY 18

"Ignorance has no beginning but it ends. Enlightenment has a
beginning but it never ends."~Osho

Ignorance is one of the primary causes of suffering according to
Eastern thought. Also, while the opening quote's wording is attributed
to Osho, it represents a very ancient idea. Right knowledge helps us
to attain the enlightenment that will lead to our liberation. Think
about all the lies that you believed about yourself in the depths of your
traumatic wounding. Until you learned a different truth, the ignorance
kept you stuck. Recall all of the lies you may have believed about
yourself as a person with an addiction—how did right knowledge help
to set you free?

My favorite part of this teaching is that we never stop learning—
gaining knowledge is a process. Enlightenment is a process. Consider,
however, that this process must begin when we accept the first truths
that will lead us from the darkness of ignorance into the light of
awareness. For those of us who struggle with traditional concepts
of Higher Power, you may also consider using right knowledge or
enlightenment and guidance for Step 2.

Invitation: Spend at least 5 minutes in this reflective writing practice.
Make two columns. Can you list 5 things that you believed about
yourself or the world before choosing to get well (as part of any recovery
path) that are untrue? That kept you stuck in ignorance? What new,
correct knowledge have you gained since? Write those down in the
opposite column.

Prayer or Intention: Today I value that enlightenment has no
end—may I always remain open to gathering new knowledge about
myself and the process.

FEBRUARY 19

"Love wins. Love always wins." ~Morrie Schwartz

Struggling with Higher Power or spirituality can be a normal part of the recovery process. You may be someone who identifies as atheist or agnostic and the concept of a Higher Power that so many of us yap about doesn't resonate. Of course it can be difficult to hang around 12-step contexts when this is the case, especially if your beliefs do not feel honored. You may be someone who fundamentally believes in God or a Higher Power but because of where you are at in your journey right now, you feel cut off from accessing this power. Or you just may be angry, hurt, and not feeling God right now. There are countless reasons why the Second Step may not feel alive for you at the moment.

Instead of relying on language like God, Higher Power, or anything spiritual, consider using *love* as your Higher Power. While there are any variety of constructs that can work for Higher Power, for many of us, faith in the power of love is accessible. Even if we've been hurt by love before, notice if there is evidence in your life of love's healing power, especially since stepping on the path of recovery. If you are frustrated with the state of the world and all of the hatred you witness, hold the hope that universal love for mankind can be the opposite of hate and be open to those small acts of kindness you see around you that testify to love. If you are stuck, consider making this love your higher power or inner power.

Invitation: Spend 3-5 minutes in a practice of your choice (e.g., sitting meditation, walking meditation, or an expressive practice) and bring to mind an example of love's power over hatred, no matter how small it may seem. When you find something you can use, notice what you are feeling in your body, whether it is a sensation in your heart or a general feeling all over your body. Might it be doable for you to use this experience and the love it represents as your higher power or inner power today?

Prayer or Intention: Today I am open to recognizing the healing power of love.

FEBRUARY 20

"Roots of reality, supplanting the neurotic underbrush, will hold fast despite the high winds of the forces which would destroy us, or which we would use to destroy ourselves." ~Bill Wilson, *As Bill Sees It*, p.204

Bill Wilson did not have the literature related to trauma recovery, and yet he intuited some of what we now know to be best practice wisdom today. Our spiritual serenity is built through the formal and informal therapeutic experiences that give us the ability to have insight into our day-to-day lives. The "neurotic underbrush" consists of those unprocessed memories of trauma and adverse life events that make us unable to take root in the reality of the moment.

As we continue our recovery actions, the forces of ongoing trauma and adverse life events that are part of daily living will not have the same ability to toss us around, and our survival brain will no longer hijack our insightful mind's ability to take care of ourselves. It used to be that the cycle of being destroyed by forces or destroying ourselves was seen as weakness or lack of willingness. Now we know that trauma recovery allows us to bring the darkness into the light and have agency over the memories of the past, the thoughts and actions of the present, and our preparation for the future.

Invitation: Using whatever practice feels right for you today, whether it be still or in motion, spend a few minutes noticing a part of your body that feels either neutral or pleasant. Then notice what thoughts are present or are arising. Then, regardless of the nature of the thoughts, return to the pleasant or neutral body sensations. This is an exercise in getting roots in reality.

Prayer or Intention: Today please let me lean into and even appreciate reality. Let me notice how my efforts to not try and escape are starting to pay off.

FEBRUARY 21

"Music was my refuge. I could crawl back into the space
between the notes and curl my back to loneliness."
~Maya Angelou

The celebrated poet Maya Angelou, herself the survivor of childhood
and adolescent trauma, expresses a sentiment that many of us can
echo. Music possesses a mystical power to comfort, to soothe, and to
heal. Whether you are listening to it or playing it, for you, music may
be the ultimate resource.

Music comes from the same Greek root as the word *muse*, and
that root suggests a quality of inspiration. What can music inspire in
your recovery today? How can you align music as a healing resource
that will serve you on the journey? You may also consider that if you
struggle with a conventional concept of a Higher Power, some quality
of music may work for you to represent some power or some hope
greater than yourself.

Invitation: For this practice, you are invited to select a piece of music
that you find particularly healing in your recovery today. All genres are
acceptable, as long as the song meets this description as serving your
recovery. If you don't directly have access to music today, consider
singing or humming the song to yourself, even if it's in your head.
Commit to mindfully listening to the whole piece of music, coming
back to the music even if outside distractions pull you away. After the
song or piece of music is finished, scan your body and notice what you
are noticing. What are you learning about yourself right now?

Prayer or Intention: I will be kinder to myself today by recognizing
that I am not perfect and my recovery doesn't have to be either.

FEBRUARY 22

"The spiritual experience isn't one of filling ourselves up— with either religious or intellectual beliefs—but of emptying ourselves so that we can experience what is, directly, unfiltered."~Kevin Griffin

Many of us have been taught through consumerist culture to fill ourselves up with all kinds of things in order to make ourselves happy. And then in our spiritual lives, a variety of spiritual and psychological traditions have encouraged us to fill ourselves up with ideas and practices with a hope to counteract this drive toward escaping or soothing ourselves with behaviors or substances. In reality, the goal really is to empty ourselves sufficiently so that we might experience reality directly. We fear emptiness, we fear reality. This makes sense.

Our histories have taught us to fear these things. But now we can utilize the program, the steps, our trauma recovery professionals and community to develop a new relationship with reality. We don't need to fill ourselves up to distraction. We can live in this moment.

Invitation: Spend 3-5 minutes in a practice of your choice (e.g., sitting meditation, walking meditation, or an expressive practice). When breathing in during the meditation, feel yourself filling up. On the out breath, see if you can notice an emptying of any ideas, thoughts, feelings, and sensations. We will not do this perfectly. It is a practice. Notice what you notice.

Prayer or Intention: Today let me know that the spiritual journey is not about gathering up ideas and practices, but rather an emptying of myself to greet life as it is.

FEBRUARY 23

"Don't be spiritual, be honest." ~Byron Katie

Whether we make a commitment to grow spiritually or we have a sudden spiritual awakening, there may exist a pressure to "do it right." There have been so many times in my journey where I am faced with a choice and I can feel the pressure to respond in the most "spiritual" way possible. That can mean "letting go and letting God," releasing the entanglements of attachment, or praying on a resentment and forgiving. While all of these activities can be powerful, they can keep us more stuck if they are not approached with a spirit of honesty.

When faced with a situation you may need to truthfully express your feelings even if those include things like anger or disgust. You are still human, and healthy recovery requires rigorous honesty. One time I was embarrassed to admit what I needed to a good friend of mine who is a solid yoga practitioner. I feared that what I had to express showed a lack of faith. It turned out that being honest about my human experience eventually allowed me to lean in to my faith even more. Perhaps being honest, no matter how unpleasant or uncomfortable our expressions, is the most spiritual practice of all?

Invitation: Spend 3-5 minutes in a practice of your choice (e.g., sitting meditation, walking meditation, or an expressive practice) and bring out the Byron Katie teaching that opens this meditation. Notice what it means to you. Is there something you may need to get honest with yourself about at the moment that you have been blocking, especially based on fear of not being spiritual enough?

Prayer or Intention: May I recognize the importance of honesty with myself about the fullness of my human experience. This is spiritual practice.

FEBRUARY 24

"Despite my firm convictions, I have always been a man who tries to face facts, and to accept the reality of life as new experience and new knowledge unfolds." ~Malcolm X

Working a 12-step program of recovery in a trauma-informed way recognizes the power of flexible structure. Yes, the steps and the principles of the program give us a structure and a design for living. These are available to us as the foundation on which we can build our recovery.

Yet, there are many qualities in the steps that allow for flexibility—flexibility that is necessary for people in modern times, especially if our traumatic wounding left us riddled with triggers. One such example is the phrase, *as we understood* in the Second Step. This step gives us full permission to create a power greater than ourselves to be whatever we need that power to be for the sake of our own healing. If anyone inside the program tries to force their view of Higher Power on you, remember that nowhere in the step is this permitted. If someone outside of the program tried to convince you that the 12-step path is too rigid, consider this example of flexible structure offered in the Second Step.

Invitation: Spend 3-5 minutes in a practice of your choice (e.g., sitting meditation, walking meditation, or an expressive practice) and notice what the phrase *as we understood* stirs within you as you consider a Higher Power, inner power, or anything else that may work for you in this step. Do you like having this degree of flexibility, or is this new for you? Take some time to reflect on all of the possibilities.

Prayer or Intention: I need both structure and flexibility to thrive in my recovery today; teach me what I need to know in order to achieve the necessary balance.

FEBRUARY 25

"It takes a village to raise a child." ~African proverb

The notion of "it takes a village" gained widespread popularity when then First Lady Hillary Clinton published a book honoring the wisdom of this African proverb. The notion of *it takes a village* applies very powerfully to both the idea of support system and seeking outside help if needed in the recovery process. Too often people seeking recovery are looking for the quick fix, the magic bullet that will heal us. However, most of us doing this successfully have found that it takes more than one than thing. Whether it's people or other healing resources, it truly does take a village.

The idea of building a support system and network of resources to support you in your recovery may feel scary—especially if your trauma is defined by other people having let you down or hurt you. It can feel risky to reach out for help in this way. If you are feeling stuck, maybe consider reaching out to someone you've met at a meeting or in your immediate circles who seems to have a solid sense of a support system. Consider asking them what steps they took to build such a network and how they overcame any fears about the process.

Invitation: Spend 3-5 minutes in a practice of your choice (e.g., sitting meditation, walking meditation, or an expressive practice) and engage in a bit of self-inquiry about the quality of your support system. Do you feel well supported in your recovery right now, or is something lacking? If something feels lacking, where can you reach out in your extended "village"—whether in recovery circles or in the larger community—for help and support?

Prayer or Intention: May I be open to the idea of widening my support networks, or further leaning into the ones I have, to help me grow today.

FEBRUARY 26

"Do not fight the dark, just turn on the light, and breathe into the
goodness that you are."~Swami Kripalu

Living with untreated trauma can feel like we are stuck in a state of
perpetual darkness. Although many of us initially find comfort in
drinking, using drugs, or engaging in other activities, we also find that
after the effects wear off, the darkness remains. In fact, the darkness
can even feel more piercing. We may even feel perpetually cut off from
any source of light.

Learning the tools of recovery is like having the presence of a
light switch revealed to us. When we turn on that light, we receive the
guidance of a Higher Power or inner power greater than ourselves,
the assistance of healthy resources, or any combination of the two.
When we first discover or are shown how to turn on the light, it can
feel a bit overwhelming at first, especially if we've long been used to
darkness. The temptation could be very real to just turn off the light
and go back to sleep. You may have even done that at some point in
your recovery. Know that the light is still there; it is your decision and
your responsibility to get up and turn on the switch. When you realize
that help is available and you choose not to access it, you are essentially
sitting in a dark room with a perfectly working light. What's keeping
you from getting up and turning it on?

Invitation: Take 3-5 minutes and reflect on what may be keeping
you from getting up and turning on the light of awareness today. You
can engage in seated practice, walking meditation, journaling (visually
or with standard writing), or you may even choose to dance with the
reflection. There are a variety of reasons why we may elect to stay
stuck in the darkness when we know that there's a perfectly good light
available to us—fear of change, lack of motivation, paralysis resulting
from years of being let down. What are you noticing about your own
patterns today?

Prayer or Intention: Help me to turn on the light of awareness
today and on the path ahead.

FEBRUARY 27

"There are two means of refuge from the misery of life —
music and cats." ~Albert Schweitzer

One of the trauma-informed ways that I like to frame the notion of a
Higher Power is viewing this Higher Power as a resource. Early in my
recovery I was encouraged to have a conception of a Higher Power,
and I immediately turned toward my cat. For some cats are a resource,
for others it may be a dog. For some music is a resource, for others,
it is silence. Every time I looked at Kitty (that was her name), I saw
a being that didn't think about record deals or relationships or what
people thought of her. I saw a furry being who ate, pooped, purred,
and crawled on my chest to go to sleep.

To my mind, she was a genius and a Zen Master. She knew the
answers that I needed. So I tried to be more like Kitty. And it helped
me to begin a new relationship with life that was more relaxed, more
accepting. And for sure, it helped me to Keep It Simple.

Invitation: Spend 3-5 minutes in a practice of your choice (e.g., sitting
meditation, walking meditation, or an expressive practice). Without
judgment, visualize your current conception of a Higher Power. If it is
your cat, so be it. If it is your fellows in the program, that is great. And
for this meditation period, truly be with this resource.

Prayer or Intention: Whatever my conception of a Higher Power,
it is mine. I can draw on this resource whenever I choose.

FEBRUARY 28

"A dreamer is one who can only find his way by moonlight, and his
punishment is that he sees the dawn before the rest of the world."
~Oscar Wilde

Many people in recovery experience *using dreams* and become very
concerned with what they mean. Even in long-term recovery, they can
still happen. Some of them can be so frighteningly real, you may wake
up wondering, "Wait, am I still sober? Did I use?" When you are able
to answer that question with a definitive "No," consider using that as
an opportunity to express gratitude for your continued sobriety.

As Oscar Wilde observes, dreams can feel like a punishment,
especially if dreams of this variety torture us. We can choose to
approach all of our dreams, even our using dreams, as an opportunity.
Typically when I have a using dream my brain is trying to get my
attention about something. Maybe I've grown complacent, or perhaps
there is a larger feeling that I've been avoiding to which the dream is
alerting me? Often there is a recurrent theme in my using dreams that
is worth exploring with my sponsor, my therapist, and my network
of recovering friends. Unpacking this theme and all of the emotions
and sensations that accompany it is generally critical to my continued
growth in recovery.

Invitation: Spend 3-5 minutes in a practice of your choice (e.g.,
sitting meditation, walking meditation, or an expressive practice) and
contemplate your experiences with using dreams. If you have them
often, does there seem to be a recurrent theme or pattern? Might the
feelings at play in this larger theme alert you to what you need to work
on next in your recovery process?

Prayer or Intention: I appreciate that using dreams can be a
very normal part of the recovery process. I am prepared to respond
accordingly when they happen.

FEBRUARY 29

"Love and compassion are the true religions to me.
But to develop this, we do not need to believe in any religion."
~His Holiness the Fourteenth Dalai Lama

Every four years we get an extra day. Some in recovery would tell us to just treat it like any other day, and that is valid. Another option is to use its rare nature to do a spot check inventory or an inventory of some kind of the last 4 years. What has changed? What would I still like to change? What have I had to learn to accept? What new phase might I be heading into? What was my conception of a Higher Power back then? How has it shifted over these years, and where is it now? What is my perception of love? Of compassion?

As Bill Wilson noted in *Twelve Steps and Twelve Traditions*, these inventories can be done any time, so if today is not that day, then no worries, on with February 29th! If you are moved though, utilize this day perhaps as a spiritual assessment and growth day, with or without religion attached.

Invitation: Spend 3-5 minutes in a practice of your choice (e.g., sitting meditation, walking meditation, or an expressive practice). Allow yourself to consider the last 4 years. If that is too much then shorten the length of time you are looking at. Sit with the feelings and sensations that come with this meditative inventory.

Prayer or Intention: Today I will notice the changes in the big picture of my life. It will help me notice the small changes in my day.

MARCH 1

"As we understood . . . "
~Step 3, Twelve Steps of Alcoholics Anonymous

One of the most common ways I have seen 12-step members traumatize each other is through trying to dictate the nature of a Higher Power for another person. The often italicized phrase *as we understood Him* in the Third Step was added when an early member of AA could not get sober utilizing the Higher Power that was being offered. It was the 1930s, and it was pretty clear what the Higher Power was going to be. The early members realized that unless they found a way to make the Steps inclusive of all conceptions of a Higher Power, or even a lack thereof, the fellowship would perish.

I prefer to cut the italicized phrase a little shorter, as seen above. Any pronoun at the end of the statement makes an assumption about the nature of whatever it is we find that helps us to move forward in our recovery. As trauma survivors and thrivers, we are empowered to obtain, maintain, and grow our understanding of the Second, Third, and Eleventh Steps. We each get to understand in our own way, and we are able to act upon that understanding surrounded by the support of the fellowship and the healthy boundaries of the path.

Invitation: Sitting, standing, lying down, or walking, for 5 minutes or less contemplate the phrase, "As we understood . . . " Be open to new ideas, sensations, or beliefs about your conception of spiritual matters. Notice what comes up, let it go, and see what comes up next.

Prayer or Intention: As I walk this path, moment-to-moment, let me be open to deepening and growing my understanding.

MARCH 2

"As we understood . . . " (One more time)

What does this really mean? Does this mean that we truly choose whatever conception we want of a Higher Power? Well . . . yes, it does. This element of the Third Step was created because in the early days of AA, there was one potential member who could not get the program, and it was because he was being offered only one type of spirituality, only one conception of God. He could not stay sober, which meant that there would be others in a similar predicament. He was being retraumatized and left in the cold.

These words, "as we understood," are the very first trauma-informed teaching of the Twelve Steps. We are empowered to discover our own power, or a Higher Power, or the power of connection, or no power at all. We have a choice.

Invitation: Spend 5 minutes in the practice of your choice contemplating your conception that matches "as we understood." If you already have a conception, spend 5 minutes leaning into that power.

Prayer or Intention: Today let me know that I have a choice with my spirituality. It is mine to discover and to work with.

MARCH 3

"Religion is like a pair of shoes . . . Find one that fits for you, but
don't make me wear your shoes." ~George Carlin

The italicizing or underlining of "as we understood Him" might be the
most important action taken in the long history of 12-step programs.
In order for us to have trauma-informed recovery spaces, we need to
allow for a truly inclusive effort amongst all of us. Some of us are
religious, some of us are spiritual, some of us identify as neither. All of
us are welcome. All of us are necessary.

Without an inclusive spirit and practice in recovery rooms around
this issue, 12-step programs would have withered and died. Now we
can be part of a greater renaissance of the program. I will find my
notion of a Higher Power, you will find yours, and together we can
support each other along the path of recovery.

Invitation: Spend 3-5 minutes in a practice of your choice (e.g.,
sitting meditation, walking meditation, or an expressive practice).
Notice whatever your notion of a Higher Power (or a lack thereof) is,
and allow yourself to own that, breathing into your conception.

Prayer or Intention: Today my spiritual program will be mine. I
will not expect anyone else to follow my lead on these matters. I will
walk shoulder to shoulder with my fellows.

MARCH 4

"It's hard to realize you can have any kind of relationship with God you want . . . and so I now have a punk rock relationship with God."
~Billy Corgan

The words in the Third Step, "as we understood Him," mean that we are free to choose any conception of God or a Higher Power or an atheist perspective or anything in between that we want. We also get to decide on what our relationship with that spirituality looks like.

Many people come into the program or are encouraged in the program to have one particular kind of Higher Power or spirituality, resembling perhaps the one that they were raised with or even one they found in recovery. In a truly trauma-informed program, we allow each other to have punk rock relationships with God, or any other kind of relationship that works for us.

Invitation: Spend 3-5 minutes in a practice of your choice (e.g., sitting meditation, walking meditation, or an expressive practice). Breathe into your notion of spirituality, and breathe out that same notion, letting it go. Notice any body sensations, thoughts or feelings. Notice if your relationship to your current conception is fluid or solid. Finish by coming back to your object of meditation.

Prayer or Intention: My relationship to spirituality is my business. It is mine to decide and to practice.

MARCH 5

"Our friends are our family of choice."
~Margaret Rutherford

The term *family of choice* is well known to people who identify as part of the LGBT+ and queer community. It's a devastating experience if your blood family rejected you for being who you are and loving who you love. Even if they did not outright disown you, their subtle alienations and disapproval can be wounding and heartbreaking. Thus, seeking out a family of choice—those friends and people in our lives who love us unconditionally like family is supposed to—is natural and generally very beautiful.

The concept of *family of choice* does not only apply to LGBT+ folks. In fact, many people who have grown up in addiction or other dysfunction also use this term. Some of us may have lost our families or the strength of family connections due to our addiction. When we feel rejected or belittled by our blood family who are supposed to love us unconditionally, seeking out a family of choice can be a matter of emotional survival. This is often necessary for people in recovery, and can be a critical part of what it means to have a support system.

Invitation: Spend 3-5 minutes in a practice of your choice (e.g., sitting meditation, walking meditation, or an expressive practice) and notice the people you consider to be part of your *family of choice*. What qualities do they possess that help to support you in recovery today? If possible, visualize all of them standing around you in a circle, holding space for support.

Prayer or Intention: Today I recognize that family comes in many forms, and the *family of choice* I create for myself today may be the most powerful force supporting my recovery today.

MARCH 6

"I had to learn very quickly to look further and understand that I am not capable of controlling the weather, to exercise the art of patience and to respect the fury of nature." ~Paolo Coehlo

There are many ways to describe the power of mindfulness, and its use in our recovery. Patience is a quality that most of us have to develop, after years of reacting controlled by the more impulsive parts of ourselves—not because we were dumb or immature, but rather because our survival mechanisms were working on overdrive. In recovery we have the opportunity to develop a patient attitude born out of a healthy respect for and a new relationship with reality.

Before recovery, we would, often unconsciously, create new storms and then fight with nature. Today, we can meet the truth of life, remain patient and mindful in the stormy weather, and continue on our path.

Invitation: Spend 3-5 minutes in a practice of your choice (e.g., sitting meditation, walking meditation, or an expressive practice). Notice whatever storms you are facing today. Breathe into the storm, acknowledging its presence. Breathe out one more breath, despite the storm.

Prayer or Intention: Today I will notice the development of patience. I will grow in my mindfulness, and I will grow in my ability to be with reality.

MARCH 7

"The change process is like learning to write with the left hand when you've been writing your entire life with the right." ~Jamie Marich

I recently accepted the challenge to rent a car on a trip in the United Kingdom where vehicles drive on the left (or the "proper" side as locals say). As an American, having a little experience driving left a few years prior, I decided to accept the challenge for a few days, knowing it would take a great deal of mindful focus. Although I was doing well, I noticed that with the new direction, my perception just felt off. Even though I was extra careful, the differences messed with my head. A few days into the trip I bumped a curb pretty badly due to the perception wooziness coupled with a moment of lapsed attention.

Although it wasn't the end of the world, I took pause to ponder once more at the recovery process being like changing directions or sides. You can be used to doing something for a certain way so long that when you go to change it up, your focus can feel scrambled. The bottom line is that you can do it—you can drive on the other side of the road. It will just take some practice, patience, and attention whilst everything reorients.

Invitation: Get out a piece of paper and a pen or pencil. Sign your name five times with your dominant hand, the hand you always use. If you are truly ambidextrous, pick the side that you tend to favor. Then, put the pen in the other hand and sign your name at least five times. What did you notice about how you responded to the challenge?

Prayer or Intention: May I accept the change process as a challenge today that is similar to driving on a new side of the road or writing with my other hand. I can do it with time, patience, and practice to adjust.

MARCH 8

"If you practice for a result, then it becomes a hindrance."
~Dipa Ma

Many people in 12-step programs will encourage each other to rush or even race through the steps believing that we need to have a full spiritual awakening on a limited time clock. This assumes the Twelve Steps are result oriented, and we are on a journey to a final destination. There are many hindrances on our path, and one of the biggest is when we are holding a sign that says, "Spiritual Awakening or Bust."

The Third Step implies the truth of our path—making decisions and letting go. One of the most trauma-informed slogans already in place in 12-step programs is, "take the action and let go of the result." When we practice in this way, anything is possible.

Invitation: Utilizing your current practice whether stationary or in motion, on the in breath silently say, "Action" and on the out breath, "Letting go."

Prayer or Intention: Today I will live in the spirit of the Third Step, taking actions and letting go of the results.

MARCH 9

"Whaddya talking about? I pray every day."
~Randy, Steve's first sponsor

After my first few meetings in AA, I was convinced that the Lower East Side of NYC rockers that surrounded me were working some secret program that bypassed the spiritual "angle." I finally got up the nerve to ask Randy about this secret society. His reply shocked me a bit. But I also then worked up the nerve to ask him how he prayed. He gave me the Third Step prayer and Seventh Step prayer from the "Big Book" and I began. He made it clear I didn't have to believe or understand any of the words, or even say the "G" word at the beginning of the prayers. He was suggesting more than anything that I set an intention out loud.

Prayer for the traumatized person can take many forms, from traditional petitioning of a Higher Power to an atheist's setting of an intention for the day. It is not the belief in a particular Higher Power that is important, rather it is the belief in the possibilities of the recovery process expressed in the prayer, affirmation, or meditative state.

Invitation: Write a short prayer or intention-setting statement or affirmation in your own words that is meaningful to you. Notice what your current spirituality and belief looks like, and see if you can embrace it with as little judgment as possible. Use it for today and we will see if it fits as well tomorrow.

Prayer or Intention: As I go throughout my day, I will turn to prayer and intention setting as wanted and needed to continue my journey.

MARCH 10

"When we seek daily spiritual guidance, we are guided toward the
next step forward for our art. Sometimes the step is very small.
Sometimes the step is, "Wait. Not now.""
~Julia Cameron

Part of the trauma-informed genius of the Third Step is that it is not
asking us to do anything but make a decision. That decision is based
on the willingness to consider that the answer to the question of life is
not always the same. In the Third Step in the "12 and 12," Bill Wilson
suggested that all we are trying to do in this step is bring ourselves in
alignment with our true nature. My therapist Simon told me over and
over again that my true nature was to be creative. This is true of all
of recovery.

Recovery is a co-creative process, the co-creators being ourselves,
our fellows, and whatever our notion of a Higher Power might be.
Regardless, if I approach it all with a Third Step posture of letting go
of results, there comes an opportunity to enter the flow of life more
fully, knowing when to act, when to wait, when to listen.

Invitation: Spend 3-5 minutes in a practice of your choice (e.g.,
sitting meditation, walking meditation, or an expressive practice).
Meditate upon your day to come. Notice any challenges at hand.
Notice whether you might need to act, wait or listen.

Prayer or Intention: Today I will live in the flow of letting go. I will
co-create my day by staying out of the way as much as possible and
noticing what needs to be done and what needs not be done.

MARCH 11

"Let Go and Let God."~recovery slogan

Throughout recovery you will hear people give the instruction to "let go." Many of us in early recovery and even later on in the process will sometimes struggle with what this even means. Inherent in this confusion is fear. Many of our fears have protected us for many years. Perhaps they have even contributed to some success in life. So the admonition to let go can feel counterintuitive, even dangerous. And then when I am told to let go and let God, it might become even more daunting.

Trauma recovery allows us to start letting go in a safe and healthy fashion. Trauma and adverse life event recovery allow us to integrate the fearful parts of our brain and bodies with the part of us that is able to make decisions, like the decision to let go of a fear-based life strategy that is no longer useful. Without trauma recovery, letting go is in fact very confusing and difficult. With trauma recovery, it becomes a natural process, allowing our whole selves to engage with recovery, the world, and with whatever conception of spirituality we have found.

Invitation: Spend 3-5 minutes in a practice of your choice (e.g., sitting meditation, walking meditation, or an expressive practice). When breathing in, just breathe in. When breathing out, silently repeat, "letting go." Notice body sensations, thoughts, and emotions that come up during the practice.

Prayer or Intention: Today my intention is to live in the spirit of self-care that allows me to understand and act upon the spirit of letting go.

MARCH 12

"But now it appears that there are certain
things which only the individual can do."
~Bill Wilson, *Twelve Steps and Twelve Traditions*, p. 40

In his treatment of the Third Step in the "12 and 12," Bill Wilson laid the foundation for a shift from the focus on powerlessness into a path toward a proper sense of alignment with our newfound power that we found in Step 2. When linked with "as we understood Him," personal willpower becomes foundational in our recovery. My experience is that this is an even more profound cornerstone than our powerlessness.

Rather than being intrinsically and inherently powerless at any time, in fact I am only as of yet unaware of my power, and I need to bring it into awareness. That was the work of the first two steps. It is not the powerlessness that leads to my willingness to recover as much as it is a trauma-informed, strengths-based acknowledgement of my inherent resilience that leads to my willingness to recover. Then I am able to take action on my own behalf that I can bring into alignment with the Higher Power I have identified.

This issue of alignment will be our meditation for the next few days, in all its manifestations. First, we can notice our bodies, their alignment, where my edges are, and most importantly where my strength comes from.

Invitation: Practice sitting for at least 3 minutes, being especially mindful, if you are able, of your spine and your core. No need to go into laser focus, simply notice how you support yourself from your core and your back. Notice where the strength is, where the struggle might be, and where you might need support. Know that the struggle, once brought into awareness, becomes a launching pad for mindful intention.

Prayer or Intention: Help me to notice my physical alignment. Help me to notice the space I occupy, and my strength within it.

MARCH 13

"Once we have come into agreement with these ideas, it is really easy to begin the practice of Step Three. In all times of emotional disturbance or indecision, we can pause, ask for quiet, and in the stillness simply say: "God grant me the serenity to accept the things I cannot change, courage to change the things I can, and wisdom to know the difference."
~Bill Wilson, *Twelve Steps and Twelve Traditions*, pp. 40-41

Continuing our meditation on the principles of alignment found in Step 3, we turn our attention toward our emotions. As opposed to silencing our emotions or allowing them to run our entire lives, recovery allows us to engage all three brains. My lizard brain keeps me safe, my limbic brain keeps me connected to others and to my own emotions, and my human brain helps to guide me to safety and connection.

Bill Wilson, Viktor Frankl, Thomas Merton, and thousands of spiritual teachers over the millennia have encouraged enacting a pause and entering quiet in order to allow all three brains to engage and even link. The body pauses and quiets the mind. The mind pauses and quiets the heart. Then rather than deny or squash any emotional disturbance, we can use the Serenity Prayer or the equivalent to find serenity, courage, and wisdom. Now our emotions can become fully embodied, our thought lives become more skillful, our bodies become less activated from stress. This is the ongoing process of obtaining and maintaining emotional alignment.

Invitation: Sit for a few moments and see what emotion seems to be primary at this moment. Choosing the Serenity Prayer or another prayer or mantra, ask for quiet, take a pause and notice the impact of the prayer on your emotional state. You can do this for 5 minutes, or even just 1 minute. Doing 1 minute can help develop the practice of utilizing this practice at a moment's notice.

Prayer or Intention: Throughout the day, I will seek the serenity, courage, and wisdom to maintain emotional alignment as best I can.

MARCH 14

"Sleep is the best meditation."
~His Holiness the Fourteenth Dalai Lama

Vivid dreams and nightmares can feel like torture to survivors of trauma. They can disrupt our sleep, affect our mood, and make us feel like we're growing crazy. I've worked with many people seeking recovery who engage in self-destructive behaviors simply to avoid sleep and the dreams that may come when they try to rest.

Learning to befriend all of my dream content has been vital to my healing from both trauma and addiction. Dreams are our brain's way of trying to process heavy emotions and adverse life experiences for us. They are rarely meant to be interpreted literally, rather, they happen to get our brain's attention about something that needs healing. Work with a trauma-focused professional can be a vital part of your recovery if you are plagued by what happens in your sleep. Not only can they help you be less afraid of your dreams and with strategies for returning to peaceful sleep, they can work with you on using this content in your larger therapeutic journey.

Invitation: Spend 3-5 minutes in a practice of your choice (e.g., sitting meditation, walking meditation, or an expressive practice) and think about a dream or nightmare you may have regularly that you may find distressing. What is the feeling at play in this dream? Could this be your brain's way of trying to get your attention about some feeling you may need to heal or some aspect of your healing that needs attention? Consider sharing what comes up with a sponsor, helping professional, or trusted friend.

Prayer or Intention: May I learn to befriend all of my dreams, even the ones that scare me. May I appreciate them as messages about aspects of my healing that need attention.

MARCH 15

"Nothing is absolute. Everything changes, everything moves,
everything revolves, everything flies and goes away."
~Frida Kahlo

The truth of impermanence has been spoken in hundreds of languages by thousands of artists, philosophers, spiritual leaders, and poets. Frida Kahlo spoke to this impermanence, but also said that she "painted flowers so they will not die." This is the paradox of trauma recovery, the paradox of being alive in this human form. We can live in the Third Step of making decisions and letting go, in the knowledge that all things pass.

And we can engage in expressive arts and creative living, so all that we see in this world that heals us and makes us whole does not have to disappear. We can utilize the truth of impermanence to our advantage by allowing the pain to pass. We can leverage the truth of impermanence in our art and artful living by building those ineffable structures of people, places, things and creations that allow us to live a life in recovery.

Invitation: Spend 3-5 minutes in a practice of your choice (e.g., sitting meditation, walking meditation, or an expressive practice). Using the breath or body sensations, notice the coming and going of your object of meditation.

Prayer or Intention: I will witness the truth of impermanence today. I will see that truth with as little judgement as possible. I will make decisions and turn over the results.

MARCH 16

"Being at ease with not knowing is crucial for
answers to come to you." ~Eckhart Tolle

In my own recovery, I've come to embrace *I don't know* as three of
the most special, sacred, and spiritual words in my vocabulary. The
pursuit of knowledge, especially about our recovery and what we need
to do to heal and live a more adaptive life is noble. Arguably, obtaining
knowledge on the human condition and how we can be of better
service to others is an even more valuable pursuit. Yet we all reach
those walls where we just don't know—we can't possibly know what
the future will hold or how we are to respond in any given situation.

When I say "I don't know," throwing my hands up with palms
facing towards the sky, I am surrendering. I am allowing my Higher
Power or my Higher Self (or whatever I may believe exists outside my
own ego) to take over. This is when grace can envelop us and miracles
are truly born, even if that miracle is something as simple as getting
out of my own way.

Invitation: Spend 3-5 minutes sitting, laying down, or standing. If
possible, turn your palms up in a gesture that says "I don't know." Let
this be a physical meditation on this very powerful recovery phrase and
notice what happens in your experience.

Prayer or Intention: Teach me what I need to know and help me
accept that it's okay not to know. Gratitude for allowing me to embrace
the knower under any circumstance.

MARCH 17

"How do you know when an alcoholic
has been holding on to something? When it has
claws all over it." ~recovery saying

Trauma survivors are notorious for trying too hard. We can exert too much effort at work, force outcomes in our relationships and friendships, and change ourselves so that people will like us. This sense of striving can happen for a variety of reasons. Sometimes we're never totally sure as to why this internal push to do and to be too much causes so much struggle in our lives. Yet a common thread for strivers seems to be that if we can make an outcome happen to our liking or receive validation from outside sources, we will feel better. The pain of our past will be vindicated. The struggle will all feel worth it.

The mindfulness attitude of non-striving encourages us not to try so damn hard. In fact, when we practice non-striving, we are invited to give up our fixation on outcome and the "push." Non-striving is not about becoming lazy or leaving everything to chance. When we practice non-striving we can still put in effort toward healthy living, and doing what we need to do in to keep ourselves well. We let go of our fixation on outcome or on how others will behave. By releasing these fixations, we can release all struggle and notice a greater sense of freedom in our bodies and in all aspects of our experience.

Invitation: Take a few minutes to engage in a practice of *Clench and Release*. Squeeze your hands a few times, making fists. When you have reached your edge, see if you can squeeze just a little bit tighter and notice the physical experience of holding on. Do not hurt yourself, and if you have a condition that inhibits you making fists, consider clenching your feet or another muscle group in your body. When it feels too uncomfortable for you to keep holding on, slowly release the grip, paying mindful attention to how good it can feel to release and to let go.

Prayer or Intention: Today I release all struggle. Even if I'm not able to release fully, may I release a little bit more than I was able to the day before.

MARCH 18

"What you need to do to help people to change and recover is to help them find different areas of passion and help them find better ways of coping." ~Maia Szalavitz

If we were looking for a short form definition of recovery, it might be a switching out of coping mechanisms. Using a trauma-informed approach that tells us in active addiction the brain is looking for ways to survive or at least to avoid pain and gain pleasure, we can see the overarching truth of our need to find new ways to self soothe and cope. And we need to find something even more than coping strategies. We need to find passion. We need to find ways to create new meaning in our lives.

This is what it means to go from surviving to thriving. Simple survival will absolutely bring us through portions of our recovery journey. But we will also need to find ways to take that to the next level if we are to sustain our recovery.

Invitation: Spend 3-5 minutes in a practice of your choice (e.g., sitting meditation, walking meditation, or an expressive practice). Meditate on actions and thinking that you utilize to survive. Next meditate on those actions and thoughts you use to thrive. Notice any body sensations, thoughts, or feelings that go with these two objects of meditation.

Prayer or Intention: I have the tools to cope and survive. I have the tools to go to the next level and thrive.

MARCH 19

""Thank you" is the best prayer that anyone could say. I say
that one a lot. Thank you expresses extreme gratitude, humility,
understanding." ~Alice Walker

Many of us are taught in recovery that our prayers can be simple.
When I was new in recovery, in response to my query to my first
sponsor – "How do you pray? I've never done it," I was taught the
Third, Seventh, and Eleventh Step prayers. Another lesson I was given
early on was that my prayer in the morning could be simply, "Please,"
and my evening prayer could be "Thank You." Like Alice Miller
suggests, over the years I've used the "Thank You" prayer over and
again throughout the day and evening.

This practice fits with the notion of Radical Acceptance, while also
pointing us toward greater humility. Just intoning or contemplating
"Thank You" is a simple act of gratitude, regardless of whether you
see it as a formal prayer.

Invitation: Spend 3-5 minutes in a practice of your choice (e.g.,
sitting meditation, walking meditation, or an expressive practice).
Focus during this period on the words "thank you,' and notice whatever
resistance or acceptance of this gratitude arises. Look for your edges as
to what you are willing to be thankful for.

Prayer or Intention: "Thank you."

MARCH 20

"May what I do flow from me like a river. No forcing,
no holding back, the way it is with children."
~Rainier Maria Rilke

We often hear the phrase *turning it over* in the rooms of recovery fellowships. It's one of those sayings that can be very confusing, especially if we're new or never really stopped to consider what it means. Moreover, the idea of *turning it over* can be very scary, especially if we don't know to whom or what we are turning it over. This prospect is even scarier if so much of our lives have been defined by surrendering our power.

There is an aspect of turning it over that has long resonated powerfully for me, especially in my work. Every morning before starting my day I pray the Third Step prayer, and ask that my Higher Power speak through me in my work and my other actions that day. This is an especially powerful way of stepping out of my own ego and letting something more powerful work through me. To use the Rilke metaphor that opens this meditation, I let myself flow with the river of spirit. Ultimately, I've been able to live a freer life as a result. This idea of the river, or the force of nature and time, that we cannot stop or control, may also work for you if you struggle with traditional concepts of a Higher Power. Learning to surrender in this way has allowed me to practice *turning it over* in other aspects of my life much more easily.

Invitation: Spend 3-5 minutes in a practice of your choice (e.g., sitting meditation, walking meditation, or an expressive practice) and bring up the notion of surrender. Notice the immediate response that emerges in your body and spend some time with it, without trying to stop it, just as you would not try to stop the flow of a river. How might this experience better help you to embrace the wisdom of the Third Step?

Prayer or Intention: May what I do flow from me like a river.

MARCH 21

"No person is expendable, and no one is without worth.
Can we make our treatments so comprehensive and so robust
that no one will be lost?" ~Francine Shapiro

There are many instances where Francine Shapiro, the developer of EMDR Therapy, and the Twelve Steps intersect. One is this area of inclusivity. Shapiro desperately wanted to make EMDR therapy available to everyone in the world. Bill Wilson and Dr. Bob Smith along with the other early founders of AA, wanted their program to be inclusive. When they discovered elements that made it less so, they put in the words, " . . . as we understood Him", into the Third Step.

This made the issue of God or a Higher Power one that each person could decide for themselves. This was a way of making the AA "treatment" more robust, so that no one would be lost. This is the spirit of a trauma-informed application of the Twelve Steps. No one is expendable. No one is without worth. And as a result of inclusivity, no one is lost.

Invitation: Spend 3-5 minutes in a practice of your choice (e.g., sitting meditation, walking meditation, or an expressive practice). Meditate upon your favorite 12-step group. Notice the faces and the stories that go with the faces. Notice the diversity. Notice the interconnectedness. If none of these emotions or thoughts is present, just notice what you notice.

Prayer or Intention: Today I will know that I have worth. I will know that I am not expendable. I will go toward people and things that build on that self-worth.

MARCH 22

"Don't wear your shoulders like earrings." ~Johnny Weir

Not until I began practicing yoga did I realize what I problem I had with spiking my shoulders, clenching them so tightly that they were close to my ears. This phenomenon no doubt results from years of constantly being hypervigilant in my home—always on guard for something bad to happen. When I heard figure skater Johnny Weir make the statement that opens this meditation in television commentary, I instantly related. In thinking about how certain manifestations of trauma have played out in my body over the years, it's no doubt that my shoulders have suffered.

To this day, noticing my shoulders creeping up towards my ears is still something that I work on, a chance to accept the invitation I've received countless times to soften my shoulders. It still amazes me how when I allow them to soften, I often hear creaks and crunches in my bone structure, a sign to me of just how bad my hypervigilence can get. When I am cognizant of this experience, I often ask the question: What is this really about? What am I reacting to today? What are the fears that I believe may attack me at any moment?

Invitation: Practice sitting for at least 3 minutes, being especially mindful to soften your shoulders when you sit. Notice if your shoulders start to creep up towards your ears. If they do, please refrain from judging yourself. Rather, use this awareness as an invitation to practice softening your shoulders, and notice what happens next. This exercise may take some time and practice, yet it is with time, practice, and awareness that we are able to rewire our brains and ultimately our bodily responses to stress and reminders of trauma.

Prayer or Intention: Help me to soften my shoulders today; literally and figuratively.

MARCH 23

"Pain is not wrong. Reacting to pain as wrong initiates the trance of unworthiness." ~Tara Brach

In the Third Step we are often encouraged by people in the program to "let go." But what is it exactly that we are letting go of? Tara Brach and others teach us that the most important thing to let go of is our opinions about our pain. Her idea of Radical Acceptance is not one of passive engagement with our reality. It is the active letting go of our old operating system which tells us to fight our pain or to forge an identity from it.

So, this is the decision the Third Step talks about. We get to make a choice about whether or not to judge our pain. When we stop judging our pain, we get to feel our pain. When we get to feel our pain, we get to move toward the healing available in the rest of the steps and with our fellows in recovery.

Invitation: Spend 3-5 minutes in a practice of your choice (e.g., sitting meditation, walking meditation, or an expressive practice). Notice any judgements you are currently holding. Like clouds in the sky, see if you can allow them to pass. Notice what is left once the judgements about yourself have passed. There may be pain. See if you can sit with the pain with as little judgement as possible.

Prayer or Intention: Today let me acknowledge the shared pain of being human. Let me seek the healing that allows me to have radical acceptance of this fact, and then let me act on my own behalf and on behalf of others.

MARCH 24

"One important key to success is self-confidence.
An important key to self-confidence in preparation." ~Arthur Ashe

In EMDR therapy, the main trauma-focused healing modalities that both of us practice as clinicians, one of the phases is called preparation. The preparation phase is a vital step where we teach our clients a wide variety of meditations, skills, and techniques to handle what might come up in terms of emotion or sensation in later work. Bolstering existing recovery and lifestyle skills for wellness and health is also a vital component of preparation.

When many people in recovery express their concern about doing deeper trauma work and/or moving on to the Fourth and Fifth Step, they often say they don't feel ready. Indeed, many people do plunge into this deeper work without adequate preparation. The solution is not to avoid the work or the steps, but rather to engage in the necessary preparation to handle the intensity that may surface. The first three steps are vital in this process, as is work with a sponsor, and hopefully a trauma-informed professional who can equip you with the skills you need to be prepared.

Invitation: Spend 3-5 minutes in a practice of your choice (e.g., sitting meditation, walking meditation, or an expressive practice) and ask yourself how prepared you are feeling right now to take your recovery work—step work and/or trauma work—to a deeper level. Remember, not feeling prepared is not an excuse. Rather, what is it that you would need to feel more prepared to go further, and how can you access both professional and non-professional resources to help you.

Prayer or Intention: Today I recognize the importance of preparation for taking my healing to a deeper level. Grant me what I need to feel prepared today.

MARCH 25

"When pleasure and pain arise how are we going to use the Dharma
to be free of them? This is the point of practice." ~Ajahn Chah

What have we chased all these years with our addictive minds? We
could probably sum it up as the chase for pleasure and then running
away from pain. The historical Buddha actually noted this either/or
dynamic as central to the human experience: our seeking pleasure,
avoiding pain, and believing that successful navigation of this binary
will lead us to happiness. It's no wonder we became addicted! This
teaching from Ajahn Chah, reveals that our addiction problem is
actually just a human problem. Buddha, without brain scans or other
research material, saw the truth of our survival-oriented brain, and
how it could get into a trauma-infused cycle of mindlessness.

Ajahn Chah also spoke about formal meditation practice being
important. But the real practice is this—in each moment, what will
we do when pleasure or pain arise? He says to use the Dharma, also
known as the truth or the teachings. So here we consider using the
truth of the Twelve Steps. Moment to moment, how will we use the
steps to guide our response to pleasure and pain? All of the steps are
available and pertinent. Perhaps one step that is the fulcrum though is
the Third Step. We make a decision to turn our responses to pleasure
and pain over to the truth of this step, moment to moment, day by day.

Invitation: Spend 3-5 minutes in a practice of your choice (e.g., sitting
meditation, walking meditation, or an expressive practice). Consider
doing a brief meditation on Feeling Tone, the practice of noticing
experiences as pleasant, unpleasant, or neutral. Such a practice is
not meant to foster judgment, rather, to train you for listening to the
messages that sensations might carry. As you practice, when sensations,
emotions or thoughts arise, note them either as pleasant, unpleasant
or neutral.

Prayer or Intention: Today I will seek to utilize the truth of the
Third Step, meeting pleasure and pain with a mindful pause.

MARCH 26

"God has arranged everything in the universe in consideration of
everything else."~St. Hildegard of Bingen

I revolt against the phrase *God's plan* and have gotten angry at many
holy people when they try to lecture me about *God's plan*. "How could
it be part of a loving God's plan that all of this happened to me!" is
a protest that I and many others have made. While that phrase can
be particularly bristling, my recovery has revealed to me that there is
something larger than my ordinary understanding at play. When I can
fully step back and consider how even my deepest sufferings have been
transformed into something good that has allowed me to be of service
to others, I am amazed.

People often tell me that I am a solid big picture thinker—that I
have an ability to see the larger context where many of my colleagues
and friends cannot. While I take this as an amazing compliment, it is
a skill that's flowed from my ability to trust in something greater than
me and working the Third Step. Moreover, my recovery thrives on a
day-to-day basis because I trust that even though I am good at seeing
the bigger picture, my Higher Power or the workings of the universe
is much better at it!

Invitation: Spend 3-5 minutes in a practice of your choice (e.g.,
sitting meditation, walking meditation, or an expressive practice)
and bring up the idea of *the big picture*. Can you think of any time in
your life when your suffering felt like it was the end of the world, yet
through some process, that suffering was transformed? Then, consider
something you are struggling with right now. How might surrendering
it to the *big picture* be helpful to you? If you are still very raw in your
trauma recovery, this may not be helpful at all so feel free to opt out of
this second part of the meditation.

Prayer or Intention: Today I am open to at least considering the
existence of a bigger picture. If possible, I will surrender to this larger
plan.

MARCH 27

"You can't make decisions based on fear and the possibility of what might happen."~Michelle Obama

The Third Step has many turnkey elements. One of the most distinctive lessons in the step is contained in the words, " . . . made a decision." How is simply making a decision such an integral part of and a turning point in the recovery journey? Because some of the hallmarks of our suffering in addiction and trauma are confusion, ambivalence, ambiguity, powerlessness, and a lack of agency. All of these are driven by our trauma and adverse life event responses.

The first two steps and then the third build up our internal resources so that we might then be able to make decisions that are not based in fearful thinking. Making a decision implies that our neocortex is back online through our work up until this point. Now we can engage with reality, let go of the control that fear creates, and allow for new recovery perspective to drive our decision making.

Invitation: Spend 3-5 minutes in a practice of your choice (e.g., sitting meditation, walking meditation, or an expressive practice). Meditate upon a situation that you have in your life today that requires a decision. Notice any fear that arises, and then notice any ability you have in this moment to let go of that fear. If you are fearful, see if you can hold that with compassion.

Prayer or Intention: Today I will notice all the small and large opportunities to make decisions. I will utilize my tools, the steps, and a Higher Power if that is part of my recovery to guide and energize me.

MARCH 28

"Easy does it." ~12-step slogan

I recently attended a gentle yoga class where the instructor said, "In this class we're going to take it easy . . . which isn't so easy for many of us." I felt like he was talking directly to me as a person in recovery who has struggled with work addiction. Over the years, hearing "easy does it" can made me bristle even though I recognize its wisdom. I even acknowledge that I need to take it easy; or at least start by taking it easier.

There are many reasons why trauma survivors struggle to embrace the art of "easy does it." For many of us, achievement was rewarded in our homes, or it was the way that we were able to make ourselves feel special and in control when so much of life was bleak. In our families of origin, we may have even been punished for taking a break or slacking off. In alcoholic and other dysfunctional homes, we can try so hard to be the perfect child so that our parents will change. Even though our attempts are futile, that *push* to be perfect and the behaviors that accompany can linger long into adulthood.

Invitation: Spend 3-5 minutes in a practice of your choice (e.g., sitting meditation, walking meditation, or an expressive practice) and ask yourself, "When is the last time that I took it easy? Really took it easy?" Notice what comes up for you. Maybe you've *never* taken it easy. Perhaps you equate taking it easy with laziness, or even with giving up and surrendering control. How can identifying the source of the struggle help you to see where you need to practice taking it easy?

Prayer or Intention: May I begin to practice taking it easy today. For me, it may very well take a great deal of practice.

MARCH 29

"Reinvent yourself over and over and over and over and over until you find home. There is no timeline for the soul." ~Malebo Sephodi

When I first started working with the Twelve Steps, I was told to just keep working the first three steps for a while. The First Step would help me to take care of myself at the bottom line. The Second Step would help me to start developing some kind of faith, whether it be in an outside Higher Power or in myself and my ability to change. The Third Step helps me to integrate my bottom line of sobriety and my faith in moving forward and then do just that: move forward.

In a sense, I am using these steps to move with the flow of the truth of impermanence. I can reinvent myself over and over and over, or I can fight the flow. The Third Step helps me to stop fighting, and instead enter a creative relationship with life. The more I do this, the more I will find that which feels like home.

Invitation: Spend 3-5 minutes in a practice of your choice (e.g., sitting meditation, walking meditation, or an expressive practice). Meditate upon your own bottom line of sobriety. Then spend a few moments touching into whatever faith you have developed thus far in your life. Then touch into the bottom line and faith working together to know what to do in this moment. Notice any body sensations, thoughts or emotions that arise.

Prayer or Intention: Today I will reinvent myself once again, as I always do, a day at a time.

MARCH 30

"Don't let other people take up *free rent* in your head."
~recovery saying

The directive that opens this meditation can feel so much easier said than done, especially when the individuals in question have wounded us. Throughout my years in recovery, I have found taking that person through the first three steps to be a remarkable help in both addressing resentments and assisting me in the difficult process of letting go.

The approach works something like this: "I am powerless over (insert the name of the person in question). He is making my life unmanageable. I believe that You (however you conceptualize Higher Power) can restore me to sanity, so I think I'll let you." If you are past the *I think I'll let you*, replace it with a simple: *I let you*. The steps have broad application to all areas of our lives and our healing journey; go ahead and use them!

Invitation: At least for today, take one person with whom you are struggling through the first three steps in this fashion. Notice whatever you notice. I generally like to engage in this strategy for at least a week to notice a significant shift.

Prayer or Intention: May I be willing to use the first three steps in all areas of my life, especially when dealing with those people who take up free rent in my head.

MARCH 31

"There is no way to happiness. Happiness is the way."
~Buddhist teaching

Addiction can develop whenever we rely on anything outside of ourselves to feel happy and content; to experience a sense of ease and comfort. Those outside forces can be drugs and alcohol. They can also come in the form of people, places, things, or experiences. We've likely fallen into the trap, at one time or another, of believing that when a person behaves exactly as we want them too, then we will feel complete. Then we will be happy. Some people may even use God or religion as this *outside force* that we rely on to feel better on the inside.

Would you consider that, even when we discuss God and spirituality, that happiness truly is an inside job? Even if you believe in God or a Higher Power, seeing them as living inside of you may help you more effectively sink into the idea that nothing outside of you will ever be the answer to wholeness. God is not some magician floating around on a cloud; they do not exist outside of us. When we elevate people, places, things, or situations onto such pedestals, we run the risk of continually replacing our addictions and unhealthy tendencies in our search for the peace that can only be found within.

Invitation: Spend 3-5 minutes in a practice of your choice (e.g., sitting meditation, walking meditation, or an expressive practice) and notice where you have the tendency in your own life to rely on people, places, or things outside of yourself in order to feel better on the inside. While some of these outside forces can prove helpful in terms of support or positive attachment, where may they prevent you from connecting with yourself and/or your Higher (or inner) power?

Prayer or Intention: May I consider that anytime I rely on something outside of myself, I set myself up for the possibility of addiction taking hold.

APRIL 1

"Foolish means slow to believe. Foolish . . . can also crack open a cover of fear and self-consciousness and lead to a whole new knowledge of being human." ~Henri Nouwen

I've clocked more hours in trauma-focused therapy than I've spent working on my advanced degrees. Yet I can still sometimes struggle with shaking the core belief that *I am stupid* as it relates to trusting myself and my own judgment. Being hopeful as it relates to anything connected to personal happiness sets off an allergic reaction of sorts in me, sending me back to the *I am stupid* and *I am cursed* beliefs that were put there by a variety of abuses, especially the ones that deeply connected to spiritual or identity issues. I often ask myself, "How can a *smart* person be so dumb? When will I ever learn?"

I am not stupid although I can be foolish, as Henri Nouwen defines it in the opening teaching. Framing it this way allows me to offer a new compassion to myself. My hesitancy to believe beautiful things about the reality of my true self, my nature, and the non-abusive nature of the Divine is a legitimate response to the impact of trauma. Untangling the knots has been a process, and I have been getting somewhere and today I can rest into this knowing.

Invitation: Spend 3-5 minutes in a practice of your choice (e.g., sitting meditation, walking meditation, or an expressive practice) and contemplate the concept of *foolish* as "slow to believe." How might this definition apply to my own growth and healing, and where have the wounds of unhealed trauma played a role in slowing down the process of believing or learning?

Prayer or Intention: Today I embrace the beauty of being foolish as something that is fundamentally positive for my recovery. It means that I am learning and unraveling the knots.

APRIL 2

"Not everything that is faced can be changed, but nothing can be changed until it is faced." ~James Baldwin

Our trauma responses over the course of our lives were our survival instincts trying to keep us alive. So often the response involved escape— often an understandable escape from reality. Trauma recovery gives us the resilience to look at our past, our present triggers and our future fears and begin to know what we can change and what we cannot. Our trauma-informed 12-step recovery leverages the power of the Serenity Prayer and other tools to help us face our reality.

We begin to know when we need the serenity of acceptance, and when we need the courage to change. We find our freedom when we are able to face our history, our present circumstances, and our fears of the future.

Invitation: Spend 3-5 minutes in a practice of your choice (e.g., sitting meditation, walking meditation, or an expressive practice). During this practice, simply pray the Serenity Prayer like a mantra, taking three breaths between each iteration.

Prayer or Intention: I pray that I have the courage to face reality and change, the serenity to be in acceptance when change is not possible, and the wisdom to know the difference.

APRIL 3

gauntlet (n.): a form of punishment, chiefly military,
in which the offender was made to run between two rows of
men who struck at him with switches or weapons as he passed

The Fourth and Fifth Steps can feel like we are about to pass through a gauntlet. If we've tried to work a 12-step recovery program before, it could be that doing the Fourth and Fifth took us down. Sometimes we become afraid about approaching these steps based on horror stories we hear from others, or out of fear that we are not ready. While the Fourth and Fifth Steps can be challenging, especially for those of us with unhealed trauma, they are not punishment. They are an opportunity.

Yes, in doing a Fourth and Fifth Step, it may feel like your past is attacking you, like those weapons that medieval nights of old flung at the person who was running through the rows. However, the earlier steps you've done and the other work you may be doing with professional or other support systems have equipped you with a coat of armor. When something from your past strikes you in working the steps, you may feel rattled by it, just as a weapon would rattle armor. However, the weapon is not going to tear flesh, it does not have to hurt you and cause further damage. What *armor* have I gathered thus far that will help me work a Fourth and Fifth Step?

Invitation: Spend at least 5 minutes in a practice of your choice (e.g., sitting meditation, walking meditation, or an expressive practice) and be prepared to write down a list of what you've discovered after you reflect in the practice. What have you gained in working Steps 1-3 so far that will help you to move further with the next steps? What other resources or skills have you learned, especially if you are in therapy, that can help you work the Fourth and Fifth Steps or whatever new therapeutic challenge you are facing? After reflecting, right down these resources that constitute your armor. If the list feels short, what else you may need to feel more prepared to move forward?

Prayer or Intention: May I strengthen my armor today so that I may face the challenges ahead.

APRIL 4

"You can be both a masterpiece and a work
in progress simultaneously."~Sophia Bush

This quote has made its way around the Internet in the form of memes and inspirational blogging. Most often attributed to Sophia Bush, the teaching is a great example of dialectics. Two things that seem opposite can, indeed, be true at the same time. This challenges the inertia that many of us have to stay in black-and-white thinking, especially when to do so feels safer after a lifetime of trauma or not knowing the rules in a dysfunctional home. Yet embracing the notion that these two opposites can be true simultaneously can be a game changer in the healing process.

You can love your parents and still hold them accountable for their unacceptable behavior. The same applies for your spouse, your children, or your friends. You can love your body and still work to make changes that will help you feel healthier on a daily basis. You can believe in the God or Higher Power of your understanding and pray to them, while being angry at them. You can respect yourself and still take responsibility for the harm you have caused yourself and others. You can be a powerful person and still admit your powerlessness over an addiction. Can you see where embracing the power of dialectics can free you from a lot of mental turmoil?

Invitation: Spend 3-5 minutes in a practice of your choice (e.g., sitting meditation, walking meditation, or an expressive practice) and bring to mind an example of where two seemingly opposite things are both true in your life right now. Feel free to use any of the examples offered in the meditation. Notice whatever you notice as you contemplate. What might be keeping you from embracing the truth of both right now?

Prayer or Intention: Today I recognize that two things can be true at the same time, freeing me from the bondage of overthinking and overanalyzing.

APRIL 5

"It is not a question of overcoming all of our particular feelings, but of acknowledging and recognizing that we have these feelings without identifying ourselves with them." ~Fr. Thomas Keating

Being afraid of our feelings is not only a problem for people in recovery. Our cultural programing and scripts learned in the family of origin may have taught us that we're weak, feeble, or otherwise defective for expressing our emotions. Even the existence of feelings and emotions can be viewed as weak. When we carry this fear of feelings into the process of recovery and wellness, we can find ourselves very stuck.

Even certain recovery slogans like *our feelings are not facts* can prove very unhelpful. The intention of such a slogan is not to let our feelings get the best of us for even they can pass, yet in a vortex of trauma reaction, our feelings seem like our factual reality. What if, instead, we can learn to embrace a teaching like the one that opens this meditation—we can recognize and acknowledge our feelings without shame, instead of trying to stuff them away or medicate them—while also realize that our feelings do not define us?

Invitation: Spend 3-5 minutes in a practice of your choice (e.g., sitting meditation, walking meditation, or an expressive practice) and notice where the fears may exist around your relationship with fears and emotions. Then, spend some time repeating the phrase (to yourself, out loud, or paired with some expressive practice) *I honor my feelings, and I am not my feelings.* Both truths can exist at the same time.

Prayer or Intention: May I honor myself as an emotional being with a right to express my feelings while also recognizing that my feelings do not define me as a person.

APRIL 6

"If someone gives you a hammer, do you use it
to build a house? Or are your hands entranced by
the drumbeat, making you shatter some glass?"
~Jamie Marich, *The Drumbeat*

The hammer offers us a fascinating metaphor—we can use it to build or to destroy. It all depends on our intention, where we focus our energy, and how we are using the tool. Many of our talents can be seen in this way. They can be used for the greater good, in the service of our recovery, or they can be used to further our addiction and unhealthy behaviors, or even destroy others.

You may have heard it said before, "If you put half as much effort into recovery as you did into scrounging together what you needed to in order to get high, you'll have no problem staying sober!" While I can struggle with this saying sometimes as being a bit condescending, it's intent is fabulous and connected to our hammer metaphor. It speaks to the idea that so many life skills and talents like resourcefulness, intelligence, motivation, and power can be used in a variety of ways. How we choose to use them today can make or break our recovery.

Invitation: Spend 3-5 minutes in a practice of your choice (e.g., sitting meditation, walking meditation, or an expressive practice) and reflect how one of your talents can be used in the service of your recovery and wellness or in the service of your active addiction. What are some examples that surface and what are you noticing about how you use them today?

Prayer or Intention: Today I recognize that, like a hammer, my skills and talents can be used to build or to destroy. May my recovery and healing help me to choose wisely.

APRIL 7

"Moral excellence comes about as a result of habit.
We become just by doing just acts, temperate by doing
temperate acts, brave by doing brave acts." ~Aristotle

The phrase *moral inventory* is one of the hang-ups for people in recovery. For many of us, the word moral comes with a great deal of religious baggage that we would rather not unpack. Moreover, people like to throw the words *moral* and *immoral* around when they are trying to feel elevated on their perspective about an issue. Everybody would like to fancy themselves *right* on any given subject.

In working a Fourth Step, please consider the importance of putting any religious connotations aside, especially if your religious or spiritual history was a major factor in your trauma. Go with right vs. wrong. Where have you done right by yourself and others? Where have you done wrong, and what can you do differently next time? Having a sponsor or professional guide you through some of these potentially tricky questions may be an asset to you right now. As Mary, our dear pal in recovery would explain, virtues and morality are developed over time and in context. Even if your tendency is to focus on the wrongdoing and what that must mean about you as a person as you do this Fourth Step, know that the healthy actions of recovery will help you to grow as a moral person. Like many things in this journey, it takes time.

Invitation: Spend 3-5 minutes in a practice of your choice (e.g., sitting meditation, walking meditation, or an expressive practice) and contemplate the word *moral*. Notice any uncomfortable connotations that come up with it and notice how any of those uncomfortable associations may block you from moving forward, either in doing a Fourth Step or growing in your recovery. Consider how developing morality is something that happens over time, and how your experiences with unhealed trauma may have stunted that process for you. What are you noticing?

Prayer or Intention: Today I am committed to grow as a moral person, in the time and in the context that doing the next right thing for my recovery will allow.

APRIL 8

"Perfectionism is the voice of the oppressor." ~Anne Lamott

The drive to be perfect is a barrier that keeps many of us stuck on our journeys towards recovery and wholeness. Too often we put off addressing tasks in recovery—whether that be step work or seeking outside help—because we believe that we have to do them perfectly. Indeed, the primary reason that people procrastinate is out of fear that they won't be perfect.

For survivors of trauma, especially if we grew up in addicted or dysfunctional homes, this perfectionism complex can develop for legitimate reasons. For me, it was the belief that if I could just be a perfect daughter, than everything would be okay at home. As I progressed through school, because I wasn't popular or seemingly likable in a conventional sense, being a perfect student got me attention. For me, the great work of my recovery has involved shedding the scripts around the importance of perfection.

Invitation: Spend 3-5 minutes in a practice of your choice (e.g., sitting meditation, walking meditation, or an expressive practice) and contemplate your relationship with the concept of perfectionism. How is it keeping you stuck in your own life? What is its origin story in your life and how can going to that root help you address your perfectionist tendencies?

Prayer or Intention: Free me from the need, the desire, and the drive to be perfect today. May this open up my path ahead.

APRIL 9

"Compassion is the basis of morality."
~Arthur Schopenhauer

Compassion is a core principle of many spiritual paths. This is critical for people working the Twelve Steps. So often there is little compassion for the self that had all those thoughts and did all those actions that resulted in our ending up in recovery. When we are faced with ourselves at the end of our behaviors and attitudes, and at the beginning of a recovery program, we may not see ourselves with kindness. The steps are built to help us recover so that we might be helpful and compassionate to others.

In order to do that we need to have enough compassion for ourselves to work the program. When we are at Step 4, face-to-face with all we have said and done, we need to face it with great self-compassion. In the first three steps and throughout all the steps, we have the opportunity to cultivate this quality. In Step 4, as we approach a moral inventory, we can approach it with morality's very foundation – compassion.

Invitation: Spend 3-5 minutes in a practice of your choice (e.g., sitting meditation, walking meditation, or an expressive practice). Bring up a being or person for whom you have great compassion. Dedicate your practice to that being or person. A couple of minutes into it, see if you can point that compassionate energy toward yourself for the rest of the practice. If not, continue with your object of compassionate awareness.

Prayer or Intention: A moral inventory is not about judgment, it is about compassion. Today, I will walk and speak in the language of compassionate care.

APRIL 10

"Spiritual bypass is a tendency to use spiritual ideas and practices to sidestep or avoid facing unresolved emotional issues, psychological wounds, and unfinished developmental tasks."~John Welwood

Buddhist teacher John Welwood coined the term *spiritual bypass* to describe the tendency he saw within Buddhist communities to use spiritual practices as a bandage alone. While we have no doubt that spiritual or other recovery practices can be vital to our health and wellness overall, if we use them to *avoid* working on our stuff instead of using them to *assist us* in working on our stuff, we are short-changing ourselves. Religious and spiritual people are known to bypass for sure, and this includes what people may do with slogans and recovery concepts. "I've let go and let God," or "I'm staying in today" can be two common offenders that may appear helpful on the surface, but may keep us blocked in the long run.

We are not saying that spiritual practice, recovery concepts, or being positive as a way to cope with the troubles of the world are inherently bad. It's how we use them that can cause problems. And yes, even this tendency towards what some call *toxic positivity* can be discussed here too. Sometimes we can be too quick to see the silver lining in a situation or make a gratitude list without letting ourselves feel the pain that we need to feel in addition to working with spiritual or positive psychology skills.

Invitation: Spend 3-5 minutes in a practice of your choice (e.g., sitting meditation, walking meditation, or an expressive practice) and recall a time (or a present experience) where a coping skill that you use has value, but may also be keeping you blocked from doing the deepest of your healing work. What would it look like instead if you could use skills like prayer, meditation, and positive affirmations to *help you* dig in to the heart of your woundedness and feel the feelings that are keeping you stuck?

Prayer or Intention: Today I accept the challenge to use my spiritual and recovery practices to help me encounter, not avoid, what needs to be healed.

APRIL 11

"As long as you keep secrets and suppress information,
you are fundamentally at war with yourself . . . The critical
issue is allowing yourself to know what you know. That takes
an enormous amount of courage." ~Bessel van der Kolk

Before we had the language of trauma recovery to go with the language of 12-step recovery, we would hear reports of many people relapsing on their substances or behaviors in the face of the Fourth Step. From a trauma recovery perspective, this makes a great deal of sense. The work of the trauma survivor before recovery consists of finding ways to avoid or suppress the memories, emotions, and body sensations that come with the trauma.

This is not only totally understandable; it is actually a way of surviving in this world. Therefore, the courage to know what we know, sit with it, work with it, admit and accept it is profound. This brings our need for support during the Fourth Step process to a whole new level. We need people, places and things to support us as we do what is essentially some of our deepest trauma work.

Invitation: Spend 3-5 minutes in a practice of your choice (e.g., sitting meditation, walking meditation, or an expressive practice). During your meditation, visualize the people, places, and things that currently support you in your recovery work. Visualize them either surrounding you in a circle or even providing you with a place to rest.

Prayer or Intention: I know now that the courage to face my trauma story is a profound courage. Let me find the support I need to do my inventory work.

APRIL 12

"If you survived your childhood you have enough to write
about for the rest of your life."~Flannery O'Connor

The Fourth Step asks us to take inventory and for many of us that
involves writing. The practice of writing can be a scary prospect
under circumstances that don't involve trauma and addiction, with the
doomed condition of "writer's block" keeping us stuck. The key to
writing is to just do it, even if the words don't make sense and start as
jibberish. Keep your hand moving and eventually the dam will break.

A helpful way for many of us on this path to reframe Steps 4 and
5 is to see them as putting our story down on paper and than sharing
it with at least one other human being. Guided by truth and intention
to recover, know that these steps are truly yours to take. Just as your
stories are truly yours to tell.

Invitation: Spend 3-5 minutes in a practice of your choice (e.g.,
sitting meditation, walking meditation, or an expressive practice) and
consider this idea of viewing the Fourth and Fifth Steps as a process of
storytelling. What are the qualities of a good story that speak to you?
Perhaps use this guiding question can assist you wherever you are at
with these steps today.

Prayer or Intention: May I be guided to write and to share my story
honestly and, if possible, with joy.

APRIL 13

"One does not become enlightened by imagining figures
of light, but by making the darkness conscious.
The latter procedure, however, is disagreeable and
therefore not popular." ~Carl Jung

I am not sure I have seen a better description of the travails of Step 4. The idea of facing our darkness, our dark sides or our dark memories seems infinitely counterintuitive to the survival mind. However, it seems that experience has borne out this truth. The good news though is that the Fourth Step is the Fourth Step, not the First Step. "Doing the waltz" of Steps 1, 2, and 3, as suggested by my sponsor Jim early on, not only prepares us for the difficulty of doing inventory, but provides some of the foundational content we will be looking at.

We cannot help but see some of the darkness that we exacerbated through our pre-recovery behaviors or perhaps we ignored it, trying to make it invisible to ourselves. The awareness, acceptance, and call to action of the first three steps gives us a daily practice that at a certain juncture in our recovery give us the knowledge and the strength to investigate the darkness. We can safely shine the light, with the help of others lending their light to it as well through support and identification.

Invitation: Spend 3-5 minutes in a practice of your choice (e.g., sitting meditation, walking meditation, or an expressive practice). Notice where you are in your program, and if you are ready to do Step 4. If you have already started it or done it, see what you find are the benefits of doing so or having done so.

Prayer or Intention: Today, let me not be afraid of the darkness, as turning toward it will bring me to health and recovery.

APRIL 14

"Underneath anger is pain, your pain . . . Anger is strength
and it can be an anchor, giving temporary structure to
the nothingness of loss." ~Elisabeth Kübler Ross

Many trauma survivors have found themselves in a great deal of
difficulty when confronted with Step 4. One difficulty—it asks us to do
trauma work, sometimes without proper support for such a deep and
difficult process. Another major problem is the perceived demonization
of anger found in some of the 12-step literature. Indeed, resentment
is the number one offender. However, resentment is just one form of
anger, a form that has coagulated and become habitual. It is not the
anger that is the problem, it is the maladaptive processing of the anger
that has allowed it to fester and wreak havoc. Resentment is born not
of anger as much as it is developed through repressing it or habitual
unhealthy expressions of it.

A critical component of a trauma-informed Fourth Step is an
exploration of our personal relationship to anger. If we don't find
where it is useful as an anchor or a way to set boundaries, and we go
straight to finding "our part," we will be leapfrogging over the true
trauma work that can bring sustainable healing.

Invitation: Spend 3-5 minutes in a practice of your choice (e.g.,
sitting meditation, walking meditation, or an expressive practice).
Notice any anger that you are holding. Utilizing your practice, notice
where the edges of the anger are. Notice what the anger is doing
to protect you. Notice the beginning, middle, and end of the angry
feeling or sensation.

Prayer or Intention: Today let me honor the power and importance
of my anger as a setter of boundaries and a way of getting important
needs met. Let me find healthy ways to channel, heal, and express
anger.

APRIL 15

"Resentment is the number one offender."
~*Alcoholics Anonymous*, p. 64

This well-known teaching from the "Big Book" of *Alcoholics Anonymous* can be worded another way: unhealed trauma is the number one offender. When our traumatic wounding remains unaddressed, we set ourselves up for a variety of misery, which could include the possibility of relapse. We can better understand the reason for this link by breaking down what the word resentment means. *Resentment* comes from the Latin root combinations of *re* (again) + *sentire* (to feel). So when we have a resentment, we are feeling something all over again.

Looking at resentments through this lens can be less shaming and fundamentally more productive. When we notice that a resentment toward someone or something is brewing, it's either because we are being hurt in the moment or cannot stop feeling the hurt. More likely, the source of the hurt is something very old, of which the current person or situation is reminding us. While the resentment prayer suggested in *Alcoholics Anonymous* can be helpful in dealing with resentment, it may not be a viable solution if prayer is not part of your daily practice due to your belief system. The resentment could also be so caught up in an unhealed experience, addressing that origin may be a vital part of the trauma work you need to explore.

Invitation: Spend 3-5 minutes in a practice of your choice (e.g., sitting meditation, walking meditation, or an expressive practice) and notice how resentments affect you in recovery. If you are actively in a resentment today, use that for your reflection. Consider asking yourself the question, "What is this really about?" Allow the time in silence to reveal more of the answer to you.

Prayer or Intention: Show me what feelings I need to feel today and what wounds I need to heal in order to be free of resentment.

APRIL 16

"We need the courage to learn from our past
and not live in it." ~Sharon Salzberg

Indeed, Step 4 calls for a great deal of courage. Where do we get that courage? Is it all from faking it until we make it? That may not be enough or even doable for trauma survivors. The hope is that we have garnered some new courage from working the first three steps. The first three steps orient us into the present with an eye toward the future. The Fourth Step encourages us then to look into our past for the lessons and the blessings, so that we might chart a new course going forward. Those of us who use the Serenity Prayer regularly know that we have been in a process of building acceptance, courage, and wisdom.

The courage to change the things we can, in the arc of the steps, is well represented by the courage to begin the process of Steps 4 through 9. Through these steps we are able to identify the things we can change. Step 4 thus allows us to begin to leave those no longer useful aspects of our past behind in a trauma-sensitive way. Yes, all of that happened, all of those resentments have been felt, and now in Step 4 we are looking at it all with compassionate awareness, built from the courage we see in our fellows and our own new courage to grow and change.

Invitation: Spend 3-5 minutes in a practice of your choice (e.g., sitting meditation, walking meditation, or an expressive practice). Let yourself breathe in acceptance. Let yourself breathe out courage. Consider adding lion breath, the practice of fully releasing the tongue out and opening the eyes fully as you make a roar, to your courageous out breath!

Prayer or Intention: I have new courage brought by both faith and awareness. I will go through this day leaning into my courage.

APRIL 17

" . . . courage can seldom be manifested in simple ways."
~John F. Kennedy, *Profiles in Courage*

Making the choice to get sober and well is a courageous act. Continuing to stay the course with your healing requires a daily, courageous commitment. Many individuals in recovery are quick to shame themselves as cowards because of choices they made in the past. In taking inventory, it's possible that when we reflect back, there are things we could have done differently. Consider that it takes courage to even look at oneself in this manner and recognize that we now have the power to act differently in the future.

We've heard it explained in the rooms of recovery that courage is feeling afraid and yet doing it anyway. That "it" can be whatever needs to be worked on in your recovery today. The "it" can also mean stepping up and taking a risk on tasks like becoming a full and present parent again, going back to school, or starting a new career opportunity. There are many ways to practice courageousness, sometimes in ways that aren't obvious on the surface. It's natural to be afraid. As a person committed to recovery, armed with a set of skills and resources to handle life more effectively, you are empowered to live with courage.

Invitation: Spend 3-5 minutes in a practice of your choice (e.g., sitting meditation, walking meditation, or an expressive practice) and contemplate the saying that *courage is feeling the fear and doing it anyway.* Then ask yourself, what are five ways in which I have put courage into action this week? Consider jotting your responses down in your journal or notebook. You can also consider putting what you came up with on your phone (notes section or lock screen) or on a piece of paper to keep somewhere strategic. These can serve as reminders of your ability to practice courage on days when you are feeling afraid.

Prayer or Intention: If courage is feeling the fear and doing it anyway, may I be empowered with the resources that I need today to put courage into action.

APRIL 18

"Your heart is a sacred place, not a dustbin.
Let the garbage be out of it." ~Priyanka

There is a very important reality I learned about garbage removal as a kid growing up in the west. The garbage man is no going to come into the house to remove it for you. One of my chores was to remove the garbage from the kitchen to the garage each day where a larger bin resided. Then once a week we took the garbage out to the curb. The bottom line? It's our responsibility to move the garbage so that it can be taken away.

So what happens if we don't take the garbage out? The cans overflow, it smells, it rots, flies swarm, and it's an all-around gross experience. All of these things will happen if the garbage is left to fester. There is a very powerful lesson here for recovery that speaks to the power of the inventory steps. These steps are designed to help us take the garbage out so that it can be removed, clearing the way for us to live a more comfortable life. To be clear, these steps are never about seeing yourself as garbage. Rather, they help us work to remove the accumulations that no longer serve us.

Invitation: Come into a seated position that you can sustain for the next 3-5 minutes, although lying down is an acceptable modification. Bring into focus a picture of a garbage can, bin, or basket that you use in your living space. If you have a difficult time visualizing, do this meditation actually looking at the can, bin, or basket in your living space. Imagine that the can is overflowing with one week of garbage. Then two weeks of garbage. Then three. What are you noticing?

Prayer or Intention: May I be motivated today and every day to take the garbage out.

APRIL 19

Brahmacharya: conduct consistent
with Brahma (the creative life force)

Trauma survivors in recovery generally have a great deal of healing required in the area of sex and sexuality, particularly if our trauma involved us being harmed in this way. Whether it was due to sexual abuse or being torn to shreds by your religious background for your sexual conduct or your sexual preference and identity, the potential blocks are numerous. Many of us come to recovery very ashamed of our sexual conduct. Sometimes simultaneously, we may also have little awareness about how our sexual behavior or withdrawal from the sexual aspects of ourselves is related to unhealed trauma and addiction.

The "Big Book" of *Alcoholics Anonymous* offers an inventory style called the sex ideal, although in our experience, this can trip up many trauma survivors because it can feel a little too much like the rigid morality of many a religious institution. This is where the yogic *yama*, or lifestyle observance, of *Brahmacharya* can come in handy. *Brahmacharya* is not about celibacy—rather, it challenges us to ask ourselves if our sexual conduct is *stilling* or *not stilling* to us in any given moment. Other ways to look at this include, is my current relationship to sex and sexuality causing me peace or causing me stress? Is my current relationship to sex and sexuality serving my recovery growth or blocking it?

Invitation: Spend 3-5 minutes in a practice of your choice (e.g., sitting meditation, walking meditation, or an expressive practice) and use any of the questions offered in the meditation to engage in an inventory about your current relationship with sex and sexuality. Even if you are not sexually active, bear in mind that you are still a sexual being and all of the same questions apply. Notice what you notice and consider going over your inventory with a sponsor, helping professional, or other trusted member of your support network.

Prayer or Intention: Today I honor that I am a sexual being and this creative life force can enrich my recovery, if I am willing to ask the hard questions of myself.

APRIL 20

"A man should never be ashamed to own that he has been
in the wrong, which is but saying in other words that he is
wiser today than he was yesterday." ~Alexander Pope

The Fourth Step is revolutionary for those of us in recovery. There
is so much shame wrapped up in trauma, addiction, and our other
difficulties. So, the idea of finding our way out of the shame related
to the admission of our dilemmas, and moving into a process of
admitting all of it to others as a way of building wisdom, is an earth
shaking, life altering event. The first three steps are like going to the
gym and developing the muscles of admitting, accepting, and taking
action.

And then in Step 4, we take profound action on our own behalf.
We let go of the shame, we admit the worst, and then in the Fifth Step
we are able to further reduce the shame by sharing it all with a trusted
other. All of this is in the spirit of building a new wisdom, the wisdom
of the recovery path.

Invitation: Spend 3-5 minutes in a practice of your choice (e.g.,
sitting meditation, walking meditation, or an expressive practice).
Notice whatever shameful feelings you might still have. Notice where
they are in your body. Focus on the body sensations and see if there is
movement of any kind. If not, see if you can notice it all with as little
judgment as possible.

Prayer or Intention: Today I will try to let go of shame. I can do
this through action, the action of building wisdom through admitting
my difficulties.

APRIL 21

"Some days I feel like I have a foot in both worlds,
yet never really belonging to either." ~Kate Brown
(first openly bisexual governor in U.S. history)

Feeling divided is a common experience for many of us. These feelings can show up in a variety of ways depending on where we are at in our recovery journey. Sometimes we can feel torn between our old life and our new one. At other times, the different aspects of ourselves can feel at war with each other. Perhaps you've struggled with conflict between honoring your free spirited rebellious soul and accepting a need for discipline in your spiritual or recovery practice. Maybe you feel deep connection to your family of origin with its triggers and dysfunctions while also recognizing a need to nourish new connections outside of that sphere.

There are no easy answers to this one. Many people discover that when they feel torn, the pain is too great and they have to pick a side. This choice may be critical if your sobriety and mental health are at stake. Other times the answer may be to learn from what both sides of a struggle have to say and work toward building a bridge of wisdom between the conflicting sides. This is often the best solution when we're dealing with disagreements between our parts of self, because they can all contribute something valuable. Usually the people who have worked the hardest to reconcile their inner divisions are those who know how to build bridges of connection in the world at large. The conflict can be transformed into a gift.

Invitation: Working with your internal splits and divides lends itself well to inventory. Evaluating these areas of conflict can help prepare you for Step 4. Similarly, doing an inventory in the style of the Fourth Step can be useful as you address these divisions. To prepare, spend 3-5 minutes in a practice of your choice (e.g., sitting meditation, walking meditation, or an expressive practice) and contemplate how you may be feeling pulled or torn today. How can recognizing these divides help to prepare me for deeper inventory?

Prayer or Intention: Today I recognize that the areas where I feel torn, split, or divided have a great deal to teach me about myself. May I take the best course of action to address based on what I learn.

APRIL 22

"Sometimes I wake up in the morning before going
off to a shoot, and I think, I can't do this. I'm a fraud."
~Kate Winslet

Many people in new recovery and long-term recovery alike describe themselves as having *impostor syndrome*. This term has become quite popular in the vernacular to reference the feeling many of us have— what if they find out that I'm not really good enough? What if they find out I'm faking it, that I don't really know what I'm doing? What if they regret putting their faith in me? Trust us, no one is immune to imposter syndrome. If you don't believe us, go to your favorite Internet search engine and look up celebrity quotes on imposter syndrome. You'll see that Kate Winslet is just one of many talented, successful people who struggle.

In our experience, the people who are most plagued by imposter syndrome generally are very talented, smart, or capable. The legacy of long-term, unhealed trauma and its impact has riddled them (and us) with fear. Fear is what keeps us paralyzed. Fear is what tells is that we are not good enough and that people will regret choosing us. How would our lives be different if we could let the fear dissolve and transform into spirit of faith and trust? Faith in ourselves, and trust in the process?

Invitation: Spend 3-5 minutes in a practice of your choice (e.g., sitting meditation, walking meditation, or an expressive practice) and notice where fear may be keeping you stuck. If you specifically relate to having impostor syndrome, what is the direct connection you see between the fear and the doubt you can have in yourself and your abilities? If you are able and willing, notice where fear tends to show up in your body, and then see if you can take a few deep breaths and send breath to that place or those places in your body. Feel free to share your discoveries on this invitation with a trauma-friendly sponsor, support group member, or a professional.

Prayer or Intention: May the fear that keeps me stuck dissolve and be replaced with faith and trust—faith in myself and trust in the process.

APRIL 23

"It's not what you look at that matters, it's what you see."
~Henry David Thoreau

Many of the great conflicts in the world happen because of conflicting perspectives. Even in the presence of facts, people's telling of history is based largely on their perspective. Their lenses can be colored by their own belief systems, resentments, or a combination of the two. As students of history, we are both amazed by the power of perspective and its influence on how narratives get told in certain settings.

However, perhaps the greatest conflict that skewed perspective can cause is an internal one. Unhealed trauma can adversely impact how we see ourselves based on the negative or maladaptive things we learned about ourselves at the time of an experience. We may take responsibility where it is not our responsibility to take. We may believe that we are unsafe in the present, even if all the evidence around us suggests we are safe. We may feel like we have no choices now because we have no choices then. The Fourth and Fifth Steps are ideally designed to help us realign our perspectives, helping us to take responsibility for harms we have caused while also seeing that not everything is our fault. However, if we've not started the journey of trauma healing, approaching Steps 4 and 5 can feel too overwhelming because when we look at ourselves, we only see the bad.

Invitation: Many sponsors and recovery guides emphasize that part of taking a moral inventory in the Fourth Step is to recognize that you are not *all bad*. Part of taking an inventory is to look at the good stuff—where you have done right by people in life, how you have shared your good qualities with others, and when you have been aware of the good within you but have been hesitant to show it. For this exercise, consider taking an inventory of positives. If it feels like you can't, start with looking at the evidence of where you have been resilient to survive this far. Consider seeking out support from a trauma-friendly sponsor, member of your support group, or a professional if you find yourself stuck with this invitation. Take it from us, though; there are things you will be able to identify if you don't fight the process.

Prayer or Intention: May I see my life and myself with new perspective today.

APRIL 24

"Extract the quack grass for the good plants to grow."
~Leonardo DaVinci

Approaching the inventory steps conjures up doom for a lot of people in recovery, especially if you have a history of unhealed trauma. You may have heard horror stories from others about how tough it is to work Steps 4 and 5, or the sheer legacy of shame resulting from your traumatic experiences may make these steps feel impossible. A different way to approach them is to think of a gardener or farmer who needs to do some necessary weeding or pruning. Such practices are vital in order for richer growth to take place.

How might my attitude towards Steps 4 and 5 differ if I can think of the inventory in Four and the practice of sharing in Five as clearing away what is standing in the way of my growth?

Invitation: Spend 3-5 minutes in a practice of your choice (e.g., sitting meditation, walking meditation, or an expressive practice) and reflect on what your intentions and goals are for growth in your recovery process. What needs to be cleared away in order to achieve this growth? Can framing Steps 4 and 5 in this manner assist me in more fully and less fearfully approaching them?

Prayer or Intention: Let the legacy of my past that is blocking my growth be cleared away today and on the path ahead. Grant me the willingness to take the action required for the clearing.

APRIL 25

Recovery Capital: the quality of internal
and external resources that one can bring to bear
on the initiation and maintenance of recovery.
~William Cloud & Robert Granfield

Recovery capital is everything positive, good, or adaptive that you have going for you in the service of your recovery. Recovery capital can be tangible (e.g., a place to live, a job, transportation, insurance, access to meetings and a sponsor) or intangible (e.g., motivation, willingness). This concept is vitally important as we widen the scope of recovery resources past the Twelve Steps alone. In taking a strengths-based perspective with ourselves and with individuals we serve, assessing for recovery capital can be a helpful adjunct to the Fourth Step.

This strengths-based approach can be described as *this is what I have done right and what I have going for me*. It's vital to people in recovery from traumatic wounding as we tend to see ourselves as totally worthless or defective,—at least at first. Making a simple inventory of one's assets and debits in recovery can be a solid skill. You may even consider doing it in advance of taking or writing out a formal Fourth Step.

Invitation: Take out a sheet of paper or your journal and make an assets and debits column. Whether you are new to recovery or have been at this a while, taking an inventory of this nature can be useful to see where you stand. You may even surprise yourself. If your tendency is to beat yourself up or be unkind to yourself, if you notice that your assets column is smaller than your debits, try to focus on at least one thing in that column and build from there. Be assured that many people come in to recovery feeling like they have little.

Prayer or Intention: Today I appreciate that the things I have going for me in the service of my recovery can come in many forms. I will build from what I have.

APRIL 26

"We become traumatized when our ability to respond
to a perceived threat is in some way overwhelmed. This inability
to adequately respond can impact us in obvious ways, as well
as ways that are subtle." ~Peter Levine

Often we are advised to attend "the meeting after the meeting." It is here in the less boundaried environment that we can hear less trauma-informed talk. One common misconception heard these days is a feeling that trauma or PTSD are overused to describe what we are healing from. The good news in this case is that trauma has entered the mainstream discussion, and people are using the verbiage. The bad news is that some people hold onto the old belief that one must be in a natural disaster or in combat to experience trauma.

Traumatic stress is a function of the nature of the event. It describes the subtle or not so subtle ways that we become overwhelmed by perceived threats. This can lead to, amongst other things, the cycle of addictive behaviors. Don't let anyone tell you that your trauma or adverse life events are not real, or that their effects are not real. This kind of shaming could add another level of trauma to your experience. Find those in the program and outside help that can honor this aspect of your journey. Allow yourself the space and integrity to work through your Fourth Step with these guides, not those who would judge how painful your pain is. Together we can heal from the traumatic stress that both causes and is caused by addiction.

Invitation: Utilizing your current practice whether sitting, lying down, or in motion, allow yourself to acknowledge the trauma or adverse life events that brought you to recovery. If it helps to visualize your fellows on your journey, bring them into your meditation.

Prayer or Intention: As I journey through Step 4, I will look for those guides who will honor my trauma recovery. These may be sponsors, therapists, spiritual guides, and/or friends on the path.

APRIL 27

"When a person offended us we said to ourselves, 'This is a sick man. How can I be helpful to him. God save me from being angry. Thy will be done'." ~*Alcoholics Anonymous*, p. 67

This passage from the "Big Book" of *Alcoholics Anonymous* is sometimes called the Fourth Step prayer. While the word *sick* has always struck me as a little judgmental, I do find the prayer to be useful overall when I am struggling with a resentment toward another. Instead of brewing in the resentment, what if I could channel that energy in the direction of goodwill? Such an action is far bigger than simply taking the higher ground; it's a step in reclaiming our power.

One of the greatest powers that we have as human beings is deciding where we direct our energy. The next time you feel overwhelmed in resentment and hurt at the hands of another (which may be happening for you today), notice how much energy it seems to be zapping out of your body. The more we focus on the hurt or resentment, the more our energy depletes. If you have the willingness, spend a fraction of that energetic focus sending a prayer or good wish to the person who has offended you. Use this prayer from the "Big Book" to help you if you need more structure, or proceed to the Invitation.

Invitation: In the practice of Loving Kindness meditation, we use four main verses: *May I be free from suffering, may I have physical happiness, may I have emotional happiness, may I have ease of well-being.* Spend some time in a sitting position, taking a few breaths to center, and say these verses for yourself. After a period of time to reflect, see if you can send the same verses to a person you resent or find challenging today: *May you be free from suffering, may you have physical happiness, may you have emotional happiness, may you have ease of well-being.* If this feels like too much for where you are at today, consider praying for or sending out an energetic intention for the willingness to do this practice for the other at some point in the future.

Prayer or Intention: Today I am empowered to send my Loving Kindness to the people who offend me. In so doing, I will loosen the grip of resentment.

APRIL 28

"Spiritual practice is about transformation, but it's also, and more importantly, about working with what is."
~angel Kyodo williams

The word recovery has a number of meanings and applications. One way to look at recovery is as a process of recovering what was already ours. Due to traumatic and adverse experiences throughout our lives, we may have a sense of a fractured self. What the Twelve Steps can be helpful with is giving recovery a simple structure. First, we find the fractured pieces. Then we examine them. Finally, we come to accept all of these parts of ourselves: those that we like and those that we don't like as much. And then, we can continue the process of transformation.

The process of transformation is informed and created by, as Reverend angel says, "working with what is." It is only through this wholehearted examination and acceptance of what is that we can continue on with the life-long transformation project.

Invitation: Spend 3-5 minutes in a practice of your choice (e.g., sitting meditation, walking meditation, or an expressive practice). Notice what your truth is in this moment. What is your true emotion? What is your true body sensation? Notice these and notice any movement in them during your meditation.

Prayer or Intention: I will walk on the path of transformation. I will notice, examine, accept, and act upon what is.

APRIL 29

"What you resist not only persists,
but will grow in size." ~Carl Jung

In the change process, resistance is normal. Even if our lives have spiraled down to a miserable place, a great deal of fear can be involved in taking the steps toward doing something different. The words resist and resistance can feel particularly ugly to us, especially if professionals, sponsors, or family members have constantly labeled us *resistant*. As one of our colleagues observed when she came into the field, "I don't particularly like the word *resistance* because all resistance is about something underneath."

The original Carl Jung teaching, often abbreviated in modern usage as *what resists, persists* nicely aligns with our teachings on trauma healing. Another way to look at this idea is what you do not heal will remain, and will likely grow into more of a problem. Just as a wound that doesn't get treated may get infected and cause complications, our resistance can fester. When we notice resistance, instead of judging ourselves for it, can we learn to look at what we resist as an opportunity for healing a wound?

Invitation: If movement is available to you today, come up to your feet (although this sequence can also be done in a seated position). Stand tall and look straight ahead. Move your right arm out to the side and shoulder height. Then, move the right arm across your body but keep the hips and shoulders square in front of you as you continue to look straight ahead. Then take the left arm and press it into the top of the right arm to create some resistance. Hold this stretch as long as you are able to today, then release it, noticing every sensation along the way. Really take some time to savor the aftereffect of the release. Did sinking into the resistance *and* letting it go allow for something pleasant in your body? Be sure to repeat this process on the other side.

Prayer or Intention: Today may I learn what my areas of resistance have to teach me and also be open to the healing power of letting them go.

APRIL 30

"The wound is the place where the light enters you."
~Rumi

While addiction can be a form of self-injury, there are scores of people in recovery who have hurt themselves in a variety of other ways. Cutting, head banging, and self-mutilation of various kinds may be a part of your story. We often develop these behaviors in reaction to traumatic wounding in order to feel something, or to give an outward expression to our internal pain. In my experience, hurting myself was a way of inflicting my own punishment before others could.

Now that you are getting sober or have been sober a while, there may be a struggle with some of these behaviors as you work to heal your trauma. This experience can be normal, especially when emotions heighten. Even if you do not directly struggle with the forms of self-injury mentioned here, you may relate to being unkind or harmful to yourself in order to cope. How can I send kindness and love to the hurts that need healing, instead of further harm?

Invitation: Spend 3-5 minutes in a practice of your choice (e.g., sitting meditation, walking meditation, or an expressive practice) and notice where you may still be punishing, harming, or otherwise injuring yourself in recovery. Picture yourself, however that may look for you, sending love and kindness to those areas of your body, heart, and soul.

Prayer or Intention: Today I commit to sending love and kindness to those parts of me I have traditionally harmed and punished.

MAY 1

"Always tell the truth, and you'll never be afraid
of anything in your life." ~Neem Karoli Baba

So much of Step 5 is about telling the truth. Telling the truth about how drinking, drug use, or other problematic behaviors affect ourselves and others can be very difficult. After all, addiction and its many manifestations generally flourish in a petri dish of lies and deceit. So while telling the truth may feel like hell to start with, it is a simple—if not easy—act that can go a long way. The Twelve Steps are guides for helping us tell the truth.

Rest in the assurance that you are exactly where you need to be at right now, whether you are just starting your recovery journey or taking on a new challenge in recovery. If your change process is built on a foundation of truth, as the wise sage says, you will have nothing to fear.

Invitation: Spend 3-5 minutes in a practice of your choice (e.g., sitting meditation, walking meditation, or an expressive practice) and bring up the word truth. Perhaps notice your breath as you hang out with the word truth, resting into the idea that "I am breathing. That is true." If this is where you need to start, this is where you need to start. Any time you feel yourself struggling with being truthful or admitting the truth in the next few days, come back to the breath.

Prayer or Intention: May the challenge to change that I am accepting today be built on a foundation of truth.

MAY 2

"Shame needs three things to grow exponentially in our lives: secrecy, silence, and judgment."~Brené Brown

This Brené Brown teaching is becoming a modern classic, as it describes the perfect recipe for the cocktail of shame. The shame cocktail impacts everyone I've ever met in recovery (and I rarely use such absolute language). It impacts us more than any mixed beverage. While I reject some of the shaming language around the slogan "we are only as sick as our secrets," a solution does exists in the act of naming the things we carry inside.

The key seems to be voicing or otherwise expressing what we hold in corners of our hearts to someone we trust. As Brené Brown indicates in her teaching, this needs to be someone who will not judge us; someone who will respect our human-ness; someone who, although they may hold us accountable and challenge us, will honor our vulnerability above anything else.

Invitation: Spend 3-5 minutes in a practice of your choice (e.g., sitting meditation, walking meditation, or an expressive practice) to examine the Brené Brown teaching that inspires this meditation. What ingredients (secrecy, silence, judgment) seem to be the strongest in your shame cocktail today? Is there anyone in your life or circle of support right now that seems safe and non-judgmental enough to witness as you express something you've been holding inside?

Prayer or Intention: May breaking the silence with a safe, non-judgmental witness begin to heal the impact of shame in my life. If such a person does not yet exist, may I be open to let them showing up in my life.

MAY 3

"Confront the dark parts of yourself, and work
to banish them with illumination and forgiveness.
Your willingness to wrestle with your demons will
cause your angels to sing." ~August Wilson

Recovery asks a lot of us. However, in comparison to the work required the payoffs are profound. Trauma work has traditionally been considered a dive into the darkness involving wrestling with demons that has no end. And the notion that our dilemmas and difficulties are what define us is absolutely false. In fact, it is our resources and resilience that actually define us—what August Wilson might call our singing angels.

We have a birthright of resources and resilience, though much of that might have been covered up by the trauma and despair in our lives. Now we can meet that story and those parts of ourselves with the assistance of the steps and our fellows, and come out the other side with our internal resources identified and strengthened, and with new resilience born of the reprocessing of our trauma.

Invitation: Spend 3-5 minutes in a practice of your choice (e.g., sitting meditation, walking meditation, or an expressive practice). Notice just one dark part of yourself you are working on today. And then illuminate it with one positive resource you have at your disposal at this time.

Prayer or Intention: Today, let me notice my resilience and cultivate my resources so that I might be able to safely and successfully move past my past.

MAY 4

"Sometimes people let the same problem make them miserable for years when they could just say, *So what*. That's one of my favorite things to say. *So what*." ~Andy Warhol

I had a sponsee who used to call me every day. Almost every day, she would download her difficulties of the day, and I would just listen. Eventually she would run out of things to tell me. There would be a pause. And then she would say, "Oh well." That was her way of proclaiming acceptance. All these things happened, all of them had an impact on her, and there was nothing she could do to change the fact that they had indeed happened. But she could change her relationship to them by sharing them, and then proclaiming *Oh well*. This is similar to Warhol's *So what*.

They both represent acceptance of what is, and change the relationship to the information. This is not about denial, this is actually leaning into the reality and seeing how we can build resilience and move on. Dedicated trauma recovery helps us to organically arrive at an embodied state of, *Oh well, So what*.

Invitation: Spend 3-5 minutes in a practice of your choice (e.g., sitting meditation, walking meditation, or an expressive practice). On the in-breath, use the mantra, *Oh Well*. On the out-breath, *So What*.

Prayer or Intention: Today, I will allow acceptance to guide my relationship to what has happened, what is happening, and how I respond to it all.

MAY 5

"The saint, therefore, is sanctified not only by fasting
but also by eating when he should eat. He is not only
sanctified by his prayers in the darkness of night,
but by the sleep that he takes . . ." ~Thomas Merton

What is true for the saint is true for us as well. When we take care
of our basic needs, we are taking holy recovery action. Many people
in recovery can get the idea that we have to become saints. They
believe that a saint is one who fasts, prays, and meditates for hours,
and is somehow able to engage only in acts considered by the general
populace to be holy and spiritual. What a relief when we realize that
naps are spiritual! Merton points us toward a notion that has been
expressed in many different ways in many different spiritual and
psychological traditions: that we are perfect just as we are, that we
are all children of God, that we are all spiritual beings living a human
experience, that we are not horrible people.

When in doubt about my recovery, I can always take a simple
action toward self-care. We can find our resilience, our internal
resources. We can take another small step on our path, knowing that
both our prayers and our sleep are essential.

Invitation: For 5 minutes (or more or less if you like) do a modified
walking meditation. Begin by walking the traditional 6 to 8 feet in one
direction. Meditate on the theme of "action." When you get to the
end of your path, stand in mountain pose for at least 10-20 breaths,
contemplating "rest." Then turn around and continue walking. Notice
the rhythm of action and rest.

Prayer or Intention: Today may I notice the spirituality inherent in
my simple self-care actions.

MAY 6

"There is something about catharsis
that is very important." ~Glenn Close

You've likely heard the word *catharsis* thrown around recovery and healing circles a time or two. Your therapist or sponsor may have spoken about the healing power of catharsis. Your vision of it may be from a movie, seeing a character scream and shout, or having a huge emotional release like Matt Damon in *Good Will Hunting*. Catharsis is one of those words that people tend to evaluate based on what they think it *should* be. In reality there are many different avenues for having a catharsis—through art, through writing, through movement, through therapy, through conversation, through tears, through prayer, through step work, or through screaming your lungs out, or any combination of these—all plausible avenues. And this is a short list.

A cathartic experience is anything that helps you *to cleanse*. Like many words we explore in the *Trauma and the 12 Steps* work, the word origin of catharsis is telling. It simply comes from the Greek meaning *to cleanse*. By this insight, you may do some of your deepest work taking a bath or immersing yourself in water! Either literally or metaphorically, you can approach whatever helps you cleanse yourself—body, mind, and soul—as an experience in catharsis.

Invitation: Spend 3-5 minutes in a practice of your choice (e.g., sitting meditation, walking meditation, or an expressive practice) and focus on the word *cleanse*. What helps you to feel cleansed physically? A good shower? A work out where you sweat away the toxins? Make this personal for you, then reflect on how you can translate that metaphor to the emotional healing work you must do today and on the path ahead.

Prayer or Intention: Today, I appreciate the power of cleansing in all of its contexts. This is the healing power of catharsis.

MAY 7

"When we honestly ask ourselves which person in our lives means the most to us, we often find that it is those who, instead of giving advice, solutions, or cures, have chosen rather to share our pain and touch our wounds with a warm and tender hand." ~Henri Nouwen

Henri Nouwen, the priest who coined the term *the wounded healer*, gave us a great deal to contemplate about the nature of wounds and wound healing. This teaching of his is one of my favorites that helps us to live in the solution about how to work with others who have been wounded. As a reminder, trauma simply means wound. So in embracing our work with others in a more trauma-sensitive way, we can ask the question, "How can I more effectively be with wounded people? Especially if I am privileged enough to hear a Fifth Step?"

Indeed, a major part of the solution is to consider the ministry of your own presence. The kind of person you are, how you are able to *just be* with others is imperative. So often our focus is on what we need to do or say. As Nouwen suggests, these pieces of advice, solutions, or cures are not what is most helpful. The person you *are*—absent any forcing, striving, or trying too hard—can be the most powerful force in helping another to heal. If you are in the other role and are currently seeking someone to hear your Fifth Step, do you have someone available who meets Nouwen's description?

Invitation: Spend 3-5 minutes in a practice of your choice (e.g., sitting meditation, walking meditation, or an expressive practice) contemplating the opening teaching from Henri Nouwen. As he prompts, honestly ask yourself: Who have been the people in your life who have meant the most in your healing journey? In considering their presence in your life, what is it or was it about their presence that most impacted you? How can you translate this into your work with others?

Prayer or Intention: May I be a healing presence in the lives of others today, just as others have been a healing presence for me.

MAY 8

"The moral inventory is a cool examination of damages
that occured to us during life and a sincere effort to look at them
in a true perspective. This has the effect of taking the ground
glass out of us, the emotional substance that still cuts and inhibits."
~Bill Wilson, *Daily Reflections*

The first three steps are a way to find our resilience and our resources. Then Step 4 allows us to pierce through the dust with a loving eye, and Step 5 helps us to have it witnessed in that same spirit. Then we are able to work Steps 6 and 7 to integrate our resilience, resources, and the new found healing of our trauma and adverse life events.

All of this begins with our building resilience and trauma-resistant skills in Steps 1 through 3, looking toward reality in Step 4, and then accepting the fact that our recovery is honored and witnessed in Step 5. The container of the steps, when worked with trauma sensitivity, allows for this to unfold safely and naturally.

Invitation: Spend 3-5 minutes in a practice of your choice (e.g., sitting meditation, walking meditation, or an expressive practice). See if you can begin the transition from Step 5 to Step 6 and notice how far you have come, while seeing one area where you want to let go of something no longer working for you. See the issue and yourself with as much compassion as you can in this moment. Breathe into the issue.

Prayer or Intention: Today let me be aware of the healing in progress and all the resilience I have built in recovery thus far.

MAY 9

risk: to expose oneself to the chance
of injury or loss; a hazard or dangerous chance

Risks are scary. Even a passing glance at this basic definition from a dictionary app is enough to make my spine shudder! When you are in recovery from any kind of traumatic injury, especially those that are prolonged, taking risks can feel so daunting. We often go to great lengths to keep from taking risks. Anything to avoid being hurt again! Even if this means that we stay stuck in a rut, paralyzed at the mere thought of moving forward if it means exposing ourselves to even the chance of further injury or loss. Haven't we suffered enough?

While the perils of risk are well-known and we can certainly validate from our own experiences just how terrifying they are, some degree of risk will be required if we wish to live a full, satisfying, and healthy life. Stepping on to the path of recovery is a risk. Forging new relationships of all kinds requires risk. Going to therapy and getting vulnerable may feel risky. Starting a new job or a new educational path can be risky. Yet what is the alternative if we completely insulate ourselves from change and the risk that comes with it?

Invitation: Spend 3-5 minutes meditating on the well-known saying that *with risk comes reward*. If sitting in meditation doesn't feel like a good fit for this practice, consider journaling on this saying (either with words or visually) or you can even make a playlist and dance with the songs you selected on this theme. In your meditation, however you engage it, notice what you notice. Is there a time in your life, even in your recent recovery, where taking a risk worked out for you? If you're feeling stuck right now at the thought of taking a risk, what would you need emotionally, physically, or spiritually to help you feel more supported in taking that risk?

Prayer or Intention: Grant me whatever it is I need today to breathe into the action of taking a risk and to be open to whatever unfolds.

MAY 10

"Instead of fleeing the pain we need to know it deeply and
acknowledge the suffering it is causing us and at the same time
balance this by developing our potential for happiness and discovery."
~Martine Batchelor

Everything in our body, mind, and spirit has told us to flee the pain
and distress rather than turn toward it. This is natural. We cannot
effectively turn toward our pain until we have a construct for it that
makes sense. The Twelve Steps are actually designed to help us find a
path toward a compassionate view of our pain, with the help of our
own insight, that of our fellows, and if a Higher Power figures into
your recovery, then with that help as well. The first five steps in a sense
help us to identify and then begin seeing our trauma and suffering
differently.

Steps 6 through 9 start a process of changing our lives to match the
new view. And then Steps 10 through 12 help us to live in this balance
of turning toward difficulty with compassion while also cultivating
joy, happiness, creativity, and discovery. When seen this way, the steps
become a tool for compassion, self-care, and a life fully lived.

Invitation: Spend 3-5 minutes in a practice of your choice (e.g.,
sitting meditation, walking meditation, or an expressive practice).
See if you notice any type of low-grade body disturbance. Turn your
attention toward it instead of away. Notice any changes in its intensity,
its shape, its color or its size.

Prayer or Intention: Today I will acknowledge the balance to be
found between turning toward my pain and cultivating an attitude of
happiness and discovery.

MAY 11

"The opposite of addiction isn't sobriety—
it's connection." ~Johani Hari

Whether or not you agree with Johani Hari's take on addiction, there is nugget of gold in this famous teaching. Recovery circles traditionally promote the power of connecting with other human beings. Recovery writings cheer the virtues of connection. Yet for many people connecting with others is traumatic, or at very least may trigger old trauma responses. Maybe you are introverted or painfully shy, and forced connections have been more harmful than helpful. Perhaps a close relationship in your past was the source of your trauma.

If such an experience was part of your story, of course the idea of fostering new relationships is scary and overwhelming. Relationships can be both a trigger and a resource. Are you willing to keep an open mind today about the difference between the two?

Invitation: Spend 3-5 minutes in a practice of your choice (e.g., sitting meditation, walking meditation, or an expressive practice) and consider what *connection* means to you. How much of your existing trauma or struggles with recovery involve lacking connection or a wounding in existing connection?

Prayer or Intention: Today I recognize the importance of connection and make an intention to heal those wounds around connection that may be keeping me stuck. I will keep an open mind about forging new connections.

MAY 12

"Life is tattooing scripture into your flesh . . .
wound becomes portal."~The Radiance Sutras
(*Vijnana Bhairava Tantra*), Yukti Verse 70

Whether you are a person in recovery like Jamie who has many tattoos to celebrate the story of her life and transformation, or someone like Steve who is skittish around needles, you can likely relate to the sentiment of this verse. Life leaves its mark. Life can be brutal.

And yet these wounds and scars can announce the path ahead for our continued growth. In the case of literal tattoos, what was once a wound in need of healing can remain forever as a work of art. How might this metaphor translate to your evolving recovery today?

Invitation: Spend 3-5 minutes in a practice of your choice (e.g., sitting meditation, walking meditation, or an expressive practice) and contemplate the idea that *wound becomes portal* expressed in the opening teaching. In what ways are the wounds you've experienced and identified revealing something more to you? Are there people you can surround yourself with to help you in this process of revelation.

Prayer or Intention: May I appreciate my wounds and scars today and notice the potential for transforming them into art.

MAY 13

"We may think we can control our grief, our terror,
or our shame by remaining silent, but naming offers the possibility
of a different kind of control." ~Bessel van der Kolk

When we have prepared ourselves with the first three steps for a period of time, the Fourth and especially Fifth Step may still look daunting. That may be because we are taking an action that defies all of the strategies our brain, body, and spirit used to survive up until this point.

With the first four steps and the help of friends in the program, sponsors, and any professional helpers we have met along the way, we can name all or some of what we have been through, and this will be the initial pathway toward freedom and community, the end of isolation.

Invitation: Spend 3-5 minutes in a practice of your choice (e.g., sitting meditation, walking meditation, or an expressive practice). Without going into details, see if you can silently name one or two of your difficulties. They can be difficulties that are still ongoing, or you may have already experienced relief. Notice any body sensations, emotions, or thoughts and then notice if they subside. If they do not, see if you can notice that fact with as little judgement as possible.

Prayer or Intention: Today I will let at least one person know what is going on with me in order that I might break the silence and isolation.

MAY 14

"The Universe is made of stories, not atoms."
~Muriel Rukeyser

Many trauma survivors are empowered to learn that they never have to tell the full details of their trauma story in order to heal. Please consider that for many, there can be great power in sharing your story. The sharing can help us release those aspects of the story that no longer serve us. Steps 4 and 5 can help us to do this, especially if they taken with a wise, trauma-informed guide who can gently guide you through the process.

Sometimes people get tripped up thinking that words or sharing out loud is the only way to tell one's story. Consider that in many East African cultures it's considered taboo to talk about traumatic experiences—literally. However, using allegory and enrolling animals and figures from nature to represent aspects of the story is a beautiful, if not preferable, alternative that's used in tribal ceremonies. Art, music, dance, and other creative measures can offer us powerful options for telling our story in a manner that feels safer and more nourishing. How might any of these variations on telling the story help me in working a Fifth Step?

Invitation: Spend 3-5 minutes in a practice of your choice (e.g., sitting meditation, walking meditation, or an expressive practice) and notice if there is a part of your story that you have yet to share with another human being. In your reflections, does it feel like there may be another way other than talking about it to share the story with someone you trust?

Prayer or Intention: Today, I recognize that there is more than one way to share my story. Opening myself in this way may be helpful to my recovery.

MAY 15

"Laughter is not our medicine, stories hold our cure. Laughter is just
the honey that sweetens the bitter medicine." ~Hannah Gadsby

How might any fears you have about sharing your Step 5 with another
human being be lessened if you could approach it as telling your story?
The art of storytelling has served as an amazing healing mechanism
since the dawn of time in cultures all over the planet. In some cultures,
allegory or using characters from nature to symbolize big themes is
the preferred way for handling the heavy themes of trauma. For many
survivors of trauma, being able to not take oneself too seriously and
see the humorous threads in the fabric of our stories can also be very
helpful, even if we still feel weighed down by shame.

In choosing someone with whom to work a Fifth Step, try to pick
someone who doesn't take themselves too seriously and will greet you
with a sense of genuineness. Laughter, even in the face of unspeakable
things we may have to share, can sweeten the medicine, as comedian
Hannah Gadsby so powerfully observes. Even if what you have to
share in your Fifth Step is no laughing matter, are you working it with
someone who can help you see the humor in life when the storytelling
is over?

Invitation: Spend 3-5 minutes in a practice of your choice (e.g.,
sitting meditation, walking meditation, or an expressive practice) and
bring up what is means to tell a story. How can approaching your Fifth
Step as telling a story, whether it's your first Step 5 or you are working
it again, help to diffuse some of the fear?

Prayer or Intention: Today I appreciate the art of storytelling as
a healing art in the human experience; if appropriate, I welcome
laughter to help sweeten the medicine.

MAY 16

"When you dig a well, there's no sign of water until you reach it, only rocks and dirt to move out of the way. 'You have removed enough; soon the pure water will flow,' said Buddha." ~Deepak Chopra

Many people see Steps 4 and 5 in tandem, and for good reason. They are two deeply interwoven aspects and stages of a process of uncovering and releasing. In the Fifth Step, often there is a sudden clearing of the consciousness due to the excavation of Step 4 and the sharing of Step 5. I had that lifting of the heavy burden during my Fifth Step as Randy helped me to clear out the last of the dirt and rocks, allowing for the new flow of the pure water of recovery.

Not everyone has this particular direct experience in Step 5, but for many who continue in their pursuit of the Twelve Steps, it arrives at another time, in another way, perhaps more subtly. So much of trauma work and recovery work is the clearing of the dirt and rubble. The Fifth Step is a deep initiation into the world of having help in clearing the path, seeing the path, and walking the path.

Invitation: Spend 3-5 minutes in a practice of your choice (e.g., sitting meditation, walking meditation, or an expressive practice). Notice whatever elements of your Fifth Step work remain, whatever dirt and stones may still be in your path. Notice any body sensations, thoughts or feelings. Notice if you can bring up a trusted other or being who has heard or will hear your Step 5. Notice again any shift in your experience.

Prayer or Intention: Today I will know that just because I still see obstacles on my path does not mean I am not successfully digging a recovery well that will reveal the new flow of recovery.

MAY 17

"I sail'd through the storm, I was refresh'd by the storm . . . "
~Walt Whitman, *Rise These Days From Your Fathomless Deeps*

One subtle way that trauma survivors have found ourselves retraumatized during 12-step recovery occurs when someone tells us that we should be grateful for our troubles, or that we should be able to see the growth that comes from our difficulties long before we are actually ready to see it ourselves. This comes from a misunderstanding of how to apply the thinking and behavior change suggested by the steps, or fear on the part of the person giving the advice. In any case, we can lean into the steps, an actual phased approach toward recovery, for help. We can see that the Fourth Step is in fact a storm we will sail through, and it will have all those challenges inherent in stormy weather. But we don't have to sail alone.

In the Fifth Step, it's essential to find someone who is trauma sensitive and will help us not only land safely on the shore of the Sixth Step, but even buoy us to be "refresh'd" when it is all done. If we are still tender and feeling the effects of the storm, we can lean into our external resources like a sponsor, therapist, friends, and meetings.

Invitation: Make a list of the people, animals, and places that help you weather the storms of life. Spend 5 minutes reflecting on any gratitude you have for them, and on the different ways they support you through difficulty. Also notice how they appreciate your joy.

Prayer or Intention: Today may I notice the support through storms and the camaraderie of joy.

MAY 18

"Only the hand that erases can write the true thing."
~Meister Eckhart

One of the most important lessons taught through the development of EMDR therapy and other trauma therapies has been the acknowledgement that the most powerful tools the therapist has at their disposal are the associative memory networks of the client in front of them. When we heal from trauma and addiction, we are the experts on ourselves. Our own brains and bodies are doing the healing, the professionals and others that we trust are only creating a healing environment so that the natural processes of healing can take place.

When we engage fully in recovery, our own brains, bodies, psyches and spirits reprocess the maladaptively stored material to an adaptive resolution. Remember when you would erase while using a number two pencil? There may be a shadow of the old version of the memory, but we ourselves get to write the new story with our new energy and insight. No longer powerless, we get to write the new story of healing and happiness.

Invitation: Spend 3-5 minutes in a practice of your choice (e.g., sitting meditation, walking meditation, or an expressive practice). Meditate on the phrase, "My own body does the healing" as you practice.

Prayer or Intention: Today I know that I am healing. I know that I am a healer, all I need to do is walk the recovery path and my brain and body know what to do to heal.

MAY 19

"The path to me seems like it's about transforming obstacles into doorways, which is good for us who have had a lot of obstacles—lots of doorways… doorways lead us home." ~Vinny Ferraro

Recovery introduces shifts in perspective. Am I able to see all the obstacles that I have been through as doorways? This describes very well the process of trauma recovery and the process of going through the steps. When we allow for the reprocessing of our maladaptively stored memories, whether through EMDR therapy, other trauma therapy, or any other trauma transforming modality, the very nature of our memories shifts, and the flow of information reboots and allows us to have access to our neocortex.

When we work the steps, it is implied throughout that we are going to reassess all the obstacles from our past, our present, and our future tripping, and we will have a new template for living. Those of us who have been through many traumas or years and years of addiction have a lot of doorways. Our obstacles become our gifts.

Invitation: Spend 3-5 minutes in a practice of your choice (e.g., sitting meditation, walking meditation, or an expressive practice). Visualize a current or past obstacle in your life. Allow it to transform into a doorway. Open the door and walk through in your mind, or if you are doing walking or movement meditation, act it out. And then notice any shifts in perception.

Prayer or Intention: My obstacles were obstacles, and now in recovery they are doorways. Today I will notice when I am walking through a door that was once an obstacle.

MAY 20

"The pessimist complains about the wind;
the optimist expects it to change; the realist adjusts the sails."
~William Arthur Ward

I spent five years of an eleven-year relationship with a sponsor, wondering whether or not another person would be a better fit. My sponsor was who I needed at the time I chose her early in my recovery upon moving back to the United States and I still respect how she guided me. In later years I spent too much time censoring myself, especially about my extracurricular recovery interests like yoga, Eastern meditation, and expanding my faith beyond the boundaries of Christianity. One of my greatest fears about switching is that I didn't want to be a "sponsor hopper"—just moving along because I didn't like what she had to say. Yet when I stepped back critically, I recognized that I did give it eleven years! I wasn't sponsor hopping; I needed a change. As soon as I found my new sponsor and noticed what it felt like to share so freely, I knew my decision was the right one.

Sometimes we have to change sponsors to better align with the style of recovery we seek. Not all 12-step sponsors are created equally and many are not trauma-informed. If the person you are working with right now does not seem supportive of you healing both your addiction and your trauma, consider seeking someone else. Making that change may be an important step.

Invitation: Spend 3-5 minutes in a practice of your choice (e.g., sitting meditation, walking meditation, or an expressive practice) and reflect on the sponsorship experiences you've had so far in your recovery journey. What has worked? What hasn't worked? Is there anything you feel you need right now that you are not getting?

Prayer or Intention: Today I recognize that I have choices in my recovery and who is guiding me.

MAY 21

"And a step backward, after making a wrong turn,
is a step in the right direction." ~Kurt Vonnegut

As an avid traveler through Europe, I've been prone to get on the wrong train from time to time. Sometimes the platforms confuse me, especially when I'm in a hurry to make a connection. One time I intended to go to Budapest and ended up stranded in the middle of some rural Hungarian village. A big lesson I've learned from my misadventures is that no matter how hard you try, you cannot stop a moving train. The best you can do is to practice acceptance, wait until you get to the next station, and then make a plan.

You will make wrong turns, bad decisions, and other errors in your recovery. Accepting that fact right now may help you to be kinder to yourself down the road. Remember that even these wrong turns can offer us amazing learning opportunities, and maybe even some delightfully unexpected changes of plan. Be open to what the journey reveals.

Invitation: Spend 3-5 minutes in a practice of your choice (e.g., sitting meditation, walking meditation, or an expressive practice) and recall a wrong turn, a bad decision, or an error that you made recently or at some point in the past. What was the larger lesson that this experience revealed?

Prayer or Intention: May I accept the wrong turns as part of any recovery path and may I learn from what they reveal.

MAY 22

"Radical acceptance rests on letting go of the illusion of control and a willingness to notice and accept things as they are right now, without judging." ~Marsha Linehan

The power of acceptance is well-known in 12-step recovery fellowships. The classic line from the "Big Book" of *Alcoholics Anonymous* informs us that "acceptance is the answer to all of my problems today." The difficulty that trauma survivors have with this phrase is well-known, especially if we equate acceptance with resignation. Remember that accepting something just means that we are going to cease fighting the reality that it happened.

Marsha Linehan, the founder of dialectical behavior therapy (DBT), uses the phrase radical acceptance to describe the power of this mindful attitude. Think about something that is totally out of your character for you to accept. Then what would it look like if you could just do it anyway? Even if you can't do it yet, can you picture yourself doing it? Even this visualization can pave the way forward for the practice of radical acceptance.

Invitation: Spend 3-5 minutes in a practice of your choice (e.g., sitting meditation, walking meditation, or an expressive practice) and bring to mind something or someone that you are struggling to accept. If you are not yet able to put radical acceptance into practice, can you visualize it? Alternately, you can write out an imaginal scene in which you write about yourself putting this acceptance into practice. Notice what happens.

Prayer or Intention: There is healing power in radical acceptance. Today I can put it into practice or at least consider what this force can do in my life.

MAY 23

"Do not stop trying because perfection eludes you."
~B.K.S. Iyengar

The path of recovery is filled with perfectionists. I've seen this drive toward the impossible standard of perfection manifest in so many ways and for so many reasons amongst my fellow travelers. For many of us the perfection drive started very early on, as a way to get our parents or other members in our family to change. Sometimes the standard of perfection was held up high for us, and other times we responded to societal conditioning that perfect is somehow ideal. Regardless of the origin, it breaks my heart to see so many people quit, relapse, or self-destruct because they are not reaching some perfect standard that they set for themselves.

Let me break it to you: perfection does not exist. You will keep setting yourself up for failure if perfect is your standard. There's no such thing as working the steps perfectly. As one of my early elder friends in recovery taught me, you work the steps as well as you can work them at the time, especially the first time through. Pursuing excellence and having commitment is healthy, especially in recovery. Trying to do this perfectly will make your head spin and your body ache! Be kind to yourself.

Invitation: Spend 3-5 minutes in a practice of your choice (e.g., sitting meditation, walking meditation, or an expressive practice) and notice how the drive to be perfect may be impacting your life adversely, in recovery and other areas. What are some small ways that you can go easier on yourself today? Remember that you can still pursue quality and commitment in your recovery, and you do not have to do it perfectly.

Prayer or Intention: I will be kinder to myself today by recognizing that I am not perfect and my recovery doesn't have to be either.

MAY 24

resolve (n.)—derives from the Latin word *resolvere*,
meaning to unfasten, loosen, and release

When we think about making a *resolve* in recovery, it generally refers to some type of strong commitment. For instance, I resolve to stop drinking or using drugs, putting my recovery first. Other people associate the word with its verb form as in, "What do I need to do in order to *resolve* the impact of this traumatic experience?" Indeed, the word *resolve* and its many forms can be important in our work as individuals in recovery.

During a recent conversation with a friend on the term *resolve* I considered the age-old question, "Can trauma ever truly be resolved?" Like I do in pondering any question of this nature, I turned to the word origin and was pleasantly surprise to find just how much connection *resolve* and *resolution* have to do with surrender-style concepts like unfastening, loosening, and releasing. Consider how strong the concept of a resolve sounds and how important it can be to recovery. When I can think of making a resolve or engaging in resolution as a process—a processing of loosening and releasing the impact of the things that no longer serve me in my life—I am in a position to be much kinder to myself. This process may not happen overnight, yet I feel solid in the knowledge that through right and healthy action on my part, it *is* happening.

Invitation: Choose one of the words highlighted in this meditation—unfasten, loosen, or release—whichever word rings or resonates most for you. Then, spend 3-5 minutes in a practice of your choice (e.g., sitting, walking, or an expressive practice) contemplating the interplay between the word *resolve* and the word that you chose. What can one teach you about the other, especially considering where you are at in your recovery today.

Prayer or Intention: In making a resolve to commit to my recovery and heal the wounds of the past, may I unfasten, loosen, and soften the areas of tension that are keeping me stuck in fear or shame.

MAY 25

"Confession of errors is like a broom which sweeps away the dirt and leaves the surface brighter and clearer. I feel stronger for confession."
~Mahatma Gandhi

Often when faced with becoming vulnerable and allowing others to see our weaknesses, we find ourselves stressed out or even terrified of telling our truth. We have good reason, as trauma survivors. In the past our perceived weakness may have been used against us in order to control us. Now, however, we are free to confess our errors as a form of strength.

We know that being true to ourselves and others is how we can live authentically, thriving through the use of our trauma recovery tools and our 12-step tools. We can create a bright and clear surface above a bright and clear internal experience. This brightness and clarity brings freedom.

Invitation: Spend 3-5 minutes in a practice of your choice (e.g., sitting meditation, walking meditation, or an expressive practice). Consider using a visualization where you notice a wrong you want to right, or an error you have made, where a broom literally sweeps it away, providing a bright and clear space in your consciousness.

Prayer or Intention: Today let me abide in the knowledge that confession brings strength rather than weakness.

MAY 26

"If I didn't sing how else would I clean out
the dark corners of my own heart?" ~Krishna Das

Cleaning out the dark corners of my heart—every time I hear Krishna Das offer this teaching in his chant workshops I get chills. This is a very powerful way to describe why we need cleansing practices as people in recovery. Steps like the Fourth and Fifth can do wonders here, allowing the fullness of light to shine through us once more.

To fully support our total recovery, other practices may also be required to guide us through the steps. Singing and chanting may do it for you. Perhaps it's drumming, playing another instrument, making art, or moving your body. Anything that feels adaptive, healthy, and in the service of your recovery may qualify. How do you clean out the dark corners of your own heart?

Invitation: Spend 3-5 minutes in a practice of your choice (e.g., sitting meditation, walking meditation, or an expressive practice) and reflect on the phrase *clean out the dark corners of my own heart*. What feels like it needs to be cleansed or cleared? How may the arts—even if it's just scribbling on a page—assist you in this process?

Prayer or Intention: I will allow the dark corners of my heart to be cleared out so that the light may shine through.

MAY 27

"The world breaks everyone and afterward many
are strong at the broken places." ~Ernest Hemingway

The Japanese practice of *kintsugi* or *kintsukoroi* is a popular topic for memes on social media—and with good reason. In this style of pottery, the broken places or cracks are filled in with gold. This adds to the value and the beauty of the vase, plate, or bowl. Such a beautiful metaphor for what the process of recovery can allow.

Sometimes we can feel too broken to fix. We may believe that we are defective or damaged goods, and that no one can ever love us or value us because of horrible things we've done or that have happened to us. What would it feel like if you could approach the healing of those cracked and broken places as an opportunity to practice *kintsugi*?

Invitation: Spend 3-5 minutes in a practice of your choice (e.g., sitting meditation, walking meditation, or an expressive practice) and contemplate the practice of *kintsugi*—filling the broken places with gold. How may have you done this in your life or recovery already, metaphorically speaking? What are some of the cracks and broken places that may still need to be healed in this way? Notice if you've had a tendency in the past to fill the cracks with people, places, and things that do not serve the true value of who you really are.

Prayer or Intention: Today I fill the cracks and broken places with gold as I continue in my healing process. May I realize that I am worth even more than gold.

MAY 28

"I am a lover of what is, not because
I'm a spiritual person, but because it hurts
when I argue with reality." ~Byron Katie

The steps are an invitation for us to begin a new dance with reality. Much of our history of trauma and/or addiction is peppered with fist fights with reality, and this makes perfect sense. Our survival mechanisms and coping strategies became active and then entrenched through repetition through no fault of our own. It was adaptive to escape or fight back. Now in recovery, having practiced the first three steps for a time, we can come face to face with any aspect of our reality that is hard for us to look at.

With the help of trusted others in the program, the literature of the program, outside literature and outside help, we are able to go through a thorough process that can lead to relief from a lifetime of trauma responses and give us new resilience, new relationships, and a new sense of mindfulness that will lead us to more recovery actions, more recovery thinking, and a reality that we can dance along with, instead of ignoring or fighting.

Invitation: Spend 3-5 minutes in a practice of your choice (e.g., sitting meditation, walking meditation, or an expressive practice). Notice the reality of yourself as a human body sitting on the ground (or in motion). Notice the simple reality of this fact.

Prayer or Intention: Today allow me to walk with a simple mindfulness of reality. I have gratitude for the program and the people in it who support my new dance with reality.

MAY 29

"We are all just walking each other home." ~Ram Dass

Many folks get tripped up doing Step 5 because they believe it must be heard by a sponsor or member of the clergy. While such individuals often hear Fifth Steps, nowhere does the literature say it has to be done with a sponsor or clergyperson. The step simply says: *another human being.*

For many survivors of trauma, especially those early in their journey, it may be ideal for a professional therapist or clinician to hear a Fifth Step. Trauma work often transitions very nicely into taking Step 5, and a professional who has worked with you will have tremendous insight into the larger context. The professional who has been guiding you, especially if the relationship is solid, may also be better able to assist you with triggers if they emerge as you share your Fifth Step. Obviously, we are not saying that a sponsor or clergyperson shouldn't hear your Fifth Step. We are saying that people in recovery deserve a choice.

Invitation: Spend 3-5 minutes in a practice of your choice (e.g., sitting meditation, walking meditation, or an expressive practice) contemplating the Ram Dass quote that opens this meditation. What does this teaching mean to you at this stage of your recovery journey? Whether you need to do Step 5 or hear one, how can the wisdom of this teaching assist you today?

Prayer or Intention: Today I honor the connection I share with other human beings walking the path home.

MAY 30

"A broken heart bleeds tears." ~Steve Maraboli

A foundational teaching in the work of *Trauma and the 12 Steps* is that the word trauma comes from the Greek word meaning wound. Understanding the wound metaphor is the heart of understanding the perils of trauma and offers us a template for healing. When we talk about trauma, we are in essence talking about the unhealed human wounds that lead to suffering and bleeding—whether physical or metaphorical. For many of us, self-injury becomes a coping mechanism we use. We may have engaged in such activities desperate to see a physical manifestation of the wounds we carry inside.

In my own trauma recovery, which includes recovery from self-injury, I've had to learn that I can cry instead of bleed. The wounds that trouble me are supposed to hurt, and I am allowed to cry out in pain! It took me many years in recovery to truly claim this truth and my right to feel hurt. My tears represent the necessary release that can keep me from destroying myself physically or emotionally. Allowing myself to cry can help me to grieve and not to get lost in it, and this clears the path for me to heal my broken heart.

Invitation: Spend 3-5 minutes in a practice of your choice (e.g., sitting meditation, walking meditation, or an expressive practice) and bring up the concept of the broken heart. What do you see visually, especially when you think about how dealing with heart break and wounding applies to your story? How can honoring your tears help you to heal?

Prayer or Intention: Today I cherish and honor my broken heart and will allow myself to cry as many tears as I need to in order to help me heal instead of bleed to the point of destruction.

MAY 31

"Anger is an energy!" ~John Lydon

Much of the AA and other 12-step literature can be very confusing to the trauma survivor as it pertains to anger. There is a great deal of language that gets (mis)interpreted as telling the person in recovery that they have to "get rid" of their anger, whether it be by throwing it across the room, squashing it back into some file cabinet in the heart and mind, or just never acting out on anger ever again through some kind of spiritual bypass, lest we immediately get struck drunk. Anger is much more complicated than that. And the truth is, without anger, we trauma survivors may have no guidebook or guideposts on how to start setting healthy boundaries.

The key to a healthy relationship with anger in trauma recovery and recovery in general is to acknowledge that it is a natural, normal response to boundary crossings and other difficulties that trauma survivors regularly face. When we see this clearly, we can use mindfulness, the steps, our relationships in the program, and with professionals to work on new ways to harness that energy to our own benefit and the benefit of others.

Invitation: Spend 3-5 minutes in a practice of your choice (e.g., sitting meditation, walking meditation, or an expressive practice). Notice any anger you are currently experiencing. Notice what sensations, thoughts and feelings go with it. Notice the energy in the anger. Notice what boundary you feel you need to set according to the anger.

Prayer or Intention: Today let me know throughout the day that anger is a natural and normal human emotion. I will learn one new way to channel that energy in a healthy direction.

JUNE 1

"You have character defects, but you are not those defects."
~Rabbi Rami Shapiro

If you are struggling with Step 6 and the language around *defects of character*, consider how the spiritual practice of *dis-identification* may help you move past this block. Used widely in the practice of yoga and described very simply by Rabbi Shapiro in the teaching that opens this meditation, *dis-identification* suggests that while you may have done things that have impacted your character in an unhealthy way, you are not those things. You are not defective.

What are the other stories that we may have learned to tell ourselves as the result of being in active addiction for so long? It breaks my heart every time I'm in a recovery setting and I hear people refer to themselves as *pieces of shit, scumbags,* or other self-deprecating descriptors. While you may have engaged in behaviors that can be described as illegal, immoral, or unethical during your active addiction (so much that they may have become ingrained in your character) you are never those things. Steps 6 and 7 empower us to begin writing a new narrative and sense into the truth of who we really are.

Invitation: Spend 3-5 minutes in a practice of your choice (e.g., sitting meditation, walking meditation, or an expressive practice) and evaluate some of the horrible things you have come to believe about yourself as a result of your active addiction. Then, practice saying or otherwise expressing, "I may have done _____, and yet I am *not* that person."

Prayer or Intention: Today may I recognize that I am *not* my character defects. I am in the process of discovering who I really am through the power of my recovery and healing.

JUNE 2

"The process of enlightenment is usually slow. But, in the end, our seeking always brings a finding." ~Bill Wilson

When Bill Wilson got sober, there was a very sudden white light experience involved. To this day, even with the guidance toward the educational variety of spiritual experience found in the Spiritual Appendix in the AA "Big Book," many get stuck on this idea of sudden, swift, and complete instant spiritual experience. In trauma recovery as in 12-step recovery, we are reminded constantly that we are on a journey, and that it is the seeking rather than the finding that brings the healing.

Our maladaptively stored memories are brought to an adaptive resolution allowing us to live a more adaptive life. And sometimes that event, the moment when we arrive at an adaptive resolution seems blindingly quick. In fact, though, it is usually the result of an ongoing willingness to find the wisdom, the practices, the outside help, and the help found in the program that works for us. Through that process, the simplicity of it all is revealed, that we are on a path, and the path itself provides the healing.

Invitation: Whether it is a formal walking practice or an informal walk about town, let your gaze go to about a 45 degree angle downward. For as many steps as feels comfortable, notice the path in front of you. Every few steps take a quick look back to see the ground covered. And then reset your intention, using a phrase along the order of, "I am willing to continue."

Prayer or Intention: Throughout the day I will notice the nature of the path that I am on. I will notice my level of willingness to continue on the path.

JUNE 3

"The more you know yourself, the more clarity there is. Self-knowledge has no end—you don't come to an achievement, you don't come to a conclusion. It is an endless river." ~Jiddu Krishnamurti

In 12-step recovery, one of the more trauma-informed slogans, in place for a long time and derived directly from the AA "Big Book" is "Progress, Not Perfection." In her book on Expressive Arts therapy, Jamie modified this saying to "Process, Not Perfection." This might actually be a more accurate and trauma-informed statement of this aspect of our recovery.

Importantly, in the above quote Krishnamurti does not call for self-perfection but rather self-knowledge. The steps help us to know ourselves, not perfect ourselves. As we go through the process, we progress. We don't achieve perfection, but rather move along the endless river that before recovery may have seemed like four walls closing in. Now we can go with the flow, learning about ourselves, and treating ourselves with some care and gentleness as we learn more about ourselves along the way.

Invitation: Spend 3-5 minutes in a practice of your choice (e.g., sitting meditation, walking meditation, or an expressive practice). Consider visualizing yourself slowly floating on a river raft, noticing the flow of the water and the scenery on land. Notice what sensations come up. If a water-based visualization does not appeal to you, choose another image that allows you to notice your progress along a path.

Prayer or Intention: Today I will stay in an attitude of process and progress, rather than striving for perfection.

JUNE 4

"Have no fear of perfection—you'll never reach it." ~Salvador Dali

Fear of failure, perfectionism, fear of success, we all tend to share some or all of these qualities. In the Sixth Step essay in *Twelve Steps and Twelve Traditions*, Bill Wilson declares that we will never achieve perfection nor need we be perfect to find healing. He says that what we are trying to do is keep our eyes on a horizon and we keep pointed toward those ideals expressed in the steps. We don't have to become perfect examples of those ideals.

If we stay on the path, these principles will become our true north, and healing will commence and continue. Trauma recovery and addiction recovery are the same in this way. We don't need to become perfect, perfectly healed, or perfectly sober. We walk the path, together in fellowship.

Invitation: Spend 3-5 minutes in a practice of your choice (e.g., sitting meditation, walking meditation, or an expressive practice). Consider keeping your eyes open and looking toward the horizon where you sit or are in movement. Notice what mental, emotional, or bodily associations come up with looking toward the horizon.

Prayer or Intention: Today I will walk the path, knowing that perfection need not be attained.

JUNE 5

"It is impossible to understand addiction without asking
what relief the addict finds, or hopes to find, in the drug
or the addictive behavior." ~Gabor Maté

The advent of 12-step recovery helped to move us out of the view that mental health and addiction challenges are moral issues. However, much of the stigma has persisted both outside and inside the rooms of the program. What Gabor Maté and others in the trauma-focused world of treatment have discovered over the years is that we need to look more deeply into the foundations of people's addictive behavior, and there we will find a survivor trying to get relief.

The interplay between any genetic components and painful circumstances, including thoughts and feelings leads to the level of addictive behavior we (consciously or unconsciously) find necessary to bring relief. This framework brings us to the understanding we are in a biological bind that requires a compassionate view, both from ourselves and others, to heal.

Invitation: Spend 3-5 minutes in a practice of your choice (e.g., sitting meditation, walking meditation, or an expressive practice). Notice, if you can, what it is you were seeking relief from in your addictions. As you contemplate this, notice what resources you already have to bring some relief differently. This may be the practice you are practicing in this moment.

Prayer or Intention: I know now that my addictive behaviors have been a solution to a problem, and I can forgive myself for any pain that has caused me.

JUNE 6

"I've only just realized how utterly exhausted and drained I am
after living in a near constant state of fight-or-flight for so long."
~Anonymous

Trauma survivors are all too familiar with hypervigilance—that
uncomfortable experience of always being on guard for something
bad to happen. Hypervigilance is one of the most common symptoms
of post-traumatic stress disorder (PTSD), and it may still affect you
whether or not you've been formally diagnosed with PTSD. Living in
any type of uncertainty or dysfunction can make you hypervigilant.
And it can literally be exhausting, depleting your body of breath and
other vital resources that it needs to heal.

Getting over hypervigilance is not an overnight process. This
reaction can be hardwired after many years of living this way, so it
may take some disciplined practice on a day-to-day basis using skills
like grounding and breathing to retrain your body. Becoming more
familiar with people and spaces where you feel safe enough to let your
guard down—at least a little bit at first—can also be a helpful part of
the process.

Invitation: If it is physically available to you without pain, scrunch
your shoulders up by your ears. See if you can hold this clenching
motion for about 20-30 seconds. When we are in hypervigilance, our
shoulders naturally creep up by our ears. Living with hypervigilance
every day means that we can do this a lot. So what's happening to your
breath when your shoulder are like this? Now release the shoulders
and notice immediately what happens to the breath. Try this several
times until you feel yourself more connected with the flowing breath.

Prayer or Intention: Today I will allow my breath to return more
fully to my body, helping me to heal from the impact of always being
on guard.

JUNE 7

"The heart is an organ of fire."
~Michael Ondaatje, *The English Patient*

The limbic brain, the seat of our emotions and learning as human beings, can be destroyed by unhealed trauma. Ancient Christian mystics, often called the desert fathers and desert mothers, referred to this brain as the *heart brain*. Our emotional world, governed by the limbic brain, can feel like a fire that is raging out of control. Some trauma survivors are affected oppositely—they become shut off to feeling altogether. Often we shut ourselves off from emotion by choice, afraid of what feeling them might do to us.

Our emotional world and other matters of the heart are much like a fireplace that keeps a cabin warm. If the fire rages, it can burn the cabin down. If the fire dies, the cabin goes cold. Recovery teaches us how to keep the fire in balance—properly tended to create for us a beautiful warmth.

Invitation: Interlace your hands together and place them over your heart. If directly touching your body feels too activating, you may hover this cross-fingered gesture a few inches away from your heart. Spend 3-5 minutes in this position and listen to what messages your heart—and the emotional world it represents—may be giving you today.

Prayer or Intention: May the emotional fire of my heart create warmth—not destruction—today and on the path ahead.

JUNE 8

"Dissociation is a state of missing mindfulness."
~Christine Forner

We dissociate in order to escape—to sever our tie with a present moment that is subjectively unpleasant. We may also dissociate to avoid being present with our full self. For many of us in trauma recovery, this tendency to dissociate developed very early and may have taken the shape of activities like day dreaming, zoning out, developing imaginary friends, or even creating the most glorious of imaginative worlds inside of us. Yet as we age and become introduced to alcohol, drugs, and other behaviors that help us to sever, those objects of addiction may become even more appealing. After all, they can help us to protect ourselves from the threats in our life, real and perceived.

For many of us, working on our recovery from our addiction is also a challenge to work on our dissociative tendencies. Sometimes after a period of sobriety, we may still notice that we are checking out or seeking to sever with great regularity. Usually those behaviors pre-dated our addiction so when the addiction begins to heal, it's normal for dissociation to show up. Dissociation recovery is typically about healing our relationship with the reality of the present moment, which is much easier said than done. Professional assistance is often required, although cultivation of a regular mindfulness, yoga, or other embodied practice can be helpful. Being mindful really is the opposite of being dissociative so it may be a real step outside of the comfort zone to start. Go gentle on yourself and know that you are on the right track.

Invitation: Spend 3-5 minutes in a practice of your choice (e.g., sitting meditation, walking meditation, or an expressive practice) and set an intention to be present with the moment. If you notice your attention wandering into the past or into the future, simply invite the attention back to the *now*. If it's helpful for you to meditate on the word *now*, use that as an anchor.

Prayer or Intention: Today I seek to repair my relationship with both myself and the present moment using presence as my guide.

JUNE 9

"The past is not simply the past, but a prism through which the subject filters his own changing self-image." ~Doris Kearns Goodwin

Although Doris Kearns Goodwin is a famous historian, she gives us some amazing insight here into how information processing works in the brain—and how unhealed trauma can affect it. Perhaps, in our study of trauma recovery, we have a great deal to learn from historians. Her use of the prism is also fascinating because this is a metaphor that we often use to describe dissociative expressions that involve *parts*. You may identify as having different *parts* of yourself, like an inner-child, and angry protector, and perhaps a plethora of others. Each part is like the cut or edge of a prism, reflecting light through its unique perspective.

In both active addiction and recovery we may have the tendency to want to cut off or shame different parts of ourselves and our experience—particularly if we feel that one of those parts causes us trouble. You may need the guidance of a professional to help you really explore your parts of self and learn that each part holds a unique aspect to your story. They have feelings to be felt and messages to send your healing self. The challenge is to listen to them and to help the affected parts of yourself heal too. Then, the prism that you are will be able to filter even more light, allowing your radiance to shine ever brighter through the world.

Invitation: Spend 3-5 minutes in a practice of your choice (e.g., sitting meditation, walking meditation, or an expressive practice) and set an intention to connect with a certain *part* of yourself. Most of us can at least relate to having an inner child, so that can work well for this exercise if you are feeling ready. What does that part of you have to share with your healing self today? If it feels appropriate, you can even allow yourself to engage in some dialogue writing with that part today. Since this exercise can be tricky, if you find yourself needing some extra support consider sharing what you discovered with a professional, sponsor, or trusted friend.

Prayer or Intention: Today I can begin to see my entire self— my parts, my history, and my recovery—as aspects of a larger prism reflecting light through the world.

JUNE 10

"Gratitude unlocks the fullness of life." ~Melodie Beattie

Gratitude can be tough medicine to swallow for trauma survivors in recovery. "How can I be grateful after everything I've experienced!" you may protest. When sponsors, therapists, and people in the fellowship encourage you to focus on gratitude, you may get especially surly. Rest assured, learning to practice gratitude does not require you to be grateful for anything that happened to you. You get to that place eventually or you may not. That does not block you from putting gratitude into action on a day-to-day basis.

Getting sober in Bosnia-Hercegovina, as I did following the war there, allowed me a lot of chances to practice gratitude. When I found myself in a place of complaint or self-pity on any given day, my sponsor encouraged me to make gratitude lists to help me focus on what I do have. And in comparison to some of the people I served, I could practice gratitude for very basic things—a place to live, food to eat, and yes, toilet paper to use. Sometimes all you can manage for a gratitude list is these basics and that's okay—they may be the life raft that keeps you from sinking in self-pity today and helps you to develop a greater sense of perspective.

Invitation: Spend at least 5 minutes and commit to writing out a gratitude list for yourself today. Try to put at least 5 items on it, although you are encouraged to try for 10. Be specific and remember it's okay to keep it basic. If you want to challenge yourself a bit further, think about a person, place, thing, or situation that you may find unpleasant today. Are you able to identify 5 things that you are grateful for about that person, place, thing, or situation today? Even the opportunity you have to learn and grow from the situation can be a point on the bonus gratitude list.

Prayer or Intention: I honor the healing power of gratitude and recognize that I can practice it in a variety of ways today and on the path ahead.

JUNE 11

"Have gratitude for the things you're discarding. By giving gratitude,
you're giving closure to the relationship with that object, and by
doing so, it becomes a lot easier to let go." ~Marie Kondo

We can have great difficulty letting go of people, places, or things.
There's an old folk saying in recovery circles that you know when an
alcoholic, addict, or co-dependent has been holding on to something
because it has claw marks all over it! While there is some truth to this
statement, like many slogans, I don't think it honors just how difficult it
can be for us, as people, to let go. Add unhealed trauma to the mix and
the attachments with which we struggle can be even more complicated.

Letting go is a process, and we generally need to start with letting
go of those people, places, and things that do not serve our recovery or
support our mental health. We may even struggle with letting go of our
own character defects, especially when we consider how they helped us
to survive at earlier times in our life. Many of us have had to let go of
family and friends just as we've had to let go of clutter in our house, or
old places where we used to hang out. I really like the advice given by
lifestyle "decluttering" expert Marie Kondo in the opening teaching.
Perhaps extending our gratitude first for what a person, place, or thing
gave us for that season of our life can make the process of letting go a
little bit easier. Gratitude, after all, is an antidote to many things that
keep us stuck in recovery.

Invitation: Spend 3-5 minutes in a practice of your choice (e.g.,
sitting meditation, walking meditation, or an expressive practice) and
bring to mind a person, place, thing, or situation where you will need
to practice the art of letting go. You can even use one of your own
character defects or negative coping skills. Notice, as you scan your
body how this might be difficult for you. Is there gratitude that you can
practice extending to that person, place, thing or situation first, even
if it is thanking them for teaching you a valuable lesson that lead you
to recovery?

Prayer or Intention: Today, may I notice the connection between
gratitude and letting go. I recognize the role that both play in my
recovery and wellness.

JUNE 12

"The light still illuminates the room and banishes the murkiness, letting you see the things you couldn't see before." ~Sharon Salzberg

The metaphor of turning on the lights is appropriate throughout a trauma-informed working of the Twelve Steps. In the Fourth and Fifth Steps, the lights were turned on by working on our inventory and sharing it. In the Sixth Step, as we look around our proverbial attic, we may see the patterns or the repetitive behaviors or attitudes that still may remain to some degree after our hard work. This is natural. We have turned the lights on, as opposed to having had surgery with a result of being squeaky clean and forever in bliss.

The Debtors Anonymous program talks about how vagueness is the source of all difficulties. Sharon Salzberg alludes to this idea here when she explains to us just how much just turning on some lights and thereby banishing the murkiness can lead us further along the path. Step 6 is a decision to keep the lights on, and to be willing to go into the next phase of our recovery.

Invitation: Spend 3-5 minutes in a practice of your choice (e.g., sitting meditation, walking meditation, or an expressive practice). As you breathe in, consider the words, "I am turning on the lights." On the out breath, "I keep the lights on."

Prayer or Intention: I am turning on the lights day-by-day, taking a look around, and seeing what more I can do to walk the recovery path.

JUNE 13

"If we wait until we're ready, we'll be waiting for
the rest of our lives." ~Amber Coulter

I hear so many people on the path of recovery declare that they are not
"ready." Not ready to work the steps. Not ready to seek outside help,
especially as it relates to trauma. Not ready to change. Step 6 is tricky
because it directly asks us to become *entirely* ready. Yet "I'm not ready"
seems to be one the great blocks that keeps us stuck in our journey,
even if that lack of readiness stems from legitimate fear.

We can conflate the terms *ready* and *prepare*, yet there are some
subtle differences between the two—and this difference holds a
powerful solution. Many people associate readiness with a mental state,
whereas preparation is more logistical. Preparation involves learning
skills, going to meetings, doing the next right thing, putting one foot in
front of the other—no matter how small the steps. Getting prepared
is the key to helping us experience a greater sense of readiness about
working any of the steps or addressing any of our recovery intentions.

Invitation: Spend 3-5 minutes in a practice of your choice (e.g.,
sitting meditation, walking meditation, or an expressive practice) and
bring to mind a step or an issue in your life where you have a tendency
to say "I'm not ready." Challenge yourself to replace "I'm not ready"
with any of these questions: "What can I do to get myself prepared?"
"What kind of support will I need to grow into readiness?" "How
will taking action and making necessary preparations help me to get
ready?" Notice what happens when you go with the question.

Prayer or Intention: Today may I recognize the link between the
action steps of preparation and the mental state of readiness. May I
take the steps I need to become ready.

JUNE 14

"All things are ready, if our mind be so."
~William Shakespeare, *Henry V*

The setting of intention is going on all the time. We set long-term intentions, whether to go back to school, learn a new musical instrument, or develop a new friendship. We set smaller intentions throughout the day. And truth be told, we set micro intentions moment-to-moment. You are setting an intention each moment that you commit to read the next sentence of this meditation. The Sixth Step is a step of setting an ongoing intention to step into the humility described in the following step.

In the moment-to-moment sense, a meditative spirit allows for a settling of the mind to allow for all things to make themselves apparent as they are. Over the long haul, we look toward the horizon, bringing our attention to the long-term goal of sustainable recovery. Each type of intention feeds the other and guides our words and actions going forward. We no longer are tossed about by our "character defects."

Invitation: Spend 3-5 minutes in a practice of your choice (e.g., sitting meditation, walking meditation, or an expressive practice). Notice the intention inherent in each breath that we take. Notice the intention inherent in setting the timer for this meditation. Notice the intention set before each action you take within the meditation if it is in motion, and the intention of staying still if seated or lying down.

Prayer or Intention: Today I will steady my mind and gaze through setting intention. Let me know that through that settling I will see more clearly.

JUNE 15

"Detachment means letting go and nonattachment
means simply letting be." ~Stephen Levine

Many people in recovery live in fear of letting go. They fear if they truly detach from anything or anyone, there will be nothing to replace it. Even more frightening can be this idea of non-attachment. Since so much of our trauma responses including any addictions or no-longer-skillful behaviors are geared to toward survival and adaptation, the idea of non-attachment and giving up a sense of some control is not necessarily appealing.

When applied in a trauma-informed manner, the Twelve Steps actually provide guideposts and boundaries for the process of detachment. We are able to let go of unhealthy relationships and situations as appropriate. And through a steady application of detachment, non-attachment can arise safely and effectively, again through the Twelve Steps.

Invitation: Spend 3-5 minutes in a practice of your choice (e.g., sitting meditation, walking meditation, or an expressive practice). Notice any relationship or situation that you feel is no longer serving you. See if you can let it go and come back to your object of meditation. If it persists, go ahead and repeat this process as many times as necessary during the meditation.

Prayer or Intention: Today, I will allow the steps to guide me to the action of healthy detachment, and the spirit of non-attachment.

JUNE 16

"The problem with winning the rat race is that even if you win, you're still a rat." ~Lily Tomlin

For many of us on the path of recovery, overworking or workaholism may be a part of our struggle. This can be especially true when unhealed trauma is a part of our story. Work may be one more thing that keeps us from feeling our feelings and truly being with ourselves. Furthermore, the praise that we earn from a job well done may help to boost our ego at times when we are feeling especially down or in need of nurturing. The dopamine released in our brains from this praise can be more soothing and, yes, more addicting than any chemical drug we ingest into our bodies.

Overworking of any kind can be tricky to address because in modern times working is generally necessary to support ourselves and our families. We even talk about the importance of "working" on ourselves or "working" on our recovery. So clearly work in and of itself is not the enemy, it's how we use it. Am I using work to escape something today?

Invitation: Spend 3-5 minutes in a practice of your choice (e.g., sitting meditation, walking meditation, or an expressive practice) and consider the role that work plays in your life today. This work can consist of your job (or series of jobs) or your tendency to overwork in the realm of service and volunteering. Is this work nourishing your recovery and wellness today or keeping you stuck in old patterns of avoidance?

Prayer or Intention: Today I ask for light to be shed on the nature of my relationship with work. May I use my work as a way to serve myself and fellow human beings, not as another way to escape.

JUNE 17

"All prayers get answered: yes, no, or wait."
~recovery slogan

The stress of waiting can cause human beings to self-destruct. Whether you're waiting in a line or waiting for an important decision to come through, frustration is likely. You may ask, "Is this ever going to end???" And while waiting is at very least annoying for most people, for trauma survivors still struggling to heal it can feel like a special kind of hell. Is this wait ever going to end? Our distorted relationships with time is generally the source of this angst.

Even if you don't pray and can't directly relate to the opening quote, please consider that most answers that we receive in life come in the form of a *yes*, a *no*, or a *wait*. Waiting is an inevitable part of the human experience yet we waste so much of our energy fighting it. In many cases, waiting may be required for proper timing to fall into place. As difficult as it can be to remain optimistic, especially if life has let you down so much, can you see the evidence today of where waiting has been a good thing for your recovery?

Invitation: This exercise makes use of life's laboratory. The next opportunity you have to wait—either in line at a store or other public venue, or on the phone holding for customer service—approach it as a meditation. You can use one of the following two sayings to help you: "I accept this wait as spiritual practice today," or "This wait is helping me to exercise my patience muscle today."

Prayer or Intention: As I wait, I practice the acceptance of what is—in doing so I practice recovery.

JUNE 18

"Slow and steady wins the race."
~English language idiom adopted from *Aesop's Fables*

There is a pull to want all the promises and all the rewards of recovery NOW! As individuals struggling with addiction, the propensity we have for instant gratification and instantaneous relief is a real thing that can translate into our recovery life. Often this desire is born out of our experiences with trauma. The temptation to seek a quick fix to healing is very real because our suffering is so great. I'm here to tell you that I've rarely, if ever, seen quick fixes work out sustainably for individuals in recovery.

There is nothing wrong with seeking some immediate relief of symptoms, which is possible through many of the treatments available in the realm of mental health care. However, this must be done with an understanding that true, deep healing takes time. St. Hildegard of Bingen, a 12th century healer, called this process *slow medicine*. This construct may also be useful to those struggling with change, fearing that we aren't doing it right and that's it not happening fast enough. As long as you are taking slow yet steady and consistent steps toward your healing intention, you are on the right track.

Invitation: Spend 3-5 minutes in a practice of your choice (e.g., sitting meditation, walking meditation, or an expressive practice) and contemplate the saying *slow and steady wins the race*. Does this describe your recovery process today? Or are you rushing ahead, exhausting yourself and getting prideful? Are you at a standstill, not moving at all? There are no right or wrong answers in this mini-inventory. This is simply a chance for you to check in and see where you are at.

Prayer or Intention: Today I am open to embracing the wisdom of *slow and steady wins the race*, knowing that the ultimate reward is sustainable health.

JUNE 19

"Step Six is still difficult, but not at all impossible. The only urgent
thing is that we make a beginning, and keep trying."
~Bill Wilson, *Twelve Steps and Twelve Traditions*, p. 68

According to an account of Bill Wilson's relationship with his sponsor,
when he was writing the book *12 Steps and 12 Traditions* he stopped
writing at Step 6 because he felt that he wasn't even sure if he had
worked that step or even knew how to work it. Once his sponsor
helped him with a reframe, he was able to see that the Sixth Step
was about the end of the paralysis of perfectionism. It was about the
importance of process over perfection. In trauma recovery terms, it
was the setting of intention, building a bridge from finding out what
needed to be healed to beginning that healing, and then moving into
the transformation of traumatic material to an adaptive resolution.

No wonder Bill W. found it daunting. It is a bridge between
all three stages of trauma recovery: stabilization and preparation,
transformation of the traumatic material, and walking into the future
with new purpose and skills. Bill's experience and the experience of
millions of others before us can make this work less daunting and more
of an adventure.

Invitation: Spend 3-5 minutes in a practice of your choice (e.g., sitting
meditation, walking meditation, or an expressive practice). Consider
keeping your eyes open, and set your gaze on the horizon at intervals.
Notice what intentions arise for your post-traumatic growth. Notice
any perfectionism that arises with it, and let it go with an out breath.

Prayer or Intention: Today let me notice my intentions for growth.
Let me let go of perfectionism, and allow for small steps in a healthy
direction.

JUNE 20

"There is a seed of the highest good in that field where such symptoms appear." ~ *Tripura Rahasya,* 5.27

In active addiction, we can go to great lengths to avoid negative or intense emotions. When such emotions are connected to unhealed trauma, the intensity at which we experience them can seem unbearable. We use substances or behaviors to numb their intensity or to simply feel better—if only for a while. Sometimes, even in recovery, we can learn to push these feelings away, too afraid that we may not be able to handle it. Some of us do this by striving to keep busy, some of us talk excessively when we really need a good cry, and others may stay cut off from connecting with other people when it seems like the dam will burst. We can go to such lengths, when the simplest solution may just be to feel the feeling and let it flow from there.

Engaging in this practice of feeling what we may ordinarily want to avoid is hard work, yet it can ultimately lead to some of the most fulfilling transformations. Could the stuff that once caused you such pain have the potential to form the foundation on which you will grow?

Invitation: Using the inspiration of the opening passage, bring into your awareness something in your recovery that you find challenging right now—a person, place, thing, situation, or uncomfortable emotion. Notice where you feel any unpleasantness as you hold that awareness, and then imagine that unpleasantness shrinking down to the size of a seed. Perhaps even hold out your hand and visualize the smallness of a seed resting there. Then, place your hand over your heart and bring to mind everything that a seed needs to grow—good soil, water, and sunlight. We also need such qualities, metaphorically and often literally—to nurture our growth in recovery. Spend some time and visualize what might grow from your seed: a flower, a tree, something more mythical? Allow this growth to represent the intention for transformation that you would like to see grow from this seed of struggle.

Prayer or Intention: Help me to realize that what I struggle with today is very likely the seed of my highest good— transformation that is in bloom and continuing to grow.

JUNE 21

"The Croatian word for *weird* or *strange* (čudan) and the Croatian word for *miracle* (čudo) come from the same root." ~Jamie Marich

In modern times, we usually regard a *miracle* as a gift and *weirdness* as a curse. What if we started to view them as one and the same? Would more of us feel comfortable coming out as weird, or more widely acknowledge that we all do some pretty weird things? Might we feel better about trying some of the recovery and wellness practices that people suggest to us without immediately condemning them as too weird?

Many people prevent themselves from getting the help they may most require out of fear that the practice seems too bizarre, or that others will judge them. In the last several years, many friends, students, and folks we mentor have shared with me their concerns about being perceived as *too weird*. Whether it's a feeling of self-consciousness about cleaning regimens, spiritual practices, or ways of seeing the world that may clash with the mainstream, people can viciously judge themselves based on the fear of how others will respond. How much more freedom could we experience if we learn to shed this judgment?

Invitation: Spend at least 3-5 minutes in sitting practice or in another expressive practice of your choosing (be as weird as you want—that's the point) noticing the interplay between the word *weird* and the word *miracle*. Both imply something supernatural or out-of-the-ordinary. Is there anything else you're noticing? What is keeping you today from accepting your own sense of *weirdness* or *differentness* as a miracle of creation?

Prayer or Intention: Help me to accept myself and all of my weirdness as a miracle today and on the path ahead.

JUNE 22

"When you sing, you pray twice." ~St. Augustine

Inherent in post-traumatic stress and addiction is the feeling or actuality of a lack of choice. In recovery, one of the things we recover is the power of choice. There may still be external and internal barriers to a sense of or an actual reality of a complete freedom, but when working the steps we can always be pointed toward a greater sense of freedom and autonomy.

One way we can exercise our freedom is by singing out, by expressing ourselves, not only in our pain, but in our joy. Just like the Cat Stevens song *Sing Out* (one of our favorites), invites us to do. In this recovery process I can sing, dance, and find joy. I can find the "million ways to be" and choose what fits.

Invitation: Spend 3-5 minutes in a practice of your choice (e.g., sitting meditation, walking meditation, or an expressive practice). Notice if there is a song, a movement, or poem that is asking to be expressed. Find time in the day to write the poem, sing the song, dance the dance.

Prayer or Intention: Today let me find freedom in the joy of expression. Allow me to discover some of the million ways to be.

JUNE 23

"Deep mindfulness arises from a view of our radical interconnectedness, that which links us each and all in our particular pain and possibility to earth, fire, wind, water, and space." ~Rhonda V. Magee

Recovery begins from a place of our being united in our pain. The moment we enter the stream of the recovery community, we are also united in our possibility. We join together in becoming more adaptively connected to our world; the physical and metaphysical world. We are people who have survived, and together we work so that we all might thrive.

This interconnectedness can be messy, but it is the source of our strength and resilience to move forward. As an old Zen teacher of mine used to say, we can walk shoulder to shoulder along our path, growing in our strength from each other's practice.

Invitation: Spend 3-5 minutes in a practice of your choice (e.g., sitting meditation, walking meditation, or an expressive practice). If you are sitting alone, visualize yourself sitting with others in your sangha or home group. Notice any sensations, emotions, or thoughts that accompany knowing you are receiving and sending mindful energy to others.

Prayer or Intention: Today I will walk shoulder to shoulder with my fellow survivors and thrivers.

JUNE 24

"Inside of you is a river of joy. Go drown in it."
~Michael Singer

I hear people talking, both in recovery circles and in the general public, about being happy. You may have said things like, "I'm not happy in this relationship," or "I just want to be happy." When you are depressed, you may wonder of happiness will ever return. I still remember discussing this topic at one of the first women's meetings I attended, and it stuck with me over the years—there is a difference between happiness and joy.

Happiness comes and goes. Like many other feelings, it can be fleeting. Due to the nature of the human experience, no one can be happy all the time. Joy, however, is a permanent state that exists deep in your heart and soul. Joy is fueled by your source—whatever you conceive that to be—and lets you know at your core that even when you are sad, angry, or depressed, you are okay and life is going to turn out okay. Have I discovered the fullness of joy in my life?

Invitation: Spend 3-5 minutes in a practice of your choice (e.g., sitting meditation, walking meditation, or an expressive practice) and challenge yourself to bring up this idea of joy being more core and permanent compared to happiness, which is more transient and fleeting. Then notice the source of joy in your life, or where you may experience joy within yourself. If you feel cut off from joy right now, this can be a normal part of the recovery or healing experience. Perhaps set an intention to get to know joy as opposed to happiness.

Prayer or Intention: May I realize the sources of joy within myself today and recognize those people, places, and things that help me feel most connection to this joy-source.

JUNE 25

"The thing is stuck . . . We can turn to the poem. We can open the book. Somebody has been there for us and deep-dived the words."
~Jeanette Winterson

One of my favorite sayings in 12-step programs is that the good part about a meeting is that not everyone is having the same terrible day on the same day. That is one way that meetings can help break isolation. Also, meetings are a place where stories are used for healing. Hearing the story of another who has had time to sort through that story and garner insights can be helpful to our own recovery. When we are not at meetings we can reach out for the poems, stories, and prayers that speak our truths for us. These can be true stories like memoirs, or it can be fiction.

Until we are ready and able to be our own storyteller, we can rely on those who have come before us to find the healing balm that can be found in story, in sharing, in words of compassionate healing. It can be the length of the novel, or a poem that can be recited in one breath. Words can hurt, but words can also heal.

Invitation: Spend 3-5 minutes in a practice of your choice (e.g., sitting meditation, walking meditation, or an expressive practice). Choose a short phrase that feels healing to contemplate like a mantra for this practice. It can even be just one word, such as peace, healing, smiling . . . anything that feels like a resource.

Prayer or Intention: Today I will look for opportunities to find my story in the stories of others.

JUNE 26

"Always be a first rate version of yourself and not a second rate
version of somebody else." ~Judy Garland

Authenticity is glorious. To live life with full abandon, not afraid of
what others will think! To approach every day as an opportunity to
shine your light of truth in the world. And it's so much easier said than
done! Consider how the author of the beautiful quote that opens this
meditation—one of the most used to describe authentic living—lost
her battle with addiction at the age of 49.

We tend to grow up in a culture of comparison, constantly being
shown how we are never as good as some other person. In our work
we've discovered that even very talented, high achieving people are
still prone to believing they are not good enough, especially when
comparing their work, their body, or their talent to another. When we
can move past the external metric of judgment, we are typically able to
grow in appreciation for who we are and what we have to offer to the
world. This is a vital opening to living a more authentic and ultimately
more serene life.

Invitation: Spend 3-5 minutes in a practice of your choice (e.g.,
sitting meditation, walking meditation, or an expressive practice) and
notice where comparisons have kept you stuck or are keeping you
stuck. What is the direct link you are noticing between your tendency
to compare and your willingness to live a more authentic life?

Prayer or Intention: Today I will focus on myself and refrain from
focusing on myself in comparison to others around me.

JUNE 27

"Have you talked to the little ones inside of you?"
~Svetozar Kraljevic, OFM

The phrase *inner child* can get tossed around quite a bit in recovery circles. So much so that talking about that inner child may feel like a corny cliché. However, getting in touch with both the wisdom and the pain of this little one (or in some cases, little ones) is vital for our overall healing. In cases of profound unhealed trauma, this will likely require the guidance of a qualified therapist or professional. Trauma-informed sponsors and others in your recovery support circles may also be able to provide you and the younger selves that remained unhealed inside of your system vital support in this process.

Our inner child or younger selves are great sources of wisdom because they may still be able to see the world with faith, optimism, and a spirit of beginner's mind. As part of our recovery journey we may also need to recognize where our younger selves are especially susceptible to hurt and pain, and especially when they can get triggered by current life circumstances reminiscent of wounding from those early days. Am I willing to help my inner child and these younger parts heal?

Invitation: Take at least 3-5 minutes in a reflection practice of your choice: sitting meditation, walking meditation, or an expressive arts practice (e.g., writing, artmaking, dancing/movement). Call on the inspiration of our opening quote and talk to the little one or little ones inside of you. Let them know that you want to hear from them today and notice what they reveal. If at any point the practice feels too overwhelming for where you are at today, come back to a basic grounding practice and consider trying again later, perhaps with the help or support of a therapist or sponsor.

Prayer or Intention: May I listen to both the wisdom and the pain of my little one(s) today and allow them to teach me what I need to know for the journey ahead.

JUNE 28

"In any moment of decision, the best thing you can do is the right thing, the next best thing is the wrong thing, and the worst thing you can do is nothing." ~Theodore Roosevelt

This hard-hitting wisdom from U.S. President Theodore Roosevelt, himself the survivor of innumerable traumas and losses, speaks to an important principle of recovery. Action is vital and critical in the process of change. There are many facets of traditional 12-step programs that encourage action when we are struggling, namely use of the telephone (or messenger/text messaging in modern times). When you go to meetings you are encouraged to get phone numbers. Picking up and dialing the telephone when you are in need of help is a major part of our history as members of 12-step fellowships. When Bill W. was tempted to drink in May of 1935, he picked up the phone in the lobby of the Mayflower Hotel and just kept calling churches until he found another alcoholic to whom he could speak. This lead him to Dr. Bob.

Even if you do not reach someone on the phone or you don't get a message back right away, consider that the action of dialing the numbers or entering the message in your phone is still proactive. You are *doing* something other than just ruminating with the obsessions in your head. Even if you don't reach anybody, keep calling and texting until you do. You may even realize that the simple action of reaching out and moving your hands to do it will create enough space and time for your obsessions and cravings to pass.

Invitation: This invitation directly corresponds to the topic of today's meditation. You are encouraged to practice reaching out, either via a phone call or text message. Even if you reach out to people on a daily basis, do it today as part of this practice. If you reach out and don't know what to say, you can simply open with, "I am practicing reaching out," or "I am practicing using the telephone." People will know what you mean!

Prayer or Intention: Today I recognize the healing power of action in my recovery and reaching out to others is part of that action.

JUNE 29

smiriti: a Sanskrit term meaning "coming back to awareness"
or the "memory of having been aware"

There are three Eastern languages that have terms from which we draw the English word *mindfulness*—Pali, Chinese, and Sanskrit. The Sanskrit word, *smiriti*, is especially powerful. The subtle meaning—coming back to awareness—suggest several things. First, awareness is our natural state. Second, it's natural and normal for us to wander away from awareness. We are always invited to return.

Many people in recovery believe that they can't practice meditation or mindfulness because they can't stay still or focused. Be kind to yourself. As this translation suggest, the heart of the practice is in the coming back to awareness once you have wandered from it. I often tell clients that even if their attention wanders ten times in a minute of attempting a sitting meditation, that's okay—come back to awareness ten times. This returning *is* the practice.

Invitation: Set aside 3-5 minutes to engage in a sitting meditation practice. If sitting upright is not physically possible for you, lie down or recline, and keep the eyes open. Find an anchor or focus of your choice—it can be your breath or an object that you can see in the room or hold in your hand. Stay committed to total focus on your breath or the object. If your attention wanders away from it, simply bring it back to your point of focus. Be kind to yourself if your attention wanders—you can always bring it back.

Prayer or Intention: May I be kind to myself if my attention wanders from my focus today. I take refuge in the assurance that I can return at any time.

JUNE 30

"Restore your attention or bring it to a new level by dramatically slowing down whatever you're doing." ~Sharon Salzberg

In our pre-recovery lives, we may have spent a great deal of time trying to move quickly with the modern pace of life, trying to accumulate things or people or experiences and get to one or another destination. Having never truly arrived at the apparently illusory Destination Perfect Job, Destination Perfect Relationship, or Destination Perfect *Anything*, we may still believe that sprinting will get us somewhere—anywhere but the here and now.

In Step 6, there is a sense of slowing down after what can be an arduous set of actions in Steps 1 through 5. There is a shift from discovery and sharing to a state of contemplation and preparation. This is a perfect time to hone in on our mindfulness skills and principles. We can slow down, take in, and appreciate what we have done in doing Steps 4 and 5. Then, we can consider our readiness to change further, and our level of humility and preparedness to both ask for help and take action in new ways. All of this is emboldened by mindfulness.

Invitation: Spend 3-5 minutes in a practice of your choice (e.g., sitting meditation, walking meditation, or an expressive practice). Take this chance to slow down and make your practice as simple as possible. Just notice your object of meditation, and notice when you are distracted from it. Then come back to it. That is the whole practice.

Prayer or Intention: Today I will try and slow down so that I might apply mindfulness to the large and small aspects of my day.

JULY 1

"This too shall pass." ~recovery saying

When we are at the height of our pain before recovery or even in recovery, this slogan seems patently untrue. Until we are able to see some light at the end of the tunnel, and we are able to assess that it is not a proverbial oncoming train, we might not believe this statement. From the perspective of the historical Buddha, *This Too Shall Pass* is the truest statement ever. He taught about the truth of impermanence, and how understanding this truth to its depths is at the heart of what we in 12-step programs call recovery.

Unhealed trauma actually defies the truth of impermanence. Because of the way our memories are maladaptively stored, we are unable to connect with the fact that things are passing. Working the steps and our trauma recovery together allows us to see the wisdom, the healing, and the power of impermanence. Indeed, this too shall pass.

Invitation: Spend 3-5 minutes in a practice of your choice (e.g., sitting meditation, walking meditation, or an expressive practice). Utilize the simplest form of meditation to notice impermanence. On the in breath, note silently "Arising". On the out breath, notice "Passing".

Prayer or Intention: Today let me flow with the path of impermanence. Let me know that this too shall pass, whatever *this* is.

JULY 2

"When I am breathing in, I know I am breathing in. When I am
breathing out, I know that I am breathing out." ~Buddha

Even Buddha chimed in on what happens when intoxication takes
over. He noted the loss of wealth, increased quarreling, disrepute, and
other well-known consequences of addiction. The one he noted as
the key to both the difficulty and the recovery was weakened insight.
Buddha taught many things, reportedly giving over 80,000 instructions
over his teaching career. Almost all of these instructions pointed us
toward achieving insight into all things, something that can only be
accomplished by moving through the stages of trauma recovery,
allowing our bodies to settle, so that we might be able to have access to
our cognitive functions.

Simple breath awareness allows us to do this. Of the Twelve
Steps, Steps 4 through 7 are the insight steps. We grow in our insight
into our difficulties by inventorying them, sharing them, and then
contemplating and shifting our awareness regarding the thoughts and
behaviors that sustained our previous life. Through this insight, we also
discover and are able to integrate the new neural pathways created,
and the new agency and ability to utilize our insight to create a new
life in recovery.

Invitation: Spend 3-5 minutes in a practice of your choice (e.g.,
sitting meditation, walking meditation, or an expressive practice).
On the in-breath, say silently, "When I am breathing in, I know I am
breathing in." On the out-breath, "When I am breathing out, I know
I am breathing out.

Prayer or Intention: Today I can notice my journey to insight,
simply from having insight into the simplicity of my moment-to-
moment experience of the breath.

JULY 3

"Freeing yourself was one thing, claiming ownership of that freed self was another." ~Toni Morrison, *Beloved*

Many people in recovery struggle with the speed of recovery, often feeling it does not proceed quickly enough. There is that feeling of, "Hey, I have given up my addiction, so shouldn't everything be awesome and shouldn't everything go my way?" This is quite natural, because the first burst of freedom that comes from giving up harmful behaviors and substances is quite profound. So, when life gets in the way and feels like a burden despite that new freedom, of course it can be frustrating.

Trauma recovery allows us to slow down and fully take ownership of our freedom. We get to go through the steps and through our other healing modalities to reprocess those memories and beliefs that drove our addictions. We then see that we are not just free, but we are reborn, remade, we are a 2.0 version of our previous selves. Our authentic selves shine through. And that is true freedom.

Invitation: Spend 3-5 minutes in a practice of your choice (e.g., sitting meditation, walking meditation, or an expressive practice). Breathe in the words, "I am free." Breathe out, "I am me."

Prayer or Intention: Today I will step fully into my freedom, owning my true self throughout the day.

JULY 4

"Freedom is what you do with what has been done to you."
~Jean Paul Sartre

The opening teaching by Sartre is one of my favorite lessons that I've embraced as a trauma survivor. This teaching helps to remind me that the greatest redemption I can experience is to not let the toll of what harmed me continue to weigh me down. Today I choose to live the experience of a survivor, a thriver, and an example of post-traumatic growth. Taking the steps is one measure of many that assists in this process.

While this insight doesn't necessarily help every trauma survivor, it helps me to think that when I do not actively take care of myself and my recovery on a day-to-day basis, I am letting the trauma win. I am letting those who harmed me and injure me continue to hold power over me. It is certainly not easy to wade through and undo the entanglements caused by trauma, yet I know it is possible through commitment to the healing process. In this healing and transformation my power continues to flourish.

Invitation: Spend 3-5 minutes in a practice of your choice (e.g., sitting meditation, walking meditation, or an expressive practice) and contemplate the quote that opens the meditation today. Notice whatever you notice, especially how the wisdom of this teaching may relate to you and your journey today.

Prayer or Intention: Today I recognize that I am a survivor of trauma and adverse life experiences. What I do with that recognition is completely up to me.

JULY 5

"An expert is a man who has made all the mistakes
which can be made, in a narrow field."~Niels Bohr

Both of us are considered *trauma experts* because of our work and what
we have contributed to the field. It's empowering to consider that what
makes someone an expert is a tally of all that you've achieved. It's also
taking a good look at where you have made mistakes and have been
able to learn accordingly. By this definition, we all qualify as experts
on our own lives, especially if we are willing to take a look at what
happened or what went wrong and commit to make adjustments.

Using the wisdom of Niels Bohr can be a fascinating way to
approach inventory of any kind. Whether you are preparing for a
Fourth Step or dealing with making a major decision in your life and
you are feeling stuck with that all too familiar sense of *I'm not good
enough*, consider that even experts make mistakes. Heck, what makes
someone an expert is that you've made every mistake in the book and
have lived to tell the tale! By sharing what you've learned from your
mistakes, you become an ideal candidate for helping others.

Invitation: Spend 3-5 minutes in a practice of your choice (e.g.,
sitting meditation, walking meditation, or an expressive practice) and
contemplate the idea that an expert is someone who has made every
mistake possible. Who is someone that you admire and look up to as
an expert? If you know them personally, consider asking them what
they have to share with you about mistake that they have made and
learned from along the way. If you don't know them personally but
had a chance to meet them someday, what is one question you would
like to ask them about mistakes?

Prayer or Intention: Help me to realize that every mistake I've ever
made can be used for a larger purpose and a greater good.

JULY 6

"Some people will see their role as a pilgrim in terms of setting up a fine family, or establishing a business inheritance. Everyone's got their own definition. Mine, I suppose, is to know myself." ~Eric Clapton

The term *pilgrimage* may conjure up some historically charged (i.e., English Separatists with funny hats landing on Plymouth Rock) or religious connotations. Many global faith traditions stress the importance of traveling to make pilgrimage. People of the Muslim faith are asked to make pilgrimage or *hajj* to Mecca at least once in their lives, and there are scores of holy sites in the Catholic-Christian world that are places of pilgrimage for many. Pilgrimage simply means to cross a threshold. All life offers us opportunities to make pilgrimage and indeed, the journey of recovery may be the most important one.

I've spent much of my life making pilgrimage, whether to actual sacred sites throughout the world or doing the sacred work of recovery in my life. I've learned that pilgrimages are meant to be challenging, and in these challenges lay opportunities for growth. Delays and setbacks can be part of the process, yet dropping expectations can open you up to a world of new possibilities that you never could have planned even if you tried.

Invitation: Spend 3-5 minutes in a practice of your choice (e.g., sitting meditation, walking meditation, or an expressive practice) and contemplate the world *pilgrimage*. This could be the first time that you've ever considered it as it relates to your recovery. What threshold are you being asked to cross today in your journey of recovery and wellness?

Prayer or Intention: May I approach my life and my recovery with the heart and soul of a pilgrim—willing to cross thresholds, however challenging they may be.

JULY 7

"Piglet noticed that even though he had a Very Small Heart,
it could hold a rather large amount of Gratitude."
~A.A. Milne

There was a joke going around in the New York City rooms of recovery in the late 80s and early 90s about a meeting on Friday nights in Soho. It was a very large meeting centered around a speaker with a topic. Once in a while, a friend of mine would ask, "What do you think the topic is tonight, acceptance or gratitude?" We would laugh, partly because it was true. A high percentage of the talks would relate to these two subjects.

There is a reason for this. Acceptance is something most of us need to learn in recovery, sometimes from scratch. And gratitude sometimes feels like it's fake when we first work with it, since life seems to have dealt us a bad hand. Cultivating gratitude, even when we feel we have a Very Small Heart, can lead to a larger heart, a deeper acceptance, and an authentic sense of gratitude.

Invitation: Spend 3-5 minutes in a practice of your choice (e.g., sitting meditation, walking meditation, or an expressive practice). Make a gratitude list of three things in your life, and meditate upon them during this session. Notice any pleasant or unpleasant sensations, thoughts or feelings that arise.

Prayer or Intention: I know today that cultivating gratitude may feel phony at times, but can eventually lead to an authentic joy, equanimity, and heart filled with gratitude.

JULY 8

"Honor the transition."
~Jamie Marich, teaching in *Dancing Mindfulness*

Hurrying from one thing to the next is the source of great frustration in life. Whether we rush to get from job to job or errand to errand, the rushed pace can keep us from breathing and can keep our heart rate elevated. Even the major transitions of life that can come with recovery will cause us stress. We may want to have years sober now (and all the wisdom and serenity that can come with it), and forget to savor the process. Both trauma and addiction recovery can prompt us to make major life changes—divorce, ending relationships, moving jobs, changing our living situation. These are all transitions. While they may be happening for our best interest, it is still important to be gentle with ourselves in the process.

Part of mindfulness practice is honoring the transition. Moving gently and slowly from one activity to the next—instead of working on a frantic autopilot—can be a key to greater sense of peace. Am I willing to slow down the pace of my existence today by learning to honor transitions?

Invitation: Think of transitions you normally make on autopilot. For many of us, it's moving from sitting down to standing up, or making our way from one room to the next. Pick any of these transitional activities in daily life and make a conscious intention to experiment with moving very slowly and noticing everything along the way. If you are choosing the sitting down to standing up option, experiment with taking at least one whole minute to come to your feet. What do you notice along the way?

Prayer or Intention: Today may I learn to honor transitions and learn what they have to teach me about enjoying the process, the journey.

JULY 9

"You are never strong enough that you don't need help."
~Cesar Chavez

The Seventh Step implores us to ask for help. Humility tells us to ask for help even when we think we have become stronger than strong. We have heard many stories in recovery from people who stopped asking for help when they gathered a number of years in the program because they didn't really think they needed the help anymore. They would stop going to meetings, or not get sponsorship or fellowship, or fall into old patterns of trying to go it alone.

As one of my recovering friends in NYC used to say, "Even the President has a Cabinet." There is no reason I should believe myself either so strong that I don't need help, or too ashamed to ask for help because I "should" be strong enough by now. Trauma-informed recovery tells me I can always ask for help.

Invitation: Spend 3-5 minutes in a practice of your choice (e.g., sitting meditation, walking meditation, or an expressive practice). Meditate upon a difficulty you are having right now, whether great or small, and then upon someone you could ask for help with this difficulty. Allow yourself to notice body sensations, feelings and thoughts that go with this process.

Prayer or Intention: Today I will not consider myself too strong to ask for help.

JULY 10

"Give credit to whom credit is due." ~Samuel Adams

When I first tried to get sober, I talked to a priest I respected to sort out what felt like a mixed message. I asked him, "On one hand people are telling me I need to love myself more, and on the other hand I'm hearing about the importance of not being prideful or conceited. Which is it?" His explanation made a world of difference.

He offered that loving yourself as a child of God or creation (depending on your belief system) is key. When it comes to the things that you "do," take pride in them while also giving credit where credit is due. This can mean honoring your Higher Power, divine guidance, or the teachers who helped paved the way for you. Doing so keeps us healthy in a humble way. The important point is to always recognize that even if you have many skills, accomplishments, and good deeds to your credit, you recognize that you are not in it alone.

Intention: Spend 3-5 minutes in a practice of your choice (e.g., sitting meditation, walking meditation, or an expressive practice) and bring to mind those who have helped you along the way. This can include spiritual resources, people, or a combination of both. Send them a prayer or sense of gratitude for what they have helped you to accomplish thus far. Are you willing to continue to draw upon their wisdom?

Prayer or Intention: Today I recognize that I am a beloved child of creation and that I am not in this alone.

JULY 11

"It's one thing to feel that you are on the right path, but it's another to think yours is the only path." ~Paolo Coehlo

One thing that Bill Wilson warned about in a letter found in *As Bill Sees It* was the possibility of 12-step philosophy becoming dogmatic. There was probably no way on Earth to stop this from happening to a certain degree, but now in the new millennium we have an opportunity to reboot our understanding of the program. An important message from the early days of AA was that you were encouraged to find a Higher Power of your own understanding. Ebby told Bill as much, actually asking him if he had ever considered coming up with his own conception.

We are empowered to come up with our version of the path. We are not empowered to demand that others follow our version of the path, or some version of the "original" path that we have determined is the one and only way. Trauma-informed recovery leans in to this aspect of the program—guidelines are provided to facilitate the creation of a personalized relationship to the Twelve Steps and all of their principles and practices.

Invitation: Spend 3-5 minutes in a practice of your choice (e.g., sitting meditation, walking meditation, or an expressive practice). Meditate for this period on your conception of the 12-step path. If that includes a Higher Power, then reflect on that conception as well.

Prayer or Intention: Today I will walk my path and not try to have others conform to my journey, but rather walk shoulder-to-shoulder, supportive of each other.

JULY 12

"Do so without judgment or comment."
~Kripalu and Amrit yoga teaching

Whenever I teach *Dancing Mindfulness* classes and my students begin to get a little chatty with each other, I say to myself, "There goes the commentary." Indeed, through much of my experience as a teacher of many practices, I notice that we have a tendency to comment, to joke, and to self-deprecate when we begin to judge ourselves. Sometimes that judgment is about the process of change, other times the experience is pure judgment of ourselves. "I'm not doing this right," "I'm not worthy," "I'm a loser." Instead of embracing the feelings that may come with that and deal with them, our tendency is to comment.

Although people in recovery are definitely entitled to opinions and to speak up when something doesn't feel right, consider how commentary is something completely different. Commentary includes the things we say to ourselves and to others in order to avoid or to change course. Commentary can be always having an opinion or having lots to say about something or someone else while neglecting to look at ourselves. How has my own tendency to *comment* kept me blocked from experiencing everything recovery and healing may have to offer me?

Invitation: Spend 3-5 minutes in a practice of your choice (e.g., sitting meditation, walking meditation, or an expressive practice) and deliberately engage in the practice without commentary. If you notice the tendency to comment arise (e.g., "How long is this going to last?" "I can't do this practice right either") see if you can notice that tendency to comment and let it pass. Once the commentary passes, experience the moment as fully as possible.

Prayer or Intention: May I recognize how my tendencies to comment when I am met with unpleasant emotions or experiences are keeping me blocked. May I let go of the judgment that fuels the commentary every time I exhale.

JULY 13

ACE: Accept, Change, Eliminate
~recovery acronym

I first received the wisdom of *ACE* in the rooms of Al-Anon. We talk a great deal about acceptance, changing the things we can, and setting boundaries as respective topics in recovery, yet we don't seem to discuss how all three of them together form this powerful acronym. When something is disagreeable or causing us stress in any part of our life, our three essential choices boil down to Accept, Change, or Eliminate.

We can accept the person or situation as being exactly who/what it is supposed to be in this moment (remembering that accepting something doesn't mean we have to like it). We can make changes—to our attitude, outlook, and approach (remembering that changing the other is generally futile). If both of these do not bring us peace, our third choice is to set the boundary and eliminate that person or situation from our lives. If eliminating just isn't feasible, we generally need to return to A and C in combination.

Invitation: Bring up some person, place, thing, or situation in your life that you would currently describe as stressful. Run it through the ACE test. You can do this via a meditation practice of your choice, or write it down on paper or in your journal. What are you noticing?

Prayer or Intention: May I realize that with every situation or stressor today, I have at least three choices—accept, change, or eliminate.

JULY 14

"Life is to be lived, not controlled; and humanity is won by continuing to play in face of certain defeat." ~Ralph Ellison

Especially in early recovery, there were many days where I looked at the prospect of doing another day without my old behaviors and substances, and all I could see was drudgery and pointlessness. Those are the days that truly built my recovery. I would have that feeling, and then do anything and everything to counterbalance it with action—particularly the action of reaching out for help. Sometimes I am having the bad day, sometimes it is one or more of my friends.

If we all keep a practice of reaching out and responding when we are reached out to, then we will always be able to find someone to give us just enough energy to get through those days that seem like certain defeat. This is the skillful combination of acceptance and action.

Invitation: Spend 3-5 minutes in a practice of your choice (e.g., sitting meditation, walking meditation, or an expressive practice). During this practice period, notice your feeling and attitude about the day ahead. If it is positive, lean into that feeling, thought, or sensation. If it feels difficult, meditate upon who you can reach out to today to help you walk through the day.

Prayer or Intention: Today let me reach out if I need help. Let me be available if someone needs me.

JULY 15

"To be yourself in a world that is constantly trying to make you something else is the greatest accomplishment."
~Ralph Waldo Emerson

You are not alone in the attempt to be true to yourself. Trauma and addiction can lead us away from ourselves. It is not our fault—our survival mechanisms were activated, and perhaps they were not able to link up with our adaptive memory networks. Over time, more and more experiences were stored in a maladaptive way, and this unconsciously encouraged more maladaptive attempts at an adaptive resolution.

Recovery gives us the gift of more adaptive behaviors, thoughts, and feelings, while the old material and behaviors are reprocessed and we let go of them. All of this then allows us to live by the saying found on many of the 12-step coins: To Thine Own Self Be True.

Invitation: Spend 3-5 minutes in a practice of your choice (e.g., sitting meditation, walking meditation, or an expressive practice). Focus on the mantra, "To thine own self be true." Notice any body sensations, thoughts, and feelings that arise from these words.

Prayer or Intention: Today I will be true to myself. When I am not sure what that would mean, I will be open to new answers.

JULY 16

"True humility does not know that it is humble. If it did, it would be proud from the contemplation of so fine a virtue." ~Martin Luther

Step 7 directs us to have humility. There is a conundrum present in that formulation, as Martin Luther points out here. How can we have humility, when it requires that we not believe that we have it, lest we fall into taking pride in our "humility?" As with much of the program, the first six steps help us to develop humility.

If we have applied ourselves through the admission of our difficulties, the acceptance of help, the ongoing process of making healthier decisions, the inventory and admission of Steps 4 and 5, and the willingness to strive for readiness in the Sixth Step, then the humility required for Step 7 comes naturally. Even though the steps are not always worked in order, the working of them in order provides a growing strength to go on to the next step, and to continue with our process of recovery in general.

Invitation: Spend 3-5 minutes in a practice of your choice (e.g., sitting meditation, walking meditation, or an expressive practice). Notice anything that makes you feel humble, whether it be Nature, your conception of a Higher Power, love, or anything that feels bigger than you. Meditate upon this thing or quality for today's meditation.

Prayer or Intention: Let me find humility through action—my action on the steps and on my recovery in general.

JULY 17

"That which we call paradise or happiness or the Dharma or
enlightenment cannot be sought outside us. It will be found only
when we notice we are innately endowed with it."
~ Shundo Aoyama, *Zen Seeds*

Often in the 12-step rooms people will say that recovery is an "inside
job." This is one of the more trauma-informed slogans uttered by
people in the program. In trauma work, we do not start by trying to
force internal resources on the person in recovery, but rather we try
to identify those resources that are already there. You may be aware
of them, or through gentle investigation you may find those that have
been dormant or hidden by difficulties in your life. These internal
resources are your innate nature, your birthright, your "original face
before your parents were born," as the Zen saying goes.

The steps provide a template for this type of self-reflection, with
several admonitions in the literature to not forget the positive when
going through the forest of the negative. This is how we build our
positive neural networks, build resilience, and then reprocess the traumatic material to an adaptive resolution. This is actually implicitly in
the steps, and now we are making it explicit so we might find our way.

Invitation: Spend 3-5 minutes in a practice of your choice (e.g.,
sitting meditation, walking meditation, or an expressive practice).
Meditate upon the current state of your internal resources. See if
you can find within yourself at least one that resonates for you in this
moment. Gently breathe your appreciation into the resource, and on
the out-breath, see if you can feel the power of the resource.

Prayer or Intention: As I go throughout this day, let me again and
again tap back into my internal resources, those resilient powers that
are mine to acknowledge, celebrate, and utilize.

JULY 18

I/E: intelligence/emotions ~recovery saying

The guidance of I/E is well-known to many of us who have attended 12-step meetings. The intention here is very good—in making a decision, we need both our intellect and our emotions and the intellect needs to be in the driver's seat. While I sometimes wrestle with this slogan, as I think healthy decision-making in recovery ought to involve a blend of intellect and emotion, I can appreciate the intention of this nugget. Don't operate on raw emotion!

This idea is much easier said than done with the traumatized brain. In fact, this guidance can be nearly impossible for a person with unhealed trauma who experiences a great deal of limbic level activation. The limbic brain is the seat of our emotions and when we are activated by a trigger the emotions naturally take over because blood flow rushes to the limbic brain and suspends flow to the left pre-frontal cortex. This is the part of our brain where processing and good decision-making happens. Having this knowledge is not meant as an excuse to act out and hurt yourself or others when you are triggered. Like much of the knowledge offered throughout *Trauma and the 12 Steps*, our intention is to empower you into healing action. What do you need to do today to heal the impact of trauma on your limbic brain?

Invitation: Spend 3-5 minutes in a practice of your choice (e.g., sitting meditation, walking meditation, or an expressive practice), although sitting is most recommended for this exercise. Keep your eyes open, especially if you are feeling a little raw in approaching this exercise. As you breathe naturally, on the inhale say to yourself: *I am not.* On the exhale say to yourself: *My emotions.* To be clear, this exercise is not about shaming or ridiculing you for having emotions as those or normal. See if you can experiment with using the power of your breath to diffuse their impact and restore the I/E balance.

Prayer or Intention: May I live my life with the wisdom of my intellect and my emotions today. Both are valuable, although neither define me.

JULY 19

"Enlightenment does not mean that your ego is suppressed or denied. It does mean that it is deconstructed, seen through, exposed, and then reeducated and reconstructed." ~Roshi Junpo Denis Kelly

The Twelve Steps do not promise enlightenment, or do they? A pamphlet from the early Akron group edited by Dr. Bob talked about the similarities between the "8-part program" suggested by the historical Buddha and the Twelve Steps. Many in the 12-step community see the program as a breaking down of the ego, but that doesn't mean it is beaten to smithereens. Rather, it is deconstructed and re-formed through education and action in a healthy manner. In trauma terms, our ego material gets reprocessed to an adaptive resolution.

In essence, Junpo Roshi describes the steps here where we come face-to-face with the constructs of our ego and survival instincts, and we reprocess through step work and outside help to arrive at our true nature. Enlightenment is therefore not an esoteric and unattainable state, but rather waiting for us every moment in the here and now for us to discover.

Invitation: Spend 3-5 minutes in a practice of your choice (e.g., sitting meditation, walking meditation, or an expressive practice). If it feels comfortable, today sit in silence. Notice thoughts, notice them arise, notice them pass like clouds. If this becomes too uncomfortable, allow yourself to notice physical grounding. But see if you can notice the temporary nature of things, with your thoughts as the focus today.

Prayer or Intention: Today I will look for evidence of the changing of my thinking. I will notice what my step work has done away with, and what it has revealed.

JULY 20

"Learning to let go should be learned before learning
to get. Life should be touched, not strangled. You've
got to relax, let it happen at times, and at others move
forward with it."~Ray Bradbury

What is the humility described in the Seventh Step in trauma-informed recovery? For many of us, working the first six steps allows us to learn how to let go. This doesn't mean an eternal release starting the moment we work the step. Rather, we develop a practice of letting go, of relaxing, of knowing which part of the Serenity Prayer is called for at any given moment. The "humble asking" of Step 7 is, in a sense, taking up a prayerful position in matters great and small, with the widest definition of prayer and Higher Power possible. And it allows us to leverage the gains of the first six steps: an ongoing practice of acknowledgement, identification, making decisions, taking inventory, letting go, becoming willing, and working as part of a community.

This makes for a holistic and trauma-informed application of Step 7. We ask, is this a relax-and-let-it-happen moment? Is this a move-it-forward moment? We have more agency and insight through our work thus far and we can answer these questions, though often still with the help of trusted others. But now we are one of the trusted others for ourselves.

Invitation: Spend 3-5 minutes in a practice of your choice (e.g., sitting meditation, walking meditation, or an expressive practice). On the in breath, notice "Touching life." On the out breath, "moving forward." Notice any thoughts, feelings or body sensations that accompany this meditation.

Prayer or Intention: I have the humility to ask, when it is time to allow and when it is time to move forward. I have the ability and resilience to answer these questions for myself today.

JULY 21

"Live and Let Live." ~recovery slogan

What is a trauma-informed interpretation of this slogan? My closest translation would be learning to set boundaries. Boundaries are not easy when we have been through a great deal of trauma and adverse life events. Many of those traumas were about boundary crossings. In addition, we may not have taught boundary setting or had it modeled for us. Our substance and behavioral addictions may have increased our tolerance for boundaryless situations and relationships. In recovery, we get to set boundaries so that we might live our lives fully, being true to ourselves.

Meanwhile, boundaries allow others around us to live as well, true to themselves. With some people and situations, we will have fluid boundaries, intimacy, and engagement. With others, it may be necessary to put some distance, disengage, and allow for space. As we become more skilled at boundary setting, we become more a more able to Live, and we become more and more able to Let Live.

Invitation: Spend 3-5 minutes in a practice of your choice (e.g., sitting meditation, walking meditation, or an expressive practice). Notice those people and situations with which you feel you can be engaged. Welcome them. If anyone arises that you need space with, go ahead and visualize the boundary or the space. Notice any changes in body sensations, emotions, or thoughts.

Prayer or Intention: Boundaries are essential, and they are not one size fits all. Today I will explore where my boundaries are with the people and situations I meet.

JULY 22

"It is a mistake to think that the practice of my art
has become easy to me. I assure you, dear friend,
no one has given so much care to the study of
composition as I. There is scarcely a famous master
in music whose works I have not frequently and
diligently studied."~Wolfgang Amadeus Mozart

Sometimes we think others can make recovery look so easy. We might compare ourselves to someone with many more years of recovery who seems so serene and knowledgeable. Or we may look at anyone in recovery and believe that their material success or spiritual prowess is something that came to them by some kind of magic or osmosis. In fact, an old recovery slogan can help here: Stick with the Winners.

When one of my first sponsors, Randy, brought that up over and over again, he was not telling me to find the people who had found a way in recovery to get a record deal and a perfect relationship. He was telling me to go toward and seek the counsel of those who were fully engaged in practice of the program. He was encouraging me to study the recovery practices of others who were dedicated to their own healing. He was encouraging me to do my own practice.

Invitation: Spend 3-5 minutes in a practice of your choice (e.g., sitting meditation, walking meditation, or an expressive practice). Meditate upon the word "practice." What practices am I fully engaged with these days? What practices might I need to add?

Prayer or Intention: Recovery is a daily practice. I will see what that means for me today, and I will build my recovery wisdom through this process.

JULY 23

"Light a candle instead of cursing the darkness."
~Eleanor Roosevelt

The process of recovery is a process of illumination. We have wandered in the darkness not necessarily out of our own choosing. Trauma and adverse life events were exacerbated by behaviors and/or substances that made it difficult or impossible to think things through. If I were to choose one metaphor to describe a trauma-informed reading of the steps, it might be this one of lighting a candle instead of shouting into or at the darkness. The first three steps wake ourselves up to our difficulty.

The inventory and amends steps help us understand ourselves and make sense of ourselves. And the maintenance steps help us to walk the path with an ever-present candle of wisdom. Now instead of resentment, hurt feelings, and further entrenched difficulties, we have a lighted path that allows us to explore and to grow.

Invitation: Spend 3-5 minutes in a practice of your choice (e.g., sitting meditation, walking meditation, or an expressive practice). Whether you have your eyes closed or open, see if you can start your meditation in darkness. Then visualize yourself lighting a candle. Notice what you see, and notice the accompanying body sensations, feelings, and thoughts.

Prayer or Intention: Today I know that I can light the candle of recovery at any time by working any of the steps.

JULY 24

"Start by doing what is necessary, then what is possible, and suddenly you are doing the impossible."
~St. Francis of Assisi

My sponsor Jim from Queens would often ask me, "What is the next right thing to do?" In my early recovery, the immediate thought in my mind was to either get a record deal, find a romantic partner, or head off to grad school. What he meant, of course, was for me to pause for a moment and determine - Was it time to eat a meal? Get some rest? Wash the dishes? Call a friend?

In order to take care of myself, I need to focus on what is necessary for survival first, and now in recovery I can go a step further and see what will take me one step further into recovery, health, and wellness. When we are told to set manageable goals, that is because we want to set ourselves up for success, to be able to do the necessary which becomes the possible. Then, over time, we find ourselves doing those things that before seemed patently impossible.

Invitation: Spend 3-5 minutes in a practice of your choice (e.g., sitting meditation, walking meditation, or an expressive practice). Think of one small action you can take today toward your wellness. See if it seems possible to you. If not, take a moment and find a new micro-goal for the day.

Prayer or Intention: As I go throughout this day, may I reflect often on the question, "What's the next right thing?"

JULY 25

"We shall be with you in the Fellowship of the Spirit, and you will surely meet some of us as you trudge the Road of Happy Destiny."
~*Alcoholics Anonymous*, p.164

Oh that word trudge. Why does it have to sound so heavy? This passage, while known quite well to many people working a 12-step recovery program, can cause many eyes to roll; especially when that word *trudge* comes up. It makes recovery sound so hard! Indeed, a close look at the word's origin suggests that *trudge* is a combination of the words *tread* and *drudge*. And who likes to drudge through life? Weighed down by meaningless tasks that have to get done and hard work that must be completed, *to drudge* is a very real part of many of our experiences.

I once heard a teaching on the phrase *trudge the Road of Happy Destiny* that put it into great perspective for me. *To trudge* is simply to walk with purpose. Now that sounds more like it! Yes, recovery is very hard work that requires me to do a lot of things I would rather not do. Yet, I work hard and do what I need to do for the larger purpose— staying sober and growing in my health and recovery. What is your purpose today?

Invitation: If physically available, you are invited to take part in a walking meditation. We suggest a more traditional walking meditation, walking slowly, one step at a time, back and forth, through a few feet of space. With each step say to yourself, "Walk with purpose," and let this saying be an anchor to keep your attention focused on the walk. As a modification you can elect to go outside and take a more standard walk. We just suggest that you do it without the distraction of headphones or music and find a rhythm to your walk where you can use the phrase "walk with purpose" as a guide.

Prayer or Intention: Today I walk with purpose. May I continue to walk with purpose on the path ahead.

JULY 26

"Nothing we see or hear is perfect. But right there in the imperfection
is perfect reality."~Shunryu Suzuki

We have heard so many times from friends, associates, clients, and
fellow travelers on the recovery path that they would love to have their
imperfections removed surgically. In our suffering and in our attempts
to escape our suffering so many of us have landed in a place of shame,
and we want it completely removed. We think our transgressions
and our imperfections make us awful, and so we must have these
imperfections completely eliminated, and we must become perfectly
new and perfectly perfect.

The truth of trauma-informed 12-step recovery is this: trauma
therapy is designed to help us bring maladaptively stored memories
and beliefs to an adaptive resolution, allowing us to have a more
adaptive life. In our 12-step recovery, it is the same. We are not made
into perfect beings or saints by working the steps. We become better be
able to meet our suffering with compassionate awareness, turn toward
the perfect imperfection of reality, and live within it, with all its joys
and challenges. This process heals us, and then we live a more adaptive
life, always in process, with all its imperfections. There is nothing to be
ashamed of. We are truly alive.

Invitation: Spend 3-5 minutes in a practice of your choice (e.g.,
sitting meditation, walking meditation, or an expressive practice).
Using your breath as the cadence, breath in gently noting "challenge."
Breathe out, noting "joy."

Prayer or Intention: Today allow me to live in the increasing peace
that comes with knowing I can live in reality with all its imperfections,
and with all its challenges and joys.

JULY 27

"We have to bring a tender, healing energy to all that is sick and torn, what is broken or lost." ~Jack Kornfield

The Twelve Steps focus keenly on the faulty processing and expression of anger and resentment. When we are in our trauma and adverse life events, we are likely to lock into fight or flight. Flight is one expression of aversion, fight is the more obvious one. Either way, fight or flight as a standard approach to all of our problems does not work over the long haul.

Recovery allows us to bring our thinking mind into the mix, and now we can compassionately and wisely tend to our own wounds and those of our fellows. We cannot angrily shout the hurt away. Instead, we can bring tenderness and empathy to our struggles and the struggles of others on the path.

Invitation: Spend 3-5 minutes in a practice of your choice (e.g., sitting meditation, walking meditation, or an expressive practice). Notice a physical or emotional discomfort you are having in this moment. Notice if you can give compassionate and tender attention to it, rather than trying to escape it or surgically remove it. Notice what happens.

Prayer or Intention: Today I can bring tender and compassionate healing to my pain.

JULY 28

"God has abundantly supplied this world with fine doctors, psychologists, and practitioners of various kinds. Try to remember that God has wrought miracles among us, we should never belittle a good doctor or psychiatrist." ~*Alcoholics Anonymous*, p. 133

In our recovery experience, we have both benefitted from the gifts of a wide variety of professionals: therapists, psychiatrists, bodyworkers, energy workers, and practitioners of Eastern medicine. Add to this the marvelous gifts we've received from meditation teachers, yoga teachers, and other spiritual practitioners, and it's safe to say were are poster children for the teaching that *outside help may be needed*.

Unhealed trauma impacts our body-mind-spirit complex in such a total way, why wouldn't we seek help from resources other than the program, especially when the program falls short?

Invitation: Take 3-5 minutes to sit quietly and meditate on the term *outside help*. As an alternative you can journal on the term, either with words or visually. What are you noticing about the outside help that you may require at this time in your recovery?

Prayer or Intention: Show me the outside help that I may require and clear the path to bring such assistance into my life.

JULY 29

"Hope is the thing with feathers that perches in the
soul - and sings the tunes without the words -
and never stops at all." ~Emily Dickinson

In certain recovery circles, the word hope takes a central role. In some trauma recovery circles, this word has a number of possible pitfalls. Perhaps we can look at hope as the amalgamation of some or all of our resources. Many times at the lowest points in my recovery I know that as long as I am still breathing, there is hope. That bottom line statement doesn't necessarily work for the long-term, but it does provide an intelligent foundation.

From there I can see that on better days I can discover and tap into my internal and external resources, thus giving me more than just breath, but also energy, creativity, recovery, even joy. This is the hope for each day, and as Dickinson points out, it "never stops at all." Our only work is to learn new ways to acknowledge our resources, build new ones, and live our lives fueled by them. This is the nature of hope.

Invitation: Spend 3-5 minutes in a practice of your choice (e.g., sitting meditation, walking meditation, or an expressive practice). As you do your practice today, see what this teaching shows you about your resources. Allow one or more of your internal resources to come to consciousness, and meditate upon it.

Prayer or Intention: Today, let me live in the hope that my resources provide. Allow me to feel their energy, their aliveness.

JULY 30

"I know where I'm going and I know the truth,
and I don't have to be what you want me to be. I'm free
to be what I want." ~Muhammad Ali

There are a number of references to freedom in the 12-step literature and the trauma recovery literature. There is good reason for this. Our survival brain does everything it can to protect us, and over time our coping mechanisms turn on us and imprison us. When we come into recovery, our new freedom becomes apparent—to ourselves and to others.

Muhammad Ali noticed that his freedom intimidated many people. He found it necessary not only to declare it for himself, but to go a step further and let the public know that they did not get to determine whether he was free or how that freedom manifested. This is in line with our own recovery. We are free to be our true selves, not anything that anyone believes we have to be. This is the real freedom of recovery.

Invitation: Spend 3-5 minutes in a practice of your choice (e.g., sitting meditation, walking meditation, or an expressive practice). Once you settle into the physical practice, notice whatever sense of freedom manifests in your mind and heart. If you notice tension or clenching, see if you can gently let it go, setting an intention to be free.

Prayer or Intention: Today I walk in this world in my freedom from the bondage of my trauma and addiction. Today I live on the path of my true being.

JULY 31

"Pride makes us artificial and humility makes us real."
~Thomas Merton

The beauty of trauma recovery is that we become real. Unfortunately, this also scares the bejeezus out of us. One of my favorite recovery slogans from my early days in New York City was, "You can't save your ass and your face at the same time." Humility seems like such a passive and even cowering act, in which case it would not be very healthy as we try to find our power so that we might live well in recovery.

Humility is filled with power in its own right. It has the power to shatter the mirror of pride, the mirror we have been trapped inside, and allow us to walk forward into our true selves. Humility expresses itself most deeply in our need for each other on this path, bolstering each other as we find our power. And then we can use that power for good, for our recovery, and to support the recovery of others. Humility is power.

Invitation: Spend 3-5 minutes in a practice of your choice (e.g., sitting meditation, walking meditation, or an expressive practice). If you like, visualize those people in your life that have bolstered you and given you power. Silently thank each one of them. Notice any body sensations, emotions or thoughts that accompany this visualization.

Prayer or Intention: Today I will walk with a humble spirit, knowing that humility is power.

AUGUST 1

vairagya: Sansrkit term often translated as
non-attachment or detachment, dispassion

The true meaning of the word *vairagya* can be hotly debated in yoga and meditation communities. A particularly sound teaching that I once heard on *vairagya* is "to live in the world and not get colored by it." This teaching may be particularly useful as we contemplate what the word detachment really means, especially in our recovery. We hear all the time how we need to detach with love, especially from toxic people or situations. How can we really do that? Especially when we are human beings with human feelings who need to live amongst other people?

Whether we are being called to detach from a loved one, from a situation, or from an outcome, the wisdom of *vairagya* can be a guide. Instead of detachment, perhaps approach that person, situation, or outcome with a spirit of, "How can I live with them (or live with this) and not be colored by it?" Typically the answer is in further working on ourselves and our own growth and spirituality/recovery. The challenge is to keep breathing and stay as unaffected as possible by the world (and the people in it) that rages around you.

Invitation: Spend 3-5 minutes in a practice of your choice (e.g., sitting meditation, walking meditation, or an expressive practice) and bring to mind the idea of living in the world without being colored by it. What are the people, places, and things in your life that most seem to be "coloring" your perceptions of the world today? These people can be in your present or your past. If you find it helpful, you can even visualize one or more of these individuals trying to ooze colors on to you that you don't particularly want today and create a visualization shield or force field that may work to keep yourself protected. Be creative!

Prayer or Intention: Today I resolve to live in the world and amongst others without being colored by what others are sending out—in this way I can detach with love.

AUGUST 2

"The purpose of EMDR is to help people live a more adaptive life."
~Francine Shapiro

There are some in the clinical community who will argue that there is no possibility of true trauma *resolution*. In fact, all trauma and adverse life events come to a resolution: either a maladaptive resolution or an adaptive resolution. The goal of the work of what we call trauma resolution is to bring those memories that have been maladaptively processed and stored to an adaptive resolution and place of storage. That means bringing the place of storage from those parts of the brain and body that cannot understand time or make meaning of things to the part of the brain that can say, "Yes, that happened, but its not happening now."

We are not calling for a *Men in Black* experience, or *Eternal Sunshine of the Spotless Mind*. We are in a process of transformation, and that transformation includes most importantly a transformation of our relationship to our memories, those memories in particular that have been driving our thoughts, feelings and behavior without our having any say over the matter. This is the work that allows us to actually work the steps, especially the maintenance steps of 10, 11, and 12 as we progress in our recovery.

Invitation: Take 5 minutes to meditate, utilizing your breath as your guide if you are able. On the in breath, silently say, "Beginning." On the out breath, silently say, "Resolution." Notice the rhythm of life with its truth of impermanence, with beginnings, resolutions, and new beginnings.

Prayer or Intention: Today, help me to know that my trauma and adverse life events can indeed be brought to an adaptive resolution.

AUGUST 3

"I teach suffering, and the end of suffering." ~Buddha

Many translations of this teaching of the Buddha say that it was *only* this that he taught. Bhikkhu Bodhi, one of the premiere translators of the early Buddhist teachings, said that it wasn't so exclusive. Buddha offered many teachings over his 40-plus year career. As it relates to our path of trauma recovery within our 12-step recovery, however, at any time we can focus on this teaching of suffering and the end of suffering. This teaching can include a Higher Power, any kind of Higher Power, or it can include nothing of the sort. This teaching when expanded into the Four Noble Truths tells us that indeed there is suffering, and it is caused by our craving and aversion, driven by our fight or flight and survival instincts.

We end suffering by taking care of this part of ourselves, so that we might have clear insight into our traumas. Then we might learn and grow from them. And in the healing process, we even get to develop a completely new relationship with our past and present difficulties. This might happen quickly or slowly, but it is an ancient truth that we can enact through taking another step into our process of recovery.

Invitation: Perhaps while having your morning beverage, or in a formal meditation posture if you prefer, notice subtle cravings and aversions. This coffee is too hot, this is my favorite mug, it's raining outside and I have no umbrella, but I love puddle jumping. Notice the cravings and aversions arise and pass for 5 minutes if you feel able.

Prayer or Intention: Today I will notice the subtle arising and passing of all that is pleasant and unpleasant, and then let those experiences and sensations go.

AUGUST 4

"Practice love until you remember that you are love."
~Swami Sai Premananda

Yogis and mystics have been teaching some variation on the theme—you are love—for millennia. Even if this teaching seems, on the surface, to clash with your own spiritual beliefs, perhaps think about how a figure like Jesus or the Prophet Mohammed empowers you with love. As people in recovery, especially as trauma survivors, we can struggle with love and all of its manifestations. So how might it change this if we can learn to see ourselves as pure love, alive in this world?

I received a beautiful idea once from one of my teachers. He shared, "When I say something like *I love you* to someone, what we are really saying is *thank you for reflecting and showing me that I am pure love*. I've never looked at love the same way again. I am in awe and grateful that seeing each other as pure love unifies us.

Invitation: Spend 3-5 minutes in a practice of your choice (e.g., sitting meditation, walking meditation, or an expressive practice) and be with the notion that *I am love*. Alternatively, you can use a statement like *I am empowered by love* if this resonates more fully with your religious beliefs. Notice what you notice as this meditation unfold.

Prayer or Intention: Today I am open to connect with the awesome power of love—may love empower me and my journey.

AUGUST 5

"Every child is an artist. The problem is how
to remain an artist once he grows up." ~Pablo Picasso

Many of us in recovery did not have a great childhood. All of us,
however, have the birthright of creativity. Trauma informing 12-step
recovery can bring us back to the creativity of our childhood if we
were able to express it back then, and if not, it can allow us to have a
do-over and live the creative life of the child as an adult. Either way,
many of us take this to be our conception of what a Higher Power is
about – we see Higher Power as a co-creative process.

Our creativity is an expression of our spirituality. Whether it is
intricately involved in one's spiritual path, or if it is just part of what
makes recovery compelling, creativity helps us to move from surviving
to thriving.

Invitation: Spend 3-5 minutes in a practice of your choice (e.g.,
sitting meditation, walking meditation, or an expressive practice).
Notice what role creativity has in your life. Notice one thing you may
have created in the last week. Meditate upon the fact that it was not
there, and then you made it manifest.

Prayer or Intention: I will notice all the creative acts that are part
of my day today. I will notice this day as a creation.

AUGUST 6

"Meditation is not a means to an end.
It is both the means and the end." ~Jiddu Krishnamurti

Some see meditation as an act; others see it as a way of life. Both of these can be true for any of us in trauma-sensitive 12-step recovery. When we are encouraged to pray and meditate in the program, we are pointed toward developing conscious contact. We don't develop that conscious contact just for the sake of having it. We develop it so that we can maintain that conscious contact and then have it become our default rather than a special circumstance. For those of us in trauma recovery, this has special meaning.

Meditation at first becomes one of the ways we try to ease our symptoms and find a way to tolerate the difficulties of the world. Then it becomes one of the most important factors in our reprocessing of the trauma of our past to an adaptive resolution. Finally, it becomes perhaps the chief maintenance tool, allowing us to live within that more adaptive life created by all of our 12-step work and our trauma work.

Invitation: For 5 minutes, utilize your current primary meditation practice to notice the power of that practice, and then notice if you are in the midst of developing or maintaining conscious contact.

Prayer or Intention: As I go throughout my day, I will notice that meditation is always with me. All I need to do is pause and notice.

AUGUST 7

"The most radical approach to resistance is acceptance—and acceptance does not mean accepting the world as it is. It means accepting *our pain* as it is." ~Melinda Gates

Trauma recovery and addiction recovery both signal a shift in our relationship to our pain. A majority of our trauma responses were driven by the survival brain that is oriented toward avoiding pain and seeking safety and pleasure. Our addictions were for the most part a more robust manifestation of these trauma responses. Much of this has happened outside of our conscious thinking. The steps, therapy, and other recovery tools put us in touch with integrative experiences that allow us to apply our cognitive abilities to our journey.

We can reprocess our trauma, we can have a new view of our painful past and our fears of the future. We can find acceptance of our pain that will allow us to then find the courage to change what we can, and further serenity to accept those things that we cannot. With the wisdom to know the difference, our lives will be more congruent.

Invitation: Spend 3-5 minutes in a practice of your choice (e.g., sitting meditation, walking meditation, or an expressive practice). During this meditation, reflect on a mantra something along the lines of, "Should I accept or should I change?" Notice what situations in your life arise during this meditation.

Prayer or Intention: Today, grant me the serenity to accept the things I cannot change, the courage to change the things I can, and the wisdom to know the difference.

AUGUST 8

"Your need for acceptance can make you invisible in this world.
Don't let anything stand in the way of the light that shines through
this form. Risk being seen in all of your glory." ~Jim Carrey

There are several reasons why people find it hard to enter recovery. One major reason is that the risk seems too great, even when life is a struggle. Sometimes the status quo, no matter how uncomfortable or even unsafe, seems more desirable to the survival brain. In particular, we may find ourselves trapped by a need for acceptance from family and friends who are in fact toxic to us, and who may be purposely or unconsciously holding us down to keep us in a box.

A trauma-informed 12-step program can help us to find our own light and to let it shine brightly, regardless of what others think of us. We build resilience and strength that allows us to break out of the status quo, and move into the full light of our own recovery. We can take this risk of shining our light on a daily basis, renewing our strength through the steps and our fellows.

Invitation: Spend 3-5 minutes in a practice of your choice (e.g., sitting meditation, walking meditation, or an expressive practice). Notice where in your body you feel most resilient. Lean into that part of your body. Notice if there are any textures, colors or other qualities to that resilience.

Prayer or Intention: Today I will let my light shine exactly as it is.

AUGUST 9

"Good for her, not for me." ~Amy Poehler, *Yes, Please!*

This constant tendency we have to compare ourselves to others can be a real roadblock on our journey to recovery and wellness. Most, if not all, of us have done it. We don't feel as pretty, as smart, as capable, or a competent as person X, Y, and Z. Even in recovery we can compare ourselves, perhaps not believing that we are as "spiritual" as someone else we meet in the program. Or we may struggle to understand why it seems so easy for some people when it feels like the hardest battle possible to even string a few days sober together.

I recently made a comment in the company of others about the plan I have in place to take care of myself as a single and very busy career woman; this involves me making a decision not to have my own children. Another person in the group pointed out another woman in our company who said, "What about her, she has three kids and she manages!" Fortunately in that moment, the opening mantra from Amy Poehler's debut book *Yes, Please!* came flooding back in response. And it felt so good to say it!

Invitation: Spend a few moments (whether sitting, lying down, or moving) saying the mantra, *good for her not for me* (you can replace *her* with *him* or *them*). Then bring up a situation where you find yourself plagued by this constant tendency to compare. It can be professional, personal, or recovery-related. Spend 3-5 minutes apply this new mantra to that situation and notice whatever may come up.

Prayer or Intention: May I recognize that the path for the people around me may not be the path I am called to. May I be free from this tendency to constantly compare myself to others.

AUGUST 10

"Everyone has some baggage, my dear, but I've never seen a suitcase
that couldn't be unpacked if it's owner was willing to start by
removing the locks." ~Samuel Decker Thompson

The metaphor of "baggage" is often used, sometimes in some very
mean ways, to describe the heavy weights that people carry. Baggage
can even refer to the wreckage of one's past or the complications that an
individual may bring to any new situation or relationship. As Samuel
Decker Thompson so beautifully expresses, let's start by recognizing
that we all have it. There is no shame in having carried the heavy
weights of trauma, frustration, pain, loss, and even the consequences
of your addiction.

The key is—are you willing to start travelling lighter? Are you
willing to begin by removing the locks with this very special key of
willingness? This is what the Eighth Step asks us to do. Don't trip
yourself up by thinking about how much there is to unpack or how
you're going to take on the Ninth Step. Stay in the moment, unlock the
suitcase, and with guidance and support, more will be revealed.

Invitation: This practice uses some real or imagined movement to
further deepen this idea of opening the lock. If you have a door with a
lock or a small travel lock available, spend about five repetitions opening
the lock. With each time that you open the lock, say to yourself, "I am
willing." If you don't have a lock and key easily available to you, mimic
the motions with your hands of what it would be like to open a lock,
also using the affirmation, "I am willing."

Prayer or Intention: May I be willing to use the keys to recovery
I've gained so far to unlock the baggage that keeps me stuck.

AUGUST 11

"As sentient beings we have wonderful backgrounds. These backgrounds may not be particularly enlightened or peaceful or intelligent. Nevertheless, we have soil good enough to cultivate; we can plant anything in it." ~Chogyam Trungpa

The Promises in the "Big Book" of *Alcoholics Anonymous* tell us that no matter how far down we have gone, we will see how our experience can benefit others. That is a wonderful beginning frame for our trauma-informed recovery. No matter what has happened to us, no matter how we have reacted or responded, we will have had experience that another person who is suffering can use to help themselves.

No matter what we have brought to the table from our pre-recovery days, we can plant an entire new life in that soil. There is nothing to be ashamed of. We can use the steps and other recovery tools to begin again, using all that we have experienced as our foundation. How strange and wonderful, to have shame and fear turn into a solid foundation for a brand new life.

Invitation: Spend 3-5 minutes in a practice of your choice (e.g., sitting meditation, walking meditation, or an expressive practice). On the in breath, notice the words *Letting Go*. On the out breath, notice the words *Planting Seeds*.

Prayer or Intention: I am planting seeds in the soil of my past. I need not be ashamed. I can build my new life with all I have done before as the soil for the seeds of the present and future.

AUGUST 12

wisdom = *knowledge* + *experience*
~recovery saying and yoga teaching

In the serenity prayer we ask for the *wisdom to know the difference*. Have we ever stopped to consider what wisdom really means? Although knowledge can be an important component of our recovery, it's not the whole picture. We can learn everything possible about the disease of addiction—how unhealed trauma impacts our system and even develop keen knowledge about our own patterns through study, step work, and therapy. Yet a crucial gap will exist if we don't put our knowledge into practice; this is how we gain experience.

Moreover, being able to draw from the well of experience, strength, and hope is a saving grace for us. All lived experiences—pleasant, unpleasant, or neutral—have something to teach us. Are we willing to learn?

Invitation: Spend 3-5 minutes in a reflective practice of your choice (sitting meditation, walking meditation, or an expressive practice) and contemplate this lesser known recovery axiom that wisdom = knowledge + experience. Do knowledge and experience both inform your recovery today or is there an imbalance you may need to address?

Prayer or Intention: May I draw wisdom from both what I know and what I experience.

AUGUST 13

"We are always looking for meaning beyond the weariness of being ourselves. We need a reason beyond mere survival to go on living."
~Dr. David Servan-Schreiber

One of the reasons that people come into recovery is that they have survived. They have survived long enough to realize that they may not have as much luck going forward along the same path they have taken, and they also get the sense that there must be something beyond the loneliness of simple survival. Servan-Schreiber wrote extensively about the power but also the limits of medicine, and the importance of helping people with their resilience in the face of waiting for medicine to do its work. He saw the breaking of loneliness as one of the most important elements of healing.

The Twelve Steps help us to break the loneliness by breaking the shame, which reduces the isolation, which puts us into fellowship with others. This is the trauma-informed reality of the 12-step approach, bringing people new resilience, offering them community, engaging in tools for healing borne of new resilience, tools, and effort.

Invitation: Spend 3-5 minutes in a practice of your choice (e.g., sitting meditation, walking meditation, or an expressive practice). Meditate upon any person or being that brings you joy or strength. Allow that joy or strength to have its place during as much of the meditation as possible.

Prayer or Intention: Let me do more than survive. Allow me to grow in community, and to live fully.

AUGUST 14

"The practice of forgiveness is our most
important contribution to the healing of the world."
~Marianne Williamson

In trauma recovery, forgiveness can seem the most difficult of our tasks. In 12-step recovery, the steps are set up to prepare a person for self-forgiveness and the forgiveness of others. Steps 8 and 9 are built upon the foundation of spiritual principles that lay the groundwork for a forgiveness that has weight to it. Not only that, it allows for us to go to others in the spirit of amends safely rather than on a high wire.

Throughout our recovery we see where the program was always trauma-informed, we just didn't have the language for it until now. Climbing this scaffolding of our inner world so that that we can practice forgiveness and then continue in that spirit through the last three maintenance steps is a powerful spiritual journey. We experience not only our own healing, but the healing of the world.

Invitation: Spend 3-5 minutes in a practice of your choice (e.g., sitting meditation, walking meditation, or an expressive practice). Choose one being, whether yourself or another, to practice sending forgiveness toward.

Prayer or Intention: Today I will heal myself and heal the world by practicing forgiveness.

AUGUST 15

"Nevertheless, we find that our thinking will, as time passes, be more and more on the plane of inspiration. We come to rely upon it."
~*Alcoholics Anonymous*, p. 87

A major goal of trauma recovery and all recovery in general is being able to regain agency over one's own life. This is not an issue of taking control and never asking for help. In reality, what we are doing is restoring the integrity of our own ability to make decisions, take actions, and live a life fueled by our own inspiration and choices. Trauma and addiction both take away this power. Recovery restores our agency, step-by-step, day-by-day.

Many people focus inordinately on the message of powerlessness in the early steps of the program. However, the truth is that our ability to utilize prayer or its equivalent, even early in our recovery, puts us back into the stream of the inspired life. We don't have to wait to be healed to be fully healed and listen to our inner voice. We can cultivate that every day.

Invitation: Spend 3-5 minutes in a practice of your choice (e.g., sitting meditation, walking meditation, or an expressive practice). Notice one challenge that is coming up today. Notice any actions or inspired thinking that become available to you during the meditation. If none arise, notice that you have placed yourself in the stream of inspiration by doing this meditation.

Prayer or Intention: Today as I go through my day, every now and then I will pause and seek inspiration.

AUGUST 16

"Rather than thinking in terms of good and bad, it is more helpful to think in terms of conscious and unconscious, aware, and unaware."
~Joan Borysenko

One of the greatest changes initiated by the development of AA and other 12-step programs was conceptualizing addiction as a health problem rather than as a moral dilemma. When looking at ourselves as bad people becoming good, we end up in a whirlwind of shame and judgment. In fact, what we are doing in our recovery is bringing the unconscious into consciousness by working the steps. We are building awareness, and then learning the tools to be able to tolerate any distress related to that new awareness.

We couldn't know what was not in our sphere of awareness. We are now bringing our inner and outer reality into the light for inspection, for healing, and for change toward greater resilience and the opportunity to thrive. We are healing through becoming conscious and aware.

Invitation: Spend 3-5 minutes in a practice of your choice (e.g., sitting meditation, walking meditation, or an expressive practice). Go back in your mind to your early recovery and notice what you knew then. Come back to the present moment and notice what you have become conscious and aware of through your step work.

Prayer or Intention: Today let me know that, rather than a bad person becoming good, I am a person healing through building a greater awareness of my truth.

AUGUST 17

"The mind is king of the senses, and the breath is the king of the mind." ~Swami Svātmārāma, *Hatha Yoga Pradīpika*

Modern yoga teachers often relay this classic yoga teaching as *the mind controls the body, but the breath controls the mind.* Making a connection to the world of therapy, you may have heard a provider tell you at some point: "Change the thinking, change the behavior." Easier said than done, right? This teaching, applied to that therapeutic instruction, would translate as: Change the breathing and that will change the thinking, and in turn the behavior will change.

While trauma survivors have been known to struggle with breath, getting over this hurdle can be incredibly important to our overall recovery. Giving ourselves that moment to breathe is a great start. Learning to spend some deliberate time deepening the breath continues the journey so that when life confronts us with stressors or our problematic thoughts attack us with what can seem like an obsessive fury, we can meet them with breath. And deepened breath can cause just enough of a shift that our thoughts may trouble us less and we'll move forward in a spirit of healthier action.

Invitation: Notice what may be bothering you today as you read this meditation page. If nothing specific is coming up, you can use a nagging thought that seems to keep emerging for you as a struggle in your recovery journey. Once you bring that thought into your awareness, take as deep a breath as you possibly can without forcing it or going past your edge. Try this a few more times, making the deliberate intention to send the breath to the thought. Think about or visualize the thought dissolving into the breath and on your next exhale, notice it release. Keep trying this as much as you need until you notice a shift.

Prayer or Intention: May the innate power of my breath cause a shift in all parts of my experience today, especially those thoughts and actions that trouble me.

AUGUST 18

"Beyond mountains there are mountains."
~Haitian proverb

The road to recovery seems so long. In fact, it is no longer than a life without recovery—minutes are minutes and hours are hours. The change that comes with recovery is the ability to see the first mountain in front of you and take it one step at a time. We are able to utilize the steps, the fellowship, and trauma recovery to bring us up and over that mountain that seemed so insurmountable.

Of course, we are then faced with another mountain, but this time we have the experience of the previous one to rely on, and we have the ability to stay in the reality of this life with its mountains made of challenges and joys. This is another opportunity to appreciate the slogan *one day at a time*. One challenge at a time, one joy at a time, one step at a time, one mountain at a time.

Invitation: Spend 3-5 minutes in a practice of your choice (e.g., sitting meditation, walking meditation, or an expressive practice). If you feel comfortable with visualization, notice a mountain in front of you. If you like, go ahead and either walk up and over the mountain or feel free to fly over it. Notice the feeling you have on the other side.

Prayer or Intention: There may be more mountains beyond the one in front of me today, but I will focus on the one in front of me, and deal with the other ones later.

AUGUST 19

"Love is at the root of everything. Love or the lack of it."
~Fred Rogers

Mr. Rogers highlights one of the most under recognized truths about the impact of unhealed trauma. We often think of trauma as something that happens *to* us. Yet all too often, especially for those of us who grew up in dysfunction, trauma is defined by a *lack of*. That could be a lack of connection, nurturing, and yes—love.

In healing from the impact of trauma as part of your recovery today, it's important to realize what you are lacking. We don't mean material things—notice what is or was missing in the areas of connection, nurturing, and love. Consider that a major part of the recovery process is to learn new ways of being in the world that involve repairing your relationship with love. How can you start by showing love to those younger, unhealed places inside of you today?

Invitation: Spend at least 5 minutes in sitting meditation, although lying down is an acceptable modification. Interlace your fingers together and then place them over your heart. In yoga this is called a gesture of supreme confidence, and it can also be a beautiful way to send some love and care to the heart. If you are not able to interlace the fingers for any reason, imagine that a protective covering is blanketing your heart. As you sit in this gesture or visualization for a few moments, ask yourself—especially your younger parts—where love needs to be healed and shown today.

Prayer or Intention: May the areas of my life where I am lacking connection, nurturing, and love be healed today.

AUGUST 20

"I'm no longer going to allow blind people
to proofread my vision." ~Anonymous

Some people see us, others don't. Some people hear us, others don't. In the program, there will be many times where you might hear conflicting messages, and you may have people shoot down your ideas about the program or any number of issues or beliefs. You may, as you go through your recovery, start to stand up for yourself and have your own vision for your life. Throughout our recovery, we need to let go of the toxic people and situations in our lives little-by-little, so that we might build our recovery world in a way that reflects our true natures.

Part of the diversity of the program is that not everyone is going to be able to help everyone else with the particulars of their lives. We have many ways of seeing and doing things. So, as we go forward, we find those people who truly see us, and we go to them for support, suggestions, acknowledgment, and recovery.

Invitation: Spend 3-5 minutes in a practice of your choice (e.g., sitting meditation, walking meditation, or an expressive practice). Reflect on the characteristics of those people that truly see you. Consider visualizing one of those people in particular. Allow them to share the space with you for the duration of the mediation.

Prayer or Intention: Today I will not expect everyone to understand my vision for my recovery. I will seek out those people who do for companionship.

AUGUST 21

"When we choose this way of being in the world, we feel at home in our own body, with no desire to leave it; because we feel at home in the body, we feel at home in the world. That is radical presence."
~Lama Rod Owens

For many in recovery, addiction and other difficulties were about escape. Sometimes this would happen organically, we wouldn't even have to engage in a behavior or take a substance in order to flee. In reality, our body was doing whatever it had to do to survive in the moment. Recovery and our work in the steps allow us to accept and embrace all of ourselves, the darkness and the light, the sadness and the joy, and all the different parts and identities that we were born with or take on.

One of Steve's Zen teachers often said that sitting meditation is a practice of the body, not the mind. In order to calm our mind and gain insight, calming the body and being able to live in this body is essential. Then we can live in radical presence, our body moving through life animated by our recovery, our love, our complexity, our very presence with others.

Invitation: Spend 3-5 minutes in a practice of your choice (e.g., sitting meditation, walking meditation, or an expressive practice). Take 3 intentional breaths, and then do a body scan meditation, noticing where you feel present, and noticing where you do not feel present with as little judgment as possible.

Prayer or Intention: Today I will notice my body moving through the world, and I set the intention to maintain radical presence as I interact with others.

AUGUST 22

"You are my place of quiet retreat,
I wait for your word to renew me." ~Psalm 119:114

Many spiritual traditions and recovery programs invite people into an experience of retreat. We commonly think of such experiences as a few days or even a few weeks where we can "retreat" from the rigors of daily life and hopefully focus on ourselves and our growth. Perhaps you've been on such retreats before. When you experience them in community with like-minded people in a setting that is deliberately crafted to set you apart from your ordinary life, it can be a magical experience. Or sometimes, because retreats bring up all your stuff, it can feel like a challenging form of hell.

Retreats do not require you to travel or even to withdrawal completely from your day-to-day life. The word *retreat* simply comes from a Middle English and Old French word meaning *to draw back*. Although for many the word comes with military connotations, that sense of drawing back or even surrendering can be very useful to as we navigate the full catastrophe of living. You can take a retreat for an hour—maybe even begin to see your meetings or the time you spend reading and meditating each day as small retreats. Allow this time of drawing back to work its restorative magic.

Invitation: Spend 3-5 minutes in a practice of your choice (e.g., sitting meditation, walking meditation, or an expressive practice) and invite yourself to view this practice as a mini-retreat. After you transition from the chosen practice, notice how you might define the word *retreat*.

Prayer or Intention: May I recognize and accept the small opportunities for retreat that exist in my day-to-day life.

AUGUST 23

"Longing is like the rosy dawn. After the dawn out comes the sun.
Longing is followed by the vision of God." ~Ramakrishna

A common struggle that we can experience at various stages of recovery is missing people, places, and things. While we may have to make difficult decisions about severing ties with the people, places, things, and ideas that no longer serve us as people seeking recovery, it is totally normal to miss them, even to long for them. As one of my friends shared with me, from his wisdom as a long-time spiritual practitioner, "It is totally okay to miss people that no longer belong in your life." I found his words validating.

You may notice that you are missing or even longing for the things that you lost as a result of your active addiction, or what you had to deliberately move away from to get well. Honor those feelings today. Feel them through, like everything else you are being asked to experience in your recovery. You may be surprised at what new dawn will clear on the path ahead as a result of being honest with yourself and honoring the truth of your experience.

Invitation: Spend 3-5 minutes in a practice of your choice (e.g., sitting meditation, walking meditation, or an expressive practice) and notice if there is a person, place, thing, or idea that you find yourself missing or longing for today, even if you recognize that this person, place, thing, or idea no longer serves you in life. Let this meditation be a period to feel whatever it is you need to feel.

Prayer or Intention: Today I recognize that it is okay to miss what no longer belongs in my life. I will validate my own feelings today.

AUGUST 24

"Do I not destroy my enemies when I make them my friends?"
~Abraham Lincoln

The Eighth Step does not intend for us to make everyone a friend. Sometimes our boundaries need to remain strong, even after going through the process of becoming willing to make amends for any pain we ourselves have caused. However, this step does so much for our reducing the number of people and institutions that we consider our enemies. The process of becoming willing to make amends for our side of things is the dismantling of our perception of others as the enemy.

This has become possible through all our work up until now in 12-step programs and with any other help we have availed ourselves of. We can now come to others in the spirit of compassion. We can mend those fences that can be mended, while simply taking care of our side of the street if that is all that is available. Living a life with a greater degree of freedom from animosity is one of the gifts of Step 8.

Invitation: Spend 3-5 minutes in a practice of your choice (e.g., sitting meditation, walking meditation, or an expressive practice). During this practice period, if you are ready to consider an amends with someone, go ahead and visualize the person, and then the words and actions of the amends process.

Prayer or Intention: Today let me see fewer enemies, more friends, and proper boundaries between me and others.

AUGUST 25

"If you chase two rabbits, you will catch neither one."
~Russian proverb

Modern times seem to emphasize the importance of multi-tasking and staying caught up in the rat race (or to honor our opening proverb, the rabbit race) of life. As a result, we feel like we're falling behind if we can't focus on many things at once. The reality is that you can't, even if you feel like you are.

A common, modern metaphor to describe the busy and anxious mind is that of a web browser that has dozens of tabs open at once. Our minds can feel like they are operating in this manner. If you are person who struggles with dissociation or having overactive internal parts, it can feel like you have several browsers open, each containing a dozen or more active tabs. Yes, all the tabs may be running simultaneously, and we can even claim this as a badge of honor, a salute to our ability to multi-task. However, having this many tabs (and browsers) open at once can strain and slow down the system. And even with all of that activity running, we can only really focus on one tab at a time. Letting the total focus remain on one tab at a time—completely and totally—is another way to describe mindfulness.

Invitation: There are many ways to practice single-pointed concentration for 3-5 minutes. You can pick one object in the room in which you sit and make an intention to focus on only that object for this set period of time. If your attention wanders to another object in the room, avoid judging yourself, notice the wandering, and bring the attention back to your designated object of focus. You may wish to take the metaphor in this meditation quite literally and actually use an open computer tab as the focus point of your meditation as a variation!

Prayer or Intention: Help me to keep my concentration and focus on one thing at a time today.

AUGUST 26

"People deal too much with the negative, with what is wrong. Why not try and see positive things, to just touch those things and make them bloom?" ~Thich Nhàt Han

This is one of the most important aspects of trauma-informed work. We are not talking about denying the negative or difficult aspects of life. We are not talking about stuffing our feelings yet again. What we are talking about here is the accessing and building of resilience and power. In order for us to be able to successfully reprocess our material, in order for us to work the inventory steps and the amends steps, we need to see the inherent goodness and power in ourselves.

We don't need to incessantly focus on powerlessness or character defects or my part in things. We need to find and nurture our resources, and where we are feeling bereft of those resources, we need to develop and nurture new ones. Leaning into the positive seems counterintuitive when we are at our low points, but in fact it is absolutely necessary.

Invitation: Spend 3-5 minutes in a practice of your choice (e.g., sitting meditation, walking meditation, or an expressive practice). Notice one aspect of yourself that you believe is good or strong. Lean into that aspect of yourself for the length of the meditation.

Prayer or Intention: I will notice and nurture my resilience and my resources today.

AUGUST 27

"The first thing you need to do is calm down."
~Saul, Steve's sponsor

This may not sound like the most trauma-informed 12-step intervention in this book! However, Saul only started using this with me when I had many years of sobriety, and took into account all the work I had done up to that point to know I had the option and the ability to engage my thinking mind when I was upset. He would say this anytime I was particularly activated during a phone call. He would wait for me to finish my fear-based rant. He made sure that I felt heard. And then he made this statement not as an admonition, but as the beginning of our strategy to help me. This actually makes it very trauma-informed. He was essentially saying, "Before we do anything else, let's use your resilience and resources to soothe our central nervous system.

Once we do that, we can do anything." Many of the Twelve Steps offer us opportunities to learn how to calm down or utilize tools to do so. Saul knew that, and he knew that I could do it. And that helped me learn for myself that I am capable of handling difficult situations and feelings.

Invitation: Spend 3-5 minutes in a practice of your choice (e.g., sitting meditation, walking meditation, or an expressive practice). Decide which practice will, at this moment, bring you the most calming effect and use that one. Use whatever mantra helps produce or accentuate that calm.

Prayer or Intention: Today I will remain aware of my need to engage resources to self-soothe throughout the day as a first step in dealing with difficulties.

AUGUST 28

"Grief can be the garden of compassion. If you keep your heart open through everything, your pain can become your greatest ally in your life's search for love and wisdom." ~Rumi

Grief can be challenging in recovery. Often memories that have never been grieved will surface in early recovery or even later recovery. Even if those memories were otherwise processed adaptively, the natural and often painful process of grieving might still present itself. It is important that we surround ourselves with people who understand that our grief is not pathological, and that we are in the midst of a normal and healthy process. Since grief contains denial, bargaining, anger, and sadness, it is tempting for those around us to try and fix us, or to worry about us and whether our recovery is steady.

If we lean into the truth of our grief, and let go of that which we need to let go of, then we will build our recovery with a foundation of authenticity. On some of our coins it says, "To thine own self be true." We can do this, supported by those that understand the relationship between trauma, recovery, and grief.

Invitation Spend 3-5 minutes in a practice of your choice (e.g., sitting meditation, walking meditation, or an expressive practice) and notice what you are currently grieving in your life. Notice the body sensations that come and go.

Prayer or Intention: As I go throughout my day, may I accept any grief that I am currently walking through. May I surround myself with people and places that will hold me through any difficult times.

AUGUST 29

"I am here. I am now. I am present."
~Jamie's favorite affirmation

As an individual in recovery, many of my day-to-day problems are caused by not living in my here and now. I obsess over things I think I should have done or should have said in the past. I regret decisions not made, chances not taken. I dwell in resentment. I project too far into the future. I catastrophize, often letting my mind wander to every possible *what if* scenario that may play out in my lifetime. I fear the future, the unknown.

For survivors of trauma, feeling stuck in past can become the norm. Fretting the future seems essential, a frantic attempt to protect ourselves from past hurts playing out again. Although addressing the root causes of these problems may require extensive outside help, as a day-to-day survival strategy, reminding myself that the only moment I really have is the present can work wonders in your recovery journey.

Invitation: Saying the three affirmations that open this meditation to yourself may help guide you to greater comfort with living in the present. They can be especially powerful when you intentionally connect your feet to the ground or sit against a wall (or some other supportive structure). If it doesn't work for you right away or you worry about whether you're doing it right, stick with it. The beauty of simple statements is that you can repeat them over and over again until they flow like a song. If these three statements don't seem to be a good fit, what are three statements you can use to anchor you back to the present moment?

Prayer or Intention: May I remain here, now, and present.

AUGUST 30

"The salvation of Man is in love and through love."
~Viktor Frankl, *Man's Search for Meaning*

Love can be a very loaded word to those of us walking the path of recovery. For many of us, love can be equated with deep pain. This pain may have been experienced in our family of origin as we were most hurt by the people who were supposed to love us. Romantic relationships or shattered friendships can also be a culprit. After a lifetime of such painful experiences, we may find ourselves flustered, wondering if we know what love really means.

Defining love can be tricky, especially since so many different types of it abound. The ancient Greeks taught about several different types of love such as brotherly love, love for all mankind, and erotic love. Even as people in long-term recovery, we can feel at a loss to define it because is love really something you can define? Or do you just know it's there when it leads you towards a deeper sense of healing? Recovery gives us a chance to reorient and redefine our relationship with the concept of love.

Invitation: Spend 3-5 minutes in a practice of your choice (e.g., sitting meditation, walking meditation, or an expressive practice) and bring up the word *love*. What feelings, experiences, or sensations does the concept of love elicit for you today. Try to notice whatever you are noticing without judgment and not push away what you are getting. What has recovery taught you so far about the true meaning of love?

Prayer or Intention: May I be open to healing my relationship with love today and in so doing be open to the healing power of love.

SEPTEMBER 1

"I never met a discontented tree." ~John Muir

Trees teach us to be grounded and flexible at the same time. Trauma-informed recovery asks this of us and draws on the inspiration from Mother Nature to inspire us. As you prepared for Step 9, which may cause you to feel a bit ungrounded at times, consider enrolling the tree as inspiration for this grounding meditation.

Grounding can take on many forms. By simple definition grounding is using all available senses to come into the here and now. If at any time during your Ninth Step work you are feeling unsteady, you are invited to come back to one of your grounding anchors like the tree visualization below, or another element of nature. Perhaps a rock or a stone in your pocket works better for you, especially as you go to make an amends.

Invitation: For this practice, come to a standing position for 2-3 minutes. If standing isn't feasible you can adapt by sitting upright. Once standing (or sitting), deliberately press down into your feet and feel an extension of energy all the way up through your body. After you've established your ground, allow yourself to sway gently, maybe making gentle circles with your body or allowing your arms to grow like branches. Notice what it feels like to be grounded *and* flexible or fluid at the same time.

Prayer or Intention: Today I draw inspiration from a tree as I discover the possibilities that grow from being both grounded and flexible.

SEPTEMBER 2

"There are no sure answers. Only better questions."
~Dick van Dyke

I am that person in a class or during a teaching on a retreat who asks lots of questions. I'm sure that I've annoyed many of my peers and more than my share of teachers with my constant inquisitiveness. Since I was a child, formulating my own questions through critical thinking, and often challenging what I heard, has been the best way for me to retain and benefit from the education process. I love asking questions and now as an educator myself, I welcome it when students ask me questions—for when they do, I know that they are not taking what I say at face value and they are engaged in critical thinking themselves.

Asking questions is one of the most important practices in our spiritual and/or recovery journey. When there is doubt, asking questions can give us an avenue to tease it out. Whether or not we are allowed to ask questions or feel welcome in asking them is also a good way to tell if we are in a healthy spiritual group or recovery meeting. I have also learned that sometimes on the spiritual path, when the questions I ask cannot be easily answered, my Higher Power/the universal flow challenges me to wait and be patient as the answer reveals itself.

Invitation: Spend 3-5 minutes in a practice of your choice (e.g., sitting meditation, walking meditation, or an expressive practice) and bring up a major question that you have right now in your spiritual or recovery journey. You are free to just be with the question or to write it or express it in some way. Is this a question you have posed to someone, like a sponsor, teacher, or therapist? If you haven't asked the question yet, what is keeping you from doing so? Or, is this the type of question that you may just need to sit with for a while?

Prayer or Intention: Today I recognize that asking questions is a form of spiritual practice. I also recognize that sometimes there are no clear-cut answers to what I seek, at least not immediately.

SEPTEMBER 3

"The best apology is changed behavior." ~recovery saying

The idea of living amends is often summarized by this teaching. The wisdom it contains is so ancient, it's no wonder that there is not an exact attribution to be found for the quote. Although making direct, verbal amends may be warranted in working a Ninth Step, amends are generally futile if we do not accompany them with behavior change. Particularly in cases where the other person does not want to accept our amends, the best way to heal that wound is through changed behavior, either to that person if they are still in your life or to others that you meet on the road ahead.

Amends are more than just saying you're sorry. They are a living, breathing extension of our commitment to healing ourselves and changing our way of life. While making amends is the good, right, and ethical thing to do toward those we harmed, also consider the impact of making amends on your own internal healing.

Invitation: Spend 3-5 minutes in a practice of your choice (e.g., sitting meditation, walking meditation, or an expressive practice) and contemplate the opening quote. Can you think of a time where someone made an amends to you through changed behavior? How did it feel? Is there anything that might be keeping you from extending that same healing outward?

Prayer or Intention: Today I recognize that the best apology truly is changed behavior.

SEPTEMBER 4

"Love lives." ~Clarence Clemons

Love is an action verb. It can be very easy to tell people that "I love you," yet consider how many people in our lives told us they loved us while also mistreating or traumatizing us. Because of this, many of us come into recovery with a skewed perception of love, or it can seem like we are allergic to the word and its very essence.

In re-learning the meaning of love and its various forms, look for the people who are putting it into action—people who treat others kindly. People who go the extra mile for others. People who accept others just as they are, even if they may be offering corrective feedback in the spirit of recovery. Love is not an action that ought to involve name calling or anything "tough," despite what we may have been told previously.

Invitation: Spend 3-5 minutes in a practice of your choice (e.g., sitting meditation, walking meditation, or an expressive practice) and consider what your working definition is of the word *love*. Then reflect on it in the practice and notice if anything different is revealed.

Prayer or Intention: I recognize that love can be a tough word for me in my recovery journey. Today I am open to seeing love and its true meaning through a new lens.

SEPTEMBER 5

"Good judgment, a careful sense of timing,
courage, and prudence – these are the qualities
we shall need when we take Step Nine."
~Bill Wilson, *Twelve Steps and Twelve Traditions*, p. 83

When Steve was about 30 days sober, he became aware that a friend from abroad was coming into New York City for a visit. Having newly heard about amends, he arranged to meet his friend at a Mexican restaurant. Steve nursed a Diet Coke while his old drinking buddy drank a margarita and listened to Steve's rambling apology for anything and everything he could think of. At the end of the monologue, the friend just stared at Steve. Finally, he exclaimed, "What on earth are you talking about? And what's with the Diet Coke?"

Judgment, timing, courage, prudence are qualities that come from the trauma recovery and spiritual experience of the previous eight steps. Of course, we can begin our living amends at any time, but utilizing the steps from a trauma recovery perspective allows us to truly prepare ourselves and those we may have harmed for this process of amends.

Invitation: Spend 3-5 minutes in a practice of your choice (e.g., sitting meditation, walking meditation, or an expressive practice). Consider one or two people who you believe you might owe amends. If discomfort arises, see if you can sit with that discomfort until it passes, knowing that new insight comes from sitting through these types of emotional states.

Prayer or Intention: Today let me know that all my amends will be made at the right time. May I develop the patience and self-compassion to allow the amends process to unfold.

SEPTEMBER 6

" . . . And the wisdom to know the difference."
~from *The Serenity Prayer,* Reinhold Niebuhr

In 12-step recovery circles we use The Serenity Prayer regularly, so it's likely you've uttered the phrase *the wisdom to know the difference* many times. So why does it feel as though wisdom is often the last thing to come online or that wisdom is always failing us? The technical name for wisdom is *sapience,* a function of your neocortex or your highest, rational brain. And as you may have learned already in your explorations with the *Trauma and the 12 Steps* work or other work in trauma recovery, this rational brain can go offline or feel like it's shutting down when we are emotionally triggered.

The key to access the full depths of our wisdom is to work on what we need to address in our trauma recovery so that we are no longer living in a state of constant, chronic activation. When we can learn to live with less reactivity and more response, the power of our own internal wisdom, which is massive, will be easier for us to access. Your wisdom, the sum total of your knowledge and experience, has never left you. Unhealed trauma can just make it more difficult to access.

Invitation: Spend 3-5 minutes in a practice of your choice (e.g., sitting meditation, walking meditation, or an expressive practice) and intentionally connect with the phrase *the wisdom to know the difference.* Instead of just praying it or saying it, see if you can breathe into it. It may help, on your inhale to say to yourself "the wisdom," and on the exhale say, "to know the difference."

Prayer or Intention: May I more actively connect with my internal wisdom as I heal from the wounds that have kept me from accessing it.

SEPTEMBER 7

"Let us be grateful to the people who make us happy; they are the charming gardeners who make our souls blossom." ~Marcel Proust

Loneliness pervades the lives of many people who have been through trauma and adverse life events. Relationships often seem like landmines rather than possible sustenance. That is why fellowship has been such an important part of the 12-step revolution. Step work is obviously critical, but so is the connection forged between members.

Our recovery tells us that we need to connect with others, our trauma recovery tells us we can do that at our own pace and in our own way. As we start to feel better and exercise greater say in regard to with whom we surround ourselves, the possibility of finding those friendships, acquaintanceships, and collegial relationships that will feed us rather than tear us down becomes a reality.

Invitation: Spend 3-5 minutes in a practice of your choice (e.g., sitting meditation, walking meditation, or an expressive practice). See if you can visualize one or more people in your life that sustain you, make you laugh, make you smile, make you happy. Allow yourself to lean into any positive or healthy feelings, sensations, or thoughts that come up.

Prayer or Intention: Today I will be grateful for any relationships that make me happy and help me grow.

SEPTEMBER 8

"The body is the last unexplored wilderness."
~Reginald Ray

How long have we, as people with unhealed trauma in recovery, been out of touch with our bodies and their wisdom? There are a variety of reasons that this can happen. Unhealed trauma can kick up such distress at the level of the body, we may do anything in our body to numb out the impact. Or to feel something different. This is a major reason that addictive substances and behaviors become appealing to us, often at a young age. Others of us grew up in religious or otherwise toxic systems where we were "warned" about the body and how body-related temptation will lead us astray.

The reality is that we must recruit our full selves—including our body—into the process of healing and recovery. The body has a great deal to teach us. The body will alert us to relapse triggers and the need for care long before our head cognitively realizes what's going on. Yes, trauma impacts the body, and learning to make friends with our body and its healing wisdom is a vital component of total healing.

Invitation: Spend 3-5 minutes in a practice of your choice (e.g., sitting meditation, walking meditation, or an expressive practice) and notice your body. Be sure to pick a practice that helps you to be most attuned to the body. See if you can practice communicating with your body today, directly asking—what do you need to teach me today? What is it you're trying to get me to see? If possible, jot down some of your reflections and share them with a trauma-informed sponsor, therapist, or trusted member of your support network.

Prayer or Intention: Today I respect the wisdom of my body and will do everything in my power to heal my relationship with my body.

SEPTEMBER 9

"Remember, a fact is a fact, no matter how hard the liars amongst you might try hushing it up." ~ Billy Childish

One very common aspect of trauma and a reason why people develop post-traumatic responses and disorders is gaslighting. Gaslighting is when people, often trusted others, lie about reality in order to manipulate those more vulnerable and under their sway due to a power differential. Over time, the person who has been gaslit will often feel like they are crazy, having been tricked into this thinking by the person doing the gaslighting. How does this relate to our trauma-informed 12-step work?

This is where we need to be very mindful of our 12-step language. Many people are instructed to "find their part in it" when looking at a situation from the past. In fact, for many trauma survivors who have been victimized by gaslighting, this is not an appropriate or useful question. When working on inventory, we are looking for our part in things, but we do not have to go there first nor do we have to have "had a part in" everything found in our inventory work.

Invitation: Spend 3-5 minutes in a practice of your choice (e.g., sitting meditation, walking meditation, or an expressive practice). Breathe in, "To mine own self be true." Breathe out, "I am true to myself."

Prayer or Intention: Today, I will know that I can live in reality, free from the any gaslighting from the past or present.

SEPTEMBER 10

"*No* is a complete sentence." ~recovery saying

The word *no* can be one of the scariest words we must learn to deal with in the process of recovery. Having people say *no* to us can feel like rejection. Needing to set boundaries and say *no* to people can bring up intense fear of rejection. The reality is that learning to receive *no* for an answer and give *no* for an answer is critical for our recovery. *No* is the building block of healthy boundary setting and learning to respect the boundaries set by others.

If hearing and/or saying "no" poses a set of problems, those generally need to be examined as part of a healthy recovery lifestyle. As with many themes explored in this meditation reader, it's very likely that unhealed wounds are at the source. What is my wounding around the word *no* that needs to be addressed?

Invitation: Spend 3-5 minutes in a practice of your choice (e.g., sitting meditation, walking meditation, or an expressive practice) with the word *no*. Keep focusing on the word as you sit or walk, or if you are in an expressive practice, use it as a prompt to create. Strong feelings may emerge that need to be felt as you meditate on the word, or you may notice quickly that you need to seek some support from a sponsor, therapist, or trusted friend to truly explore this practice. *No* is a strong word and can bring up strong feelings.

Prayer or Intention: Today I will practice receiving and saying the word *no*, recognizing the importance of both to my recovery.

SEPTEMBER 11

"No recovery from trauma is possible without attending to issues of safety, care for the self, reparative connections to other human beings, and a renewed faith in the universe." ~Janina Fisher

The journey of 12-step recovery and the path of trauma recovery both focus on creating a safe harbor. Safety doesn't imply that we live in a perfect bubble after having lived in chaos and fear. It is not about extremes, or this or that, or my way or the highway. It is about bringing the default mode to one of basic safety, the opportunity for self-care, the possibility of health and fulfilling community and family relationships, and the foundation of enough faith to keep on going.

These basics of recovery are needed to be able to dive into the deep end of the pool of repair and resilience, and enable us to move into sustainable long-term recovery. As we accumulate time in recovery it comes to us more naturally to go toward and live within our safe harbor.

Invitation: Spend 3-5 minutes in a practice of your choice (e.g., sitting meditation, walking meditation, or an expressive practice). Visualize what a safe harbor might look like for you. Notice what people or places represent safety and connection. If this does not feel possible, see if you can notice your stuck points without as little judgement as possible as you practice.

Prayer or Intention: Today I will tend to my safety, my self-care, my relationships and my faith.

SEPTEMBER 12

"Crying is one of the highest devotional songs. One who knows crying, knows spiritual practice." ~Swami Kripalu

Shedding tears can be among of the highest forms of spiritual practice. When we are in deep sorrow, tears allow us to release what we may so automatically turn inward. When we experience joy, tears may enter in to help us with the celebration. Sometimes we may cry just because we can't quite put words to our feeling or experience—we are exhausted, we don't know what else to do, or we may just feel like giving up. In 12-step recovery we are advised that rigorous honesty is a key to maintaining sobriety. The hard work of recovery may come with some tears, and shedding those tears is a way to practice this level of honesty.

So many of us have been taught to fear heavy emotion and the tears that come with it as part of growing up in abuse, neglect, or other dysfunction. We may have been told things like, "Boys don't cry," or "If you keep whining, girl, I'll really give you something to cry about." There is nothing shameful about shedding tears, for in them flows the river of your inner most truth. When we cry we can release that experience to the world, whatever it may be, so that it can be transformed into something beautiful and serving.

Invitation: Spend 3-5 minutes in a practice of your choice (e.g., sitting meditation, walking meditation, or an expressive practice) and bring up the word *tears* or *crying*. What is your relationship with those concepts today? Whether you are afraid to cry because of old messages, or your tears worry you because you cry too much, just notice any judgment that may be come up around these constructs. If possible, on every exhale, practice letting go of the judgment.

Prayer or Intention: Help me to recognize that my tears are important to the healing process and honor them as such.

SEPTEMBER 13

"Which end is up?" ~English language idiom

When you grow up in addiction and dysfunction or crippled with the aftereffects of trauma, you may find yourself asking this question quite a bit. If all three conditions defined your upbringing, you may be completely aimless when it comes to direction of any kind because you were never clearly shown how to function adaptively. You may have never been taught the best practices for managing in life. And it's very likely that you received a great deal of mixed messages.

In recovery fellowships, specifically Al-Anon, mixed messages are often described as a recipe for crazymaking. If you grew up in religious toxicity, a common mixed message is that "God loves you unconditionally," while in the next breath hearing that God would condemn you to hell. If their behavior clashed with their words, your parents or others you've loved in life may have been guilty of dealing in mixed messages. This may have spilled over over into your style of communicating in relationships, as mixed messages often flow from mixed up feelings. Who can blame you? Now that you are in recovery, it's time to sort it all out.

Invitation: Spend 3-5 minutes in a practice of your choice (e.g., sitting meditation, walking meditation, or an expressive practice) and think about a mixed message that you've received in the past or recently that caused you distress. Where do you notice that distress in your body? How can noticing the source of this distress and breathing with it help you to begin the process of unraveling the damage?

Prayer or Intention: Today I acknowledge the impact of mixed messages on my life. May I receive what I need to untangle the damage and proceed with clarity.

SEPTEMBER 14

"Travel light." –Charles R. (12-step friend of Jamie's)

If you go on your favorite Internet search engine and enter the phrase *travel light,* hundreds of websites will show up with tips from travel experts. The truth is, the more baggage you tend to schlep along on any holiday, the more work you create for yourself. You may even find that (unless you are privileged to have special help) you enjoy your trip less.

Travel light is excellent advice for recovery. Engaging in the trauma healing and completing all of the steps, especially the ninth, will assist you in this process. While it may feel like a strain at first to make amends to the people you have harmed, you will likely realize that getting it done will remove a many excess bounds from the baggage that you carry. Think of recovery as a process of unloading weight so that you can travel more freely. Working the amends steps is a major part of lightening the load.

Invitation: Spend 3-5 minutes in a reflective practice of your choice (sitting meditation, walking meditation, or an expressive practice) and visualize or draw the things that hold what's keeping you stuck. You can use boxes, backpacks, suitcases or storage containers, and then notice how heavy they feel for you at the moment. What are some very specific things, metaphorically or physically, that you can remove to lighten your load? How might making amends help with this process?

Prayer or Intention: As I work on lightening my load for the journey, help me to see the value of making amends in this process.

SEPTEMBER 15

"It is not often that a man can make opportunities for himself. But he can put himself in such shape that when or if the opportunities come he is ready." ~Theodore Roosevelt

We have spent much time preparing ourselves for our amends step. The eight steps that precede our Ninth Step amends all play a role in preparing us for opportunities. This includes finding our resilience through step work and trauma work, rebuilding trust in ourselves and others through sharing, and a greater understanding of our true nature through contemplation and action. The Eighth Step most directly prepares us, as we make an actual list and become willing to make amends to all that are on that list. Then we may go out and proactively track down those people and make our amends.

Sometimes, in our preparedness, we may unexpectedly find ourselves face-to-face with someone on our amends list. All of that preparation will allow us to continue forward with this significant aspect of our recovery, and by enacting amends we will further find our resilience, build trust, and understand our true nature.

Invitation: Spend 3-5 minutes in a practice of your choice (e.g., sitting meditation, walking meditation, or an expressive practice). Contemplate your Step 8 list, or if you have not made it yet, one person you imagine you owe amends to. You may simply visualize their presence or you might go ahead and visualize what amends to them would look like. Notice any changes in thought, emotion, or body sensations.

Prayer or Intention: I am a person in recovery. I am in preparation for my Step 9 amends, no matter what step I am on. I know that I can build the resilience to make my amends.

SEPTEMBER 16

"Change happens through movement
and movement heals." ~Joseph Pilates

In the English language the concept of *motivation* comes from the Latin word meaning "to move." So, the very concept of being motivated is rooted in movement. We don't give movement (and all the ways we can engage it) enough credit in the change process.

For many of us, learning how to move our bodies in a healthy way—free of chemicals or other impairments—can be challenging and yet ultimately healing. This can come in the form of exercise, yoga, dancing, or simply practicing movement by getting up off our behinds and getting to a meeting. Engaging in service or involving ourselves in other healthier activities in the community, whether they are 12-step related or not, can be another way we move ourselves into action. Although the *geographic cure* has been long condemned in recovery circles, for many of us, physically changing our locations to move towards something healthier and more productive is necessary. Moving locations is not all bad, as long as we recognize that we are taking ourselves with us wherever we go and accept the opportunities that the new location may offer us for growth.

Invitation: Make a deliberate attempt to move today in a way that you haven't before. Not used to taking walks? Perhaps consider taking a walk around the block. Not used to stretching your muscles? Perhaps engage in some light, gentle stretches. There are plenty of ideas for new movements on our supplemental site, referenced in the introduction. What can engaging in new invitations to move teach you about motivation overall?

Prayer or Intention: Help me to move toward those things that exist in the service of my recovery and wellness today.

SEPTEMBER 17

"There is a magnet in your heart that will attract
true friends." ~Parahamsa Yogananda

One time Steve and I were traveling together and had to go our separate ways at an airport. He left his coat behind at security and he asked me to go and get it, although his flight took off before I had time to bring it back. I was traveling elsewhere and wasn't expecting rain. Yet when the rain came one night, I was very grateful to have Steve's coat.

While it may seem like a silly story from our work in this life, I've come to embrace it as a powerful metaphor on friendship. Good friends are like a warm, protective raincoat. They give you the covering that you may need so that you can live and maybe even dance in the rain! In recovery, such friendships become very, very valuable to thriving and having support in the hard work of healing that recovery requires.

Invitation: Spend 3-5 minutes in a practice of your choice (e.g., sitting meditation, walking meditation, or an expressive practice) and meditate on the concept of friendship. Who are the friends in your life today that feel like a warm and protective raincoat? If these kinds of friendships seem to be lacking in your life, following Yogananda's teaching, consider setting an intention to attract more of what you need in terms of friendships.

Prayer or Intention: I am grateful for the friendships in my life today that are warm and protecting; open my heart to the friendships that may still be yet to come!

SEPTEMBER 18

"Freedom from remorse leads to happiness. Happiness leads to
concentration. Concentration brings wisdom.
And wisdom is the source of peace and freedom in
our lives." ~Joseph Goldstein

This brief description of the Buddhist path aligns completely with the trauma-informed 12-step path. Our goal from the beginning of recovery is to see what we can do to end any actions of harm toward self or others. We make this commitment and work the steps in order to make new actions and words manifest. This process leads to a real happiness, a happiness forged from new perspectives and actions. This feeling of happiness and freedom helps us to concentrate instead of getting pulled into monkey mind, with our thoughts going this way and that.

Concentration helps us to further develop our wisdom, and wisdom that is bolstered by happiness and concentration is our peace and freedom. Trauma recovery is a road to peace and freedom. 12-step recovery is a road to peace and freedom. And so we walk within both paths, so that we might sustain this newfound way of life.

Invitation: Spend 3-5 minutes in a practice of your choice (e.g., sitting meditation, walking meditation, or an expressive practice). Notice freedom from whatever remorse you have been freed from thus far in recovery. Notice the happiness present from that freedom. Now concentrate on an object of meditation like the breath or body for the remainder of your meditation period.

Prayer or Intention: Freedom from remorse brings happiness. Happiness brings concentration. Concentration brings wisdom. And wisdom brings more freedom.

SEPTEMBER 19

"If you always do what you've always done,
you'll always get what you've always got." ~recovery saying

The well-known recovery saying that opens this meditation is often used to cite the negative—if you keep doing the same things, you'll get more of the same results. However, there is a part of this that we don't often like to discuss in recovery, especially trauma-focused recovery . . . secondary gains. Secondary gains are the things that we get out of staying stuck or staying unwell. They can be tangible things like disability benefits, access to certain prescriptions or services, or simply an excuse for inappropriate behavior. Many times trauma survivors have made their entire identity about their trauma. While this may not have been one's faulty initially, the idea of losing this wild card whenever you are called out on unhealthy behavior or putting others in harm's way can feel scary.

We are not judging you if you are still dealing with secondary gains. Most of us have had them at one point or another throughout our journey. It can be tough to them let go of as part of a recovery process in order to take your healing even further. However, acknowledging that they exist in the first place is a major step in being able to let them go and move forward.

Invitation: Spend 3-5 minutes in a practice of your choice (e.g., sitting meditation, walking meditation, or an expressive practice) and notice whether or not the presence of a secondary gain is keeping you stuck in your recovery process right now. If so, what is that gain and are you able to admit it to yourself, a sponsor, a helping professional, or a trusted member of your support network?

Prayer or Intention: Today I recognize that some benefits—obvious or subtle—may exist as a result of me not doing the work to move forward. Show me what those may be and help me to develop a plan.

SEPTEMBER 20

"You have a right to perform your prescribed duties,
but you are not entitled to the fruits of your actions."
~*Bhagavad Gita*, 2.47

What came up for you upon reading the opening quote, one of the most famous verses from the Indian classic *The Bhagavad Gita* (The Song of the Lord)? Sometimes it's a bitter pill for many of us to swallow. What do you mean that I can try so hard, put so much effort in, and have no guarantees about what will happen? One of the most powerful recovery lessons that we can embrace—supported by spiritual practices from a variety of traditions—is that focusing on the outcome instead of taking the next right or healthy step will cause us distress. This can be a hard lesson for trauma survivors in recovery to accept because life has already dealt us so many unexpected blows. We want to feel that we are in control of something, that we have a guarantee about where our actions will lead us.

Sadly, there are no guarantees about how the fruits of our actions will grow and blossom. Yet accepting this teaching and learning to breathe into its uncertainty allows for another possibility: That the fruits of our actions will grow more beautifully and more significantly than we could have ever imagined. Great things happen when we can let go of the need to control.

Invitation: Take a few moments to move and stretch as it may feel good in your body. If you have a yoga, dance, or other movement practice, feel free to come into some of those movements for 2-3 minutes. Or you can simply stretch randomly and organically, like you would as you first wake up in the morning. After your movement, come into a place of stillness. Notice the energy, the sensation. Just be with it. This is the energy that your action generates. Breath and relax into it, and amazing things will happen. When we focus too hard on trying to control it, we lose it.

Prayer or Intention: Today I will perform my actions in accordance with what is healthy for my recovery, my wellness, and my life. I let go of the need to control how the fruits of these actions will grow in my life.

SEPTEMBER 21

"I'm sorry."

The beauty of Step 9 is that it isn't even about saying sorry. We are making amends, which literally means we are making change. Saying sorry may have been habitual and mostly annoying to the people around us before recovery. Not only that, but often we are sorry for the wrong things as trauma survivors, like sorry for taking up space or ever asserting ourselves. Now that we are in the Ninth Step, we are emboldened by all our previous work to make direct amends with those we feel we have harmed.

At this point in our recovery sorry no longer seems to be the hardest word. The real work comes with the ongoing maintenance of our spiritual condition after the apology, so that we might live in that amends. This will have a positive effect not just on the person we made amends to, but anyone who crosses our path under similar circumstances. The amends process leads to a changed perspective and a changed set of intentions. It leads to a lot of freedom to be perfectly imperfect, and to become a part of the dance of life.

Invitation: Utilizing your current practice whether sitting, lying down or in motion, visualize one or more people who you are considering for Ninth Step amends. Let yourself make the amends in your imagination. Notice any positive, negative or neutral thoughts, feelings, or body sensations.

Prayer or Intention: Today allow me to be nourished by all the work I have already done, and to know I can apologize when necessary and make real change in my life.

SEPTEMBER 22

"It's easier to act your way into better thinking than
to think your way into better acting." ~recovery saying

When I first entered recovery, my sponsor had a fabulous way of reminding me that Chapter 6 in the "Big Book" of *Alcoholics Anonymous* is called "Into Action," not "Into Thinking." A huge believer in the power of action and behaving in a way that was most likely to bring change into one's life, my sponsor's guidance never steered me wrong on this one. I can think myself up a storm and, as many of the sages and ancients observed, you can't really think yourself out of a prison made of thought! As another recovery say goes, *too much analysis leads to paralysis.*

In modern times, you may have heard therapeutic solutions like *change the thinking, change the behavior.* For some people this can work. For most people that I've known and worked with on this path of trauma-focused recovery, my sponsor's advice and the wisdom of the ancients is superior. Yes, changed thoughts can bring about changed behavior and long-term lifestyle change. However, for most people the easiest and most effective way to enter this cycle of repair is to change the behaviors first.

Invitation: Spend 3-5 minutes in a practice of your choice (e.g., sitting meditation, walking meditation, or an expressive practice) and bring to mind a time, preferably something recent, where taking right or healthy action impacted your thinking about a situation. What did this experience teach you about the power of the opening quote and its wisdom?

Prayer or Intention: Today I recognize that it may be easier to change my thinking through changing my behavior. May I be given what I need to make these necessary changes.

SEPTEMBER 23

"The lesson I learned best from her [my grandmother] was fortitude in the face of disagreeable situations. 'Where is it written,' she would say, 'that you are supposed to be happy all the time?'"
~Sylvia Boorstein

Trauma responses are extreme in nature, and for a reason. They are born from fight or flight, and are sometimes reactions and responses to a very real threat. Over time, we have come to believe that everything is dangerous and awful, all the time. It makes sense from a trauma perspective, as the maladaptively processed memories of the past link to present experience. One problem in recovery is going to the other extreme and believing that after a lifetime of misery we should graduate to being happy all the time.

However, this is neither recovery nor the way of the world. What we are building is an ability to live in reality, have agency over our lives, to develop distress tolerance—and that is what provides the room for happiness. As long as we are lost in the extremes, we are unable to live in the present moment. And with our recovery tools, we can get there, or *here* as the case may be.

Invitation: Spend 3-5 minutes in a practice of your choice (e.g., sitting meditation, walking meditation, or an expressive practice). Notice the extremes in your mind, the misery or difficulty, and the joy and hope. Let yourself gently toggle between the two, then allow yourself to go toward the joy and the hope if that feels natural and correct in this moment.

Prayer or Intention: I know now that happiness comes from rooting in reality, not trying to escape to a permanent state of ecstasy.

SEPTEMBER 24

"Before enlightenment, chop wood and carry water; after enlightenment, chop wood and carry water." ~Zen koan

The beauty of 12-step recovery is that it is a spiritual program with a focus on action. Action is not always visible. Sometimes our actions are internal, as we work on creating a new psychological and spiritual environment within us. And some of our actions are not giant steps forward, but rather simply doing the activities of daily life. In trauma-informed recovery, we add new activities of daily life such as small creative acts, going to meetings, going to therapy, anything that is part of our path. In the Zen tradition, there are many sayings like the one above to point out that the extraordinary comes from the ordinary.

We chop wood and carry water regardless of whether we are still sorting things out or we have completed the Twelve Seps and feel we are on a wonderful and amazing spiritual path. In recovery, enlightenment comes from the chopping of the wood and the carrying of the water. It comes in our showing up, and showing up for ourselves.

Invitation: Spend 3-5 minutes in a practice of your choice (e.g., sitting meditation, walking meditation, or an expressive practice). Take a moment and notice what is the wood you need to chop and the water you need to carry today. Notice if you can relax into the flow of those actions.

Prayer or Intention: Today before enlightenment I will chop wood and carry water. After enlightenment, I will chop wood and carry water.

SEPTEMBER 25

"The brain abhors discrepancies."

~V.S. Ramachandran

In the therapeutic approach called *Motivational Interviewing*, there is a concept called developing discrepancies. In the embodied version of this technique, we look at two things that don't seem to fit and allow sitting with any unpleasantness brought up by the discrepancy between them to lead us to insight. For instance, on one hand we may say that we want to be free of our past and no longer feel like an incompetent child when we talk to our parents. On the other hand, we may resistant about doing the deep therapeutic work necessary to meet this goal. Moreover, we may continue to expose ourselves to continually unhealthy dynamics with our parents.

As noted neuroscientist V.S. Ramachandran observes in the teaching that opens this meditation, the brain cannot stay comfortable with discrepancies for very long, at least without new stress being created. This resonates with another recovery teaching that once you've been exposed to a 12-step fellowship like Alcoholics Anonymous and know what you need to do to heal, it can ruin the fun you once had with drinking. The presence of discrepancies is normal to the recovery process and can be a pathway to helping us explore our resistances.

Invitation: Spend 3-5 minutes in a practice of your choice (e.g., sitting meditation, walking meditation, or an expressive practice) and notice where a discrepancy exists in your life right now. An example that applies for many is bringing up a goal that you'd like to achieve and noticing what behaviors or attitudes in your life are blocking you. Pay attention to any body-level distress brought up as you sit with this discrepancy. What can this unpleasantness teach you about taking the next steps for action?

Prayer or Intention: Today I recognize the discrepancies that exist in my being, though stressful, can illuminate the action I need to take—if I am willing to listen to my body's wisdom.

SEPTEMBER 26

"Go where it's warm." ~Anonymous

There is so much reverence for tough love in this world at times, and tough love is often abuse or neglect masquerading as love. It is not always the case, perhaps, as sometimes tough love simply means setting boundaries. But I remember early in recovery, there was a part of me, the part that was still wired for trauma responses, that would go toward the cold, toward people and situations that did not have my best interests in mind.

Hearing this admonition to go where its warm, to go to people who feed you rather than take from you, that support you rather than confront you for the sake of confronting, helped me to start to build a better radar. I found meetings and people where I could feel safe, and where there was a commitment to minimize the possibility of my being retraumatized.

Invitation: Spend 3-5 minutes in a practice of your choice (e.g., sitting meditation, walking meditation, or an expressive practice). Put on sufficient clothing or blankets that make it so that you feel warm and contained. Notice how this feels to you throughout your meditation.

Prayer or Intention: Today I can go where its warm.

SEPTEMBER 27

"One exercise that I practice is to try for a full inventory
of my blessings and then for a right acceptance of the many
gifts that are mine--both temporal and spiritual."
~*As Bill Sees It* , December 1989

Many people new to recovery bristle at the idea of looking for gratitude. That resistance makes sense. It can feel inauthentic. It can even feel inauthentic at times in later stages of recovery. We have been through so much pain and suffering that the idea of cultivating gratitude and accepting whatever blessings we can find seems like a lie. The 3 Stage Model of Trauma Treatment of Pierre Janet and even the teachings of the historical Buddha and other spiritual teachers tell us differently. We can only reprocess our trauma or work the inventory and amends steps of the program if we build resilience and resources first.

The first stage of our recovery involves a deep commitment to building our strength, and one major way to do that is to find an embodied gratitude rooted in reality. Many of us have gratitude lists that only contain the sun in the sky and a beloved pet. That is a fine place to start or to even remain. As long as we are actively cultivating these resources, we are moving forward in our recovery.

Invitation: Spend 3-5 minutes in a practice of your choice (e.g., sitting meditation, walking meditation, or an expressive practice). Notice your gratitude list for today. Whether it is short or long, lean into the energy of your gratitude for any or all of those people, places, or things on the list.

Prayer or Intention: Today I will notice my blessings and/or gratitude throughout the day.

SEPTEMBER 28

"If you are going through hell, keep going."
~Winston Churchill

There are many ways that trauma therapy, particularly EMDR therapy, and 12-step work run in a parallel or an integrated fashion. Both call for a compassionate form of perseverance. Both of them suggest that if you are in a difficult situation or phase, that the best way through is to keep going. The suggestion is not that we keep running on a hamster wheel of hell, but rather have the faith and understanding necessary to trust in the process and the guides helping us along the way. EMDR therapists are encouraged to "stay out of the way as much as possible" and allow the client's own brain do the healing, since the client's brain and body know how to do that.

Our 12-step sponsors are there to witness our hell and our recovery path, and to guide us through a process that is ours and ours alone. We don't have to walk through it without fellowship, but we are uniquely capable of doing what is required for our own health and recovery.

Invitation: Spend 3-5 minutes in a practice of your choice (e.g., sitting meditation, walking meditation, or an expressive practice). If recently you feel like you have been in a difficult phase, see if you can breathe into the difficulty and breathe yourself out to the other side of it.

Prayer or Intention: Today I will keep going, regardless of whether I am having a wonderful day or a terrible day. Either way, to keep going is the answer.

SEPTEMBER 29

"No one is ever more him/herself than when they really laugh . . .
It's very Zen-like, that moment." ~George Carlin

People in early recovery often wonder what everyone is laughing about in 12-step meetings. As trauma survivors, depending on what stage of recovery we are in, laughter can seem cruel or strange at first. The beauty of laughter, particularly in the group setting, is that it is an indicator of identification and of new perspectives.

When we are able to laugh at our shared troubles, we know that we are in the stream of healing. Laughter on its own is healing. And laughter allows for new ideas to enter in, have an impact, and be brought to bear on the road ahead.

Invitation: Spend 3-5 minutes in a practice of your choice (e.g., sitting meditation, walking meditation, or an expressive practice). Bring up a person or situation that makes you laugh. Allow yourself to laugh or smile as you meditate.

Prayer or Intention: Today I will look out for opportunities to engage in the healing power of laughter.

SEPTEMBER 30

"You drive yourself crazy when you try to reason
with a crazy person." ~recovery saying

While I'm not a big fan of how we sometimes use the word "crazy" as a slam or put-down, there's a great deal of truth in this saying. I've wasted so much energy in both active addiction and recovery trying to reason with people who are not willing or able to see my perspective. I've banked so much on trying to get them to change their minds and even their behaviors so that I feel validated. While validation can be important to healing, seeking it from such sources is largely futile. To quote another recovery saying, it's like going to the hardware store to by a loaf of bread. And it's driven me crazy!

Yes, it can be healthy to stand up for yourself and speak your mind. However, setting out to change someone's mind is what sets you up for frustration and failure. And it can heighten your stress in the process! If dialogue happens to lead to a shift on the other person's part, of course you can welcome it. Focusing on the outcome from the get-go is where the crazymaking comes in—especially if you're relying on their change to feel better about yourself. This guidance is particularly important when we deal with loved ones who are in active addiction or are ignoring their unhealed trauma or mental illness.

Invitation: Spend 3-5 minutes in a practice of your choice (e.g., sitting meditation, walking meditation, or an expressive practice) and think of a time when you tried to reason with someone who was not open to reason. How did this make you feel? What can you learn from this experience to help you change your approach next time?

Prayer or Intention: May I speak up when I need to and release any attachment to results, especially if that involves changing another person's mind or behavior.

OCTOBER 1

vis medicatrix naturae (Latin):
the healing power of the natural state

For many years, outdoor enthusiasts claimed *vis medicatrix naturae* as a slogan. They often translated it as "the healing power of nature." While this is not totally incorrect, it is not sufficiently nuanced. While the natural state can imply a return to Mother Nature and her healing powers, what is even more important is the return to the natural essence of who we really are. This means realizing that so many of the masks and pretenses that we have put on, often in response to traumatic wounding, block us from this natural state.

What does returning to your natural state mean to you today? It could mean simplifying your life and getting back to the essence of what is really important. It could also imply being open and out about a part of yourself that you've kept hidden for a long time, fearing judgment and condemnation. It could also mean the recognition of the impermanence of this life and all of the stressors that we let weigh us down as if they are the end of the world. Consider that they are most definitely not. Who we really are is so much bigger, brighter, and more wondrous than anything this petty world might have us believe. How would my life be different if I could live from that realization?

Invitation: Spend 3-5 minutes in a practice of your choosing (e.g., sitting meditation, walking meditation, or an expressive practice) and contemplate the opening phrase. Whether you are old school and want to hold the phrase in Latin or choose to go with English or your own language, really cradle the idea that there is healing power in returning to your natural state. If there is any part of you that resists that today, don't judge yourself; rather, notice where the source of that resistance may be and send your breath there. What may this resistance teach you about where you are at on your recovery journey today?

Prayer or Intention: There is healing power in my natural state— may I be open to seeing myself in that light today and living from that place.

OCTOBER 2

"What better way to honor the sacredness that I am than
to practice buying myself flowers?" ~Jamie Marich

In *After a While*, her celebrated poem revered by those of us on a path of recovery from co-dependency or co-addiction, Veronica A. Shofstall challenges us to do for ourselves what we usually wait on others to do for us. Like buying yourself flowers. In modern times, society can program us to think that we are only worthy of receiving flowers if something gets them for us. As nice a gesture as this may be, what stops you from buying your own flowers?

This is just one example. There are many ways, especially as our recovery develops and progresses, that we can learn to take care of ourselves instead of waiting on others to do it for us. If you struggle with love addiction or issues with unhealthy attachment to others, these practices of self-care may be particularly vital for you in discovering your own worth.

Invitation: Spend 3-5 minutes in a practice of your choice (e.g., sitting meditation, walking meditation, or an expressive practice) and think of what it means to *decorate our own soul*. Is there a way you can concretely put that into action today—like making art when you have feared that wasting time on it is frivolous, or buying yourself flowers?

Prayer or Intention: Today, may I learn how to decorate my own soul instead of waiting on validation from outside people, places, and things.

OCTOBER 3

"We begin to discern new paths that are body guided. We start to live in rhythms and cycles that are nourishing rather than depleting. We touch a primal joy that is our birthright." ~Christine Valters Paintner

The constructs of *nourishing* and *depleting* are particularly valuable as we engage in ongoing self-inventory. Even as people in recovery who are doing well, the fast pace of life and its demanding energies can overwhelm us with stress. This stress can adversely affect our wellness. As people in trauma recovery, even after a period of sobriety or abstinence, we often still continue to push. Frequently, this push comes from traumatic messages about not being good enough or not working hard enough that we still need to heal.

In evaluating your life and how you spend your energy, consider doing an inventory guided by the words nourishing and depleting. What in my life do I find nourishing and what do I find depleting? If the depleting column is much longer than the nourishing column, it's very likely that some adjustments need to be made. You may also notice that some people, places, or things end up in both columns. If that's the case, use this as an opportunity to explore the dynamics of time, energy, and expectation.

Invitation: Get out a piece of paper or your journal and make two columns: *nourishing* and *depleting*. Spending some time doing an examination of where your life is at right now using this tool to guide you in your inventory. What are you noticing?

Prayer or Intention: May I make the necessary changes that will allow my life to be more nourishing, today and on the path ahead.

OCTOBER 4

"Revolution is not a one-time event."
~Audre Lorde

Every day requires deliberate practice and attention to our wellness. I grow concerned when I see people seeking recovery or healing in search of the "quick fix." Whether it's through a religious experience or some miracle treatment, there have been and will always be people out there claiming to offer it. Yet, I've never known an instantaneous cure to be sustainable and ultimately nourishing.

In my travels I once met a young priest who offered this in a sermon: "Do you want to be cured, or do you want to be healed?" That stuck with me, for as soon as he offered the question, I knew that healing is what I needed—body, mind, and spirit. For me, healing has been a process that requires daily maintenance and care of my total condition. My radical transformation has been a series of small, daily revolutions.

Invitation: Spend 3-5 minutes in a practice of your choice (e.g., sitting meditation, walking meditation, or an expressive practice) and sit with the question: "Do I want to be cured or do I want to be healed?" Notice what comes up for you in your meditation experience and consider jotting down or otherwise expressing what was revealed in a journal or on paper.

Prayer or Intention: Today I recognize that deep healing requires my daily participation for its potential to unfold.

OCTOBER 5

Every day is a good day.
~Zen koan

Working through trauma and adverse life events of the past and the present can be grueling work. And having someone admonish you to buck up and try and smile and even get over it can add a new layer of rage or despair to this work. We often get mixed messages from the recovery world and the therapeutic world, but they actually don't have to be mixed at all. Early Buddhist teachings encourage by letting us know that the end of suffering will come through our diligence, and as a result we will be filled with loving kindness, compassion, empathetic joy, and equanimity. Those teachings also tell us that we can cultivate these qualities as well, even before we are at the end of the path. So, the idea that every day is a good day does not need to be a mixed message.

Going toward the positive doesn't have to mean faking it till you make it. At times where we have the insight and energy, we can cultivate the positive. It need not be big, and it need not be sustained for hours on end. We can take any internal or external resources that we notice, and acknowledge them, appreciate them, and utilize them. That is how every day can be a good day, even the most challenging ones.

Invitation: Take a few moments to see if you can identify an internal resource that you feel is attainable today. It can be as simple as petting a pet, spending some time with a friend, reading and meditating a few extra minutes, or taking a walk.

Prayer or Intention: Today help me to see the positive, no matter how small and for however short a time.

OCTOBER 6

"A bend in the road is not the end of the road . . .
Unless you fail to make the turn." ~Helen Keller

Trauma recovery and recovery in general help us to deal with the long and winding road of life. Before recovery, we were driven by our survival instincts, with good reason, and it was hard to navigate the road ahead. Now here at Step 10, we come to what many in recovery refer to as "the maintenance steps". This is where we take all the recovery garnered thus far and continue to put it into daily action. However, now we may be able to do that more skillfully.

We have learned how to bring our neocortex online to dialogue with our survival instincts and come up with more nuanced and healthy responses to life. And now when we assess a response and find we might like to do it differently we can make amends where we need to. We can engage that as an ongoing process and avoid the murky buildup of years of secrets, resentments, and other forms of pain and suffering.

Invitation: Spend 3-5 minutes in a practice of your choice (e.g., sitting meditation, walking meditation, or an expressive practice). Look at yesterday. Notice if there is anything you want to do differently. Look at today. Notice what your provisional plan is to go forward.

Prayer or Intention: Help me navigate the winding road of recovery with all the new tools and friendships I now have at my disposal.

OCTOBER 7

life style: an individual's characteristic way of
overcoming or compensating for feelings of inadequacy
(Alfred Adler, 1929)

A common denominator in the programs that we've seen work for others in getting sober and well is the importance placed on lifestyle change. Whether you are working a 12-step path or not, are the strategies you are using to recover helping you to bring about meaningful, necessary lifestyle change? Getting sober and well requires us to learn a whole new way of managing our day-to-day existence, which can translate to a whole new way of approaching our lives in general.

Alfred Adler, one of the early fathers of psychology, was the first to coin the term *life style.* His original definition connects very powerfully to the role unhealed trauma and wounding can play in forming the lifestyle patterns that we develop. How many of my lifestyle choices that are causing me problems are directly tied to past wounds—and their inferiorities they create?

Invitation: Adler further described life style as a pair of glasses through which we see the world, and the wounds of our unhealed inferiorities wrote the prescription. He described wellness as getting a new pair of glasses—or at least getting a new prescription for the existing frames. Spend 3-5 minutes in a practice of your choice (e.g., sitting meditation, walking meditation, or an expressive practice) contemplating this metaphor. What needs done with my glasses today?

Prayer or Intention: May I be open to evaluating my lifestyle as part of my recovery journey. May I receive help making the adjustments that I need to see with world through a healthier pair of glasses.

OCTOBER 8

"All of life can be a trauma trigger… or a relapse trigger."
~Jamie Marich

Life is rough. We make no excuses for that fact. Whether it's contemplating the things that have happened to us or the experiences we are enduring now, life was never meant to be an easy road. That does not mean that it can't be enjoyable and peaceful, especially if we learn to embrace the challenges that life brings our way.

The triggers generally get our attention. Keeping with the wound metaphor used throughout the *Trauma and the 12 Steps* work, when something irritates us, we generally need to do something about it to bring about relief. For many years, drinking, drugs, and other reinforcing behaviors may have been the easy answer to keep us distracted from the irritation. We inevitably notice it again when the effects of our substance or behavior of choice wears off. To truly address irritation, we need to look at its source, feel the feelings, or otherwise work it through. Using this attitude, we can approach the daily miseries of life as opportunities for growth.

Invitation: Spend 3-5 minutes in a practice of your choice (e.g., sitting meditation, walking meditation, or an expressive practice) and contemplate the idea of triggers as a growth opportunity. Notice what unfolds for you, specifically on how irritation is designed to get your attention. How can I respond once I am aware?

Prayer or Intention: Today I embrace all of life, including its triggers and irritations, as opportunities for growth.

OCTOBER 9

"You can attain many insights by looking into the past.
But you are still grounded in the present moment."
~Thich Nhàt Han

Many 12-step slogans can be confusing at first, including *One Day at a Time*. When we look at it from a perspective of getting through the difficult days, it seems to make a great deal of sense—that we can make it through one day if we just reduce our goal to that length of time. Many people in 12-step programs will push back, saying we must plan, we must be able to look to the past for clues and look to the future for next steps. All of this is true and does not require push back. The truth of One Day at a Time is the truth of mindfulness, the truth of non-judgmental present-time awareness, the truth of this moment is the only moment actually in session right now.

Achieving mindfulness one moment at a time, one day at a time, allows us to not wallow in past regrets nor worry about the future. We are able to heal the past and leverage it. We are able to face the future and walk into it with resilience. We are able to truly live in the moment, with all that it encompasses.

Invitation: Spend 3-5 minutes in a practice of your choice (e.g., sitting meditation, walking meditation, or an expressive practice). Do a simple breath tracking, where you count your breaths from 1 to 10 on the out breath. If you get to 10 or lose your place on the way, just come back to 1. Notice whether this helps place you in the moment.

Prayer or Intention: Today I will live this day only. To the best of my ability, today I will not regret the past nor will worry about the future.

OCTOBER 10

"As we go through the day we pause, when agitated
or doubtful, and ask for the right thought or action."
~*Alcoholics Anonymous*, p. 87

Sometimes the suggestions or admonitions in 12-step programs seem so simple, yet so unrealistic. We can look at One Day at a Time and think, well, what about my future? I have to plan! We can look at Live and Let Live and believe that we are great at letting everyone else live just fine, while we have no idea how to do our own living. Today's suggestion of pausing and praying in the "Big Book" can seem especially impossible when we find ourselves incapable of finding the "pause." Our traumatic response network wordlessly and powerfully tells us to be agitated and doubtful. We may feel permanently wired to follow agitation with doubt and more agitation. In fact, we may have become wired this way, but it is temporary.

Now in recovery, we can build the systems of prayer and action that rewire our ability to stop and pause—sometimes quickly, sometimes slowly. We become able to calmly hover over the agitation and doubt, and we become able to use our thinking processes to take new resilient action on our own behalf.

Invitation: Spend 3-5 minutes in a practice of your choice (e.g., sitting meditation, walking meditation, or an expressive practice). Notice what issues are upon you today. Now notice that you are in meditation, and within that find a pause. Notice what comes in to fill the pause, whether it be further doubt or perhaps a new idea or some calm.

Prayer or Intention: This recovery is about my finding the pause. My agitation and doubt is temporary. The pause is there for me to empower myself.

OCTOBER 11

"Energy wants to work for us—to heal us, to restore us—
if we let it." ~Chintan (Jamie's sponsor)

There is an art to staying out of your own way. Like many other folks in recovery, you may have heard this statement and asked, "What does that even mean?" Part of the answer is letting the healing resources you are letting into your life do their thing—they don't need your extra help or push. Too often we can force healing solutions or try too hard to bring about change, that we interfere with the natural intelligence of energy and the flow of time to work its magic.

Another part of staying out of our own way is a conscious commitment to engaging in daily recovery practices and doing the next right or healthy thing for ourselves. Sometimes it's difficult to stay the course, especially if we don't see a clear outcome ahead. Know that by daily commitment to a healthier lifestyle you are allowing the healing power of energy to do her thing. Before you may even be consciously aware of it, the impact of that healing will begin to unfold.

Invitation: Come into a seated position that you can sustain for the next 3-5 minutes, although lying down is an acceptable modification. Rub your hands together for about 30 seconds to generate some heat or some energy. Then, turn your palms so that they are facing each other but do not allow them to touch. Play with moving your hands back and forth, without letting them touch and see if you can notice the presence of energy. It may be heat, it may be an indescribable pull that keeps your hands from moving any closer together. Notice what you notice, tapping into this very experience of energy that wants to help in your healing process.

Prayer or Intention: Today I will let the healing power of energy work in my life. I will stay out of my own way.

OCTOBER 12

"Nothing pays off like restraint of tongue and pen . . . When we are tempted by the bait, we should train ourselves to step back and think. We can neither think or act to good purpose until the habit of self-restraint has become automatic."
~Bill Wilson, *Twelve Steps and Twelve Traditions*, p. 179

Bill W. and Dr. Bob were truly onto something when they noticed that anger was at the heart of the recovery dilemma. They were way ahead of their time. On the other hand, they did not have modern trauma theory and practice at their disposal when designing their program. This quote from the "12 and 12" lets me know that I need to step back and think before I act or speak out of anger.

The problem for many traumatized individuals is that the ability to think clearly when in the fight or flight state has been compromised. This has a number of implications. One is that I need to have compassion for myself when I am not always able to step back and think. I have to know this is a process that is not about perfection. Forgiveness will be important, first and foremost toward myself as I learn how to practice self-restraint.

Invitation: Without getting into details, see if you can start to mindfully track your anger and your responses. You might try a walking meditation, slowly and mindfully walking back and forth for a distance of about 6 to 8 feet. Choose one foot and label it *anger* and label the other foot *response*. And then notice how each case of anger and response brings you to the next steps in your journey. Notice if the mantra fades away at any time during the meditation, or if it stays steady.

Prayer or Intention: I will notice my anger mindfully, and I will notice my responses. I can have compassion for myself as I learn how to manage my anger.

OCTOBER 13

"Human freedom involves our capacity to pause between stimulus
and response and, in in that pause, to choose the one response
towards which we wish to throw our weight."
~Rollo May, *The Courage to Create*

Dealing with unhealed trauma and living in active addiction can feel
like our power to make choices have been ripped away. While the
opening teaching by Rollo May, echoed by many of his contemporaries
like Viktor Frankl, may feel good and right on the surface, it's so much
easier said than done! Of course, I may want to take that pause and
choose the healthy course of action, and yet if the brain feels hijacked,
do I really have that choice?

Recovery can be described as learning to widen the space between
stimulus and response. Viktor Frankl taught that in this space is our
power and our freedom. It doesn't happen overnight, especially if
we've spent most of our lives in a reactionary mode for the sake of
survival. Regular engagement in mindfulness practices and practicing
the regulation of our breath and body can be powerful ways to widen
this space. The widening doesn't happen overnight, which can be
difficult for those of us with a penchant for instant gratification to
handle. Keep practicing and the space will widen and you will notice
that choice has returned.

Invitation: Allow at least 3-5 minutes for this practice, coming into a
comfortably seated position if you are able (laying down is permissible
as a variation). Visualize the words *stimulus* and *response*. If visualizing is
difficult for you, write them down on a piece of paper. Then, with your
eyes closed or open, allow yourself to begin focusing on your breath.
With each breath, see if you can visualize the space between the words
stimulus and *response* widening. Continue to breath into the power of
this space.

Prayer or Intention: May my breath and commitment to mindful
living widen the gap between stimulus and response today, allowing
me to reclaim the power of choice.

OCTOBER 14

"For me to be a saint means to be myself."
~Thomas Merton

The point of the steps is not to be washed clean of everything forever. Just as the point of trauma recovery is not to have everything surgically removed that we find unbearable. The point of the steps is to be guided to our true selves, at least enough so that we can make daily decisions to honor that true self and set intentions from that place. The last three steps are often called the maintenance steps because they encapsulate the learning and healing of the first nine steps and create a framework for our lives going forward.

In trauma recovery terms, they provide us with the third stage of trauma treatment, that of relapse prevention, living our new healthier lives, and looking toward the future with dedicated intention. Step 10 makes clear to us that we are not made into perfect angels or saints by the process, nor should we be. Rather we are now in a state of awareness and mindfulness that allows us to continue in our self-reflection day-to-day, moment-to-moment, and make the adjustments necessary to stay true to ourselves and our recovery. That is the type of sainthood we have achieved, Merton's sainthood of becoming our true selves.

Invitation: Spend 3-5 minutes in a practice of your choice (e.g., sitting meditation, walking meditation, or an expressive practice). In the spirit of contemplative prayer, utilize your practice to ask for wisdom that will orient you toward your true self. See if you can utilize the wisdom of the Tenth Step to see your path clearly along with any adjustments that need to be made.

Prayer or Intention: Today let me live in the self-reflection of the Tenth Step, not remorseful rumination, but self-reflection that allows for me to be true to myself and my recovery.

OCTOBER 15

"Facebook has become like the boyfriend I no longer like but scared to dump because I've invested so much time in the relationship."
~Manasa Rao Saarloos

In our modern lives, portable technologies—smartphones, tablets, laptops—can be both a blessing and a curse. While social media can help us to network with like-minded people all over the world, we may find ourselves imprisoned by technology. We may feel the need to always be in the loop about what's going on in our networks, noticing the dread of being excluded. We may find ourselves obsessed with getting responses—over text, on statuses, on email, or on other messaging platforms—panicking with dread if we don't hear back from a certain party. Sometimes as a result of these obsessions, I've found myself not present to what is going on in my own life.

Modern technology and social media are not the enemy. Yet when they keep us from fully engaging with the people, places, and things right in front of us, then technology becomes a shackle. Admitting this reality is the first step in addressing it.

Invitation: Spend 3-5 minutes in a practice of your choice (e.g., sitting meditation, walking meditation, or an expressive practice) and contemplate how you use technology, especially social media in your life. What are some ways that it serves you? What are some ways that it keeps you blocked or even cut off from life?

Prayer or Intention: Help me to recognize when technology serves me and when it imprisons me and keeps me from living my life to the fullest.

MOM'S BDAY

OCTOBER 16

"There is no complexity in what is, but only
in the many escapes that we seek." ~Jiddhu Krishnamurti

One of the slogans I heard early on in meetings was that it was a simple program for complicated people. Krishnamurti points out that our brains are wired to find the escape hatches, and once we are captured in that web, we struggle in the complexity of it. Trauma-informed 12-step recovery allows us to find our way to the simplicity of finding ourselves in the moment, accepting what is, and moving forward from there.

The maintenance steps of the program are designed for us to continually look out for our further attempts at escape through old behaviors. Once we have reprocessed our traumatic memories and have had some practice at noticing what the right thing to do is in every situation, we can utilize the maintenance steps to do just that, to maintain our serenity, our courage and our sanity.

Invitation: Spend 3-5 minutes in a practice of your choice (e.g., sitting meditation, walking meditation, or an expressive practice). Bring up your day yesterday. Notice one time you felt you were trying to escape reality. Notice one time when you felt firmly planted in the moment. Notice any differences in thoughts, body sensations or emotions.

Prayer or Intention: Today I will lean into reality, into the moment. I will notice what will impede me and what will help me thrive.

overcoming situations in my mind
will help me. Not overcoming people.
situations will help me progress fwd

OCTOBER 17

"One can be the master of what one does,
but never of what one feels." –Gustave Flaubert

You feel what you feel—that doesn't mean you are going to act on your feelings, nor does it mean that you are a bad person for experiencing the emotions that you do. If I had only one teaching to impart to people in recovery, this would be the teaching. I've seen so many people needlessly torture themselves over their feelings or judging themselves for having certain feelings in particular situations. You feel what you feel.

It's clear that many of us were programmed or taught horrible things about feelings and emotions, a theme that is explored quite a bit throughout the *Trauma and the 12 Steps* work and at various places in this reader. Are you still judging yourself today based on these old messages? Consider that trying to stop yourself from experiencing your feelings is as futile as trying to stop the flow of a river, the waves of the ocean, or yes—as futile as trying to stop yourself from doing your business when your body signals that it's time to find a toilet (or at least somewhere to let it out, even if it's a roadside bush or a makeshift litter box).

Invitation: Spend 3-5 minutes in a practice of your choice (e.g., sitting meditation, walking meditation, or an expressive practice) and contemplate this very crude example if you are willing. Think about the last time you had to "go to the bathroom." What if you were told (or even told yourself) I have to hold it in—indefinitely! Consider the level of pain and distress that would ensue, and how eventually what needs to come out will come out in an even messier, uncontained way. As gross as this sounds, this is what we do when we do not allow ourselves the proper outlet to feel through our feelings, an experience of human living that is as natural as needing to do this physical business.

Prayer or Intention: Having feelings and allowing them to be expressed or at least experienced is a part of the natural flow of the human experience. May I consider that trying to stop this flow will only cause me and others more distress in the long run.

OCTOBER 18

"A voice called. I went.
I went, for it called.
I went, lest I fall."
~Hannah Senesh

Recovery requires us to engage in practices and lifestyle changes that are outside of our comfort zones. Recovery asks us to take everything that we've known as normal in the past seasons of our lives and develop new ways of looking at the world. Recovery suggests that we do some deep digging to heal the source of our wounds so that they no longer color how we interact with the world. Recovery is difficult, and at times it can feel like hell.

We've never met an individual in recovery who hasn't, at one time or another, declared that recovery is too hard. It's completely normal to have this experience. Unfortunately, this is the turning point that causes many people to stumble or even relapse. Let's face it, early in recovery drinking, drugging, or engaging in your behaviors of choice can feel like an easier way to bring about relief. Might it help if you could embrace recovery as a necessary calling to change your life, or face other consequences?

Invitation: Spend 3-5 minutes in a practice of your choice (e.g., sitting meditation, walking meditation, or an expressive practice) and contemplate the most difficult or challenging part of recovery so far. What has meeting this difficult challenge taught you about yourself?

Prayer or Intention: Today I recognize that recovery requires hard work and I ask for the strength I need to face the challenge.

OCTOBER 19

"Expectations are planned resentments." ~recovery slogan

This slogan can be a tough one, even if we recognize a lot of truth in it. Certainly, the higher we set our expectations, the more painful the fall if those expectations don't pan out. This can feel especially true as it relates to expecting other people to behave a certain way or expecting a certain outcome. The answer may seem very simple on the surface—just don't have expectations, right? If your spiritual and recovery practices are able to get you there, fabulous! On the other hand, isn't it normal and realistic to have some degree of expectations, especially of people?

For instance, if you are in a relationship or work situation, you *expect* to be treated with respect and dignity. If you are an employer, there is an expectation of how those who work for you will behave if they are going to keep their job. Of course, these expectations are realistic. The key is that if the other person involved doesn't live up to your expectations, the responsibility is yours to make adjustments— by addressing it directly or making changes in yourself to deal with your response. As a child growing up with caretakers who may have let us down all the time and which may have led to so much of our wounding, we didn't have these skills. Resentments are part of living in the human condition and fortunately now we have strategies for dealing with those too. The action is yours to take—whether it's shedding the expectations, managing disappointment, or working on the resentment.

Invitation: Spend 3-5 minutes in a practice of your choice (e.g., sitting meditation, walking meditation, or an expressive practice) and bring up the phrase *expectations are planned resentments*. Take a few moments and notice what you notice about the slogan. Then, if you are willing, draw your attention to your breath, paying deliberate attention to the exhale. On each exhale, experiment with the phrase: *I release all expectations*. Notice what you notice.

Prayer or Intention: Today may I explore what it would feel like to release all expectations, noticing whatever the opening of this release creates.

OCTOBER 20

"Memories are the key not to the past, but to the future."
~Corrie ten Boom

Driving a car provides us with a treasure trove of metaphors that we can use in the recovery process. One of my favorites is the notion that our past is just as much a part of us as a rearview mirror on any vehicle equipped for safe driving. It's vitally important that we use the rearview mirrors to navigate conditions. However, if we stay fixated on the rearview mirror and do not watch the road ahead, we will likely steer of course. Or get in an accident. Similarly, never looking back in the rearview mirrors and focusing only on the road ahead can also cause problems.

How can this metaphor of my past as a rearview mirror serve me today, especially as I continue to grow in recovery? As trauma survivors, we may have spent much of our lives being tortured by the past. With healing, that no longer has to be the case. Yet our past can provide us with tremendous insights for navigating the journey ahead.

Invitation: Spend 3-5 minutes in a practice of your choice (e.g., sitting meditation, walking meditation, or an expressive practice) and bring up the metaphor of driving a car and using your past like a set of rearview mirrors. How might this metaphor be helpful to your journey today? Do you need to look back less or more in your current stage of the journey?

Prayer or Intention: Today I recognize that my past can serve me, especially in helping me to navigate the road ahead. I do not have to remain fixated on it for this purpose to be served.

OCTOBER 21

"When you do things from your soul,
you feel a river moving in you, a joy." ~Rumi

Trauma recovery and recovery in general is not just finding new ways
to survive; these are pathways to thriving. Through our trauma, our
addictions, all of our dilemmas, many of us have lost the capacity for
joy—or so we may think. It can feel like there are many layers between
us and any joy we've experienced in the past or that may be available
in the future. Recovery shows us a new equation.

Before recovery, we may have viewed joy as the euphoria of being
high, whatever it was that helped us to get to that state. But that state
is not sustainable, nor does it constitute the deeper or genuine joy. It is
through being true to ourselves, following our vision, our insight, our
healing journey, that we find true joy. It is a longer arc to get to that joy
than taking a pill, but that joy has a longer arc of sustainability. When
we are in recovery, we are in the flow of the river—the river that can
fill us with the joy of being on the path.

Invitation: Spend 3-5 minutes in a practice of your choice (e.g.,
sitting meditation, walking meditation, or an expressive practice).
Contemplate the phrase, "To thine own self be true." Notice what
thoughts, emotions, sensations, and insights arise as you contemplate
these words.

Prayer or Intention: Today I will notice the moments of joy that
come from being true to myself and my recovery.

OCTOBER 22

"When our bubble bursts, we can recognize that we are walking through a very important doorway. Then we can experiment with hanging out on the other side of that doorway." ~Pema Chödrön

Many people feel unable to walk through the door of recovery because what is on the other side seems so daunting. This makes sense considering how in our addictions and in our other attempts to adapt to trauma, we learned to rely on our alarm system as a primary guide. So, when we look on the other side of the recovery door from afar, with everything that is unknown and the many different stories we tell ourselves about what it will be like, all our alarms go off. That is why it usually takes a very powerful bursting of the bubble to have us move into recovery.

Once we are through the door, we find that not only is there a new set of answers to the question of how to live, but a more relaxed life and lifestyle is available to us. And how does that relaxed nature come about? Through experimentation with the recovery life. We don't achieve perfection, we don't know all the answers, we just start experimenting with a new way of being and a new way of living. This is the true nature of faith—the willingness to experiment.

Invitation: Spend 3-5 minutes in a practice of your choice (e.g., sitting meditation, walking meditation, or an expressive practice). If you are comfortable with visualization, notice yourself on one side of a door to recovery, and in your meditation, walk through that door. Notice what is on the other side.

Prayer or Intention: Today let me experiment with a life in recovery, and let me notice the lessons and the blessings.

OCTOBER 23

"Bad things do happen; how I respond to them
defines my character and the quality of my life."
~Walter Inglis Anderson

As survivors of trauma we are all too familiar with bad things, even indescribable, horrible things being a part of our story. Bad things may continue to happen once we enter recovery because that is the nature of life. Accidents, disasters, misfortunes, and just plain weird twists of luck (good or bad) can happen at any time. This is part of what the slogan *life on life's term* is getting at.

Sometimes we have a tendency to personalize the bad things that happen to us in recovery, no matter how small they are. "See, no matter what I do the bad luck always seems to find me," "I'm just cursed," "I can't get a break," or "Shame on me for not being more careful," are all things that we may have said to ourselves or others. Healing the underlying wounds that cause us to say such horrible things about ourselves is a start in being able to cope with and even grow from the bad things life will inevitably bring our way. Then we can use what we have learned to respond accordingly.

Invitation: Spend 3-5 minutes in a practice of your choice (e.g., sitting meditation, walking meditation, or an expressive practice) and notice if there is a recurring statement or line you tend to say to yourself when something bad or stressful happens. Even if you are still in the middle of your healing process today, what is a more compassionate statement you can say to yourself? Essentially, what is the opposite of your normal script. Say this new statement out loud, even if you don't fully mean it, as if you are trying it on for size.

Prayer or Intention: Today I accept that bad, annoying, or otherwise stressful things may happen to me in recovery. I will be kind to myself in my response.

OCTOBER 24

"The deepest principle in human nature is the
craving to be appreciated." ~William James

The phenomenon of craving is discussed extensively in 12-step programs. Craving, especially at the biological level, is serious business. In both 12-step logic and professional diagnostic manuals, craving is a symptom of addiction or a substance use disorder. Cravings can be so powerful that we can fear them when they happen—and they will happen.

What if we could learn to use our cravings for our highest good instead of burrowing from them in fright? The body tells us that something is wrong ten steps before our rational mind can even realize what's going on. Part of a trauma-focused, embodied recovery program is to learn to recognize cravings at the body level and make a plan accordingly. This is where practices like exercise, breath, mindfulness, and getting into action can help. Also cravings can alert you to what may be wrong and reveal what is blocking you from peace and contentment. And craving states of being like peace and contentment may provide a positive spin you can put on the idea of craving, at least at this point in your recovery.

Invitation: Spend 3-5 minutes in a practice of your choice (e.g., sitting meditation, walking meditation, or an expressive practice) and notice the idea of craving. Where do you tend to feel craving the most in your body, especially where substances or unhealthy behaviors may be concerned? Now in contrast, can you bring up something positive or healthy that you may crave (e.g., peace, contentment, joy, recovery)? As you sit with that for a while, together with your breath, what are you noticing differently in your body? How can working with both types of craving at the body level serve you going forward?

Prayer or Intention: Today I recognize that all of my cravings are alerting me to action. If I allow it, my cravings will all teach me something valuable about myself and the recovery process.

OCTOBER 25

"Everyone is my teacher. Some I seek.
Some I subconsciously attract. Often I learn
simply by observing others." ~Eric Allen

We can be quick to elevate those who we believe impact us positively as our teachers. In Eastern circles, it's even common for people to identify one specific leader as their "teacher." In recovery circles, we can do this with our sponsors. While our tendency to do this may result from simple gratitude to begin with, we run the risk of being bitterly disappointed if our teacher or sponsor lets us down. Additionally, by putting too much of our focus on one person, we also cut ourselves off from what others can teach us.

On the path of recovery, *everyone* has something to teach us. Even those negative experiences we have with people offer teachable moments and valuable lessons. We both have stories of what we've learned about how *not* to stay sober or how *not* to counsel others based on the negative examples we've seen. In many cases, the negative experiences have more to teach us about ourselves and the recovery process. Our challenge is to begin seeing every experience and every person as our teacher.

Invitation: Spend 3-5 minutes in a reflective practice of your choice (sitting meditation, walking meditation, or an expressive practice) and reflect on the teachings and examples you've received in your recovery process. If you wish, you can even take this reflection into the larger course of your life. How many people do you consider to be your teachers? Are you open to learning from everyone or is your definition still rather confined?

Prayer or Intention: May I recognize today and on the path ahead that everyone has something to teach me. May I be open to the numerous lessons.

I am open to seeing everyone as
a teacher.

OCTOBER 26

"Reality is one of the possibilities I cannot afford to ignore."
~Leonard Cohen

Trauma responses are often extreme in nature and for good reason. They are born from fight or flight, sometimes very real reactions and responses to a real threat. Over time, we have come to believe that everything is dangerous and awful, all the time. It makes sense from a trauma perspective, as the maladaptively processed memories of the past link into what is happening now. One problem in recovery is going to the other extreme and believing that after a lifetime of misery we should graduate into being happy all the time.

This, however, is not recovery or the way of the world. What we are building is an ability to live in reality, have agency over our lives, to have distress tolerance built, and that is what provides the room for happiness. As long as we are lost in the extremes, we are unable to live in the present moment. With our recovery tools, we can get there—get into the present moment.

Invitation: Spend 3-5 minutes in a practice of your choice (e.g., sitting meditation, walking meditation, or an expressive practice). Notice the extremes in your mind, the misery or difficulty, and the joy and hope. Let yourself gently toggle between the two, then allowing yourself to go toward the joy and the hope if that feels natural and correct in this moment.

Prayer or Intention: I know now that happiness comes from rooting in reality, not trying to escape to a permanent state of ecstasy.

OCTOBER 27

"Science is not only compatible with spirituality;
it is a profound source of spirituality."~Carl Sagan

In recovery we no longer have to be in constant debate about spirituality, science, and everything in between. The neuroscience of trauma and the research on trauma therapies demonstrate that there is an ever-growing scientific basis that explains the impact of our trauma and adverse life event histories. And those of us who are spiritually minded see the connections and metaphysical explanations for what we have gone through and how we get better.

Both science and the spirituality are honored in the steps, as they are steeped in both elements of faith and elements of action. As Carl Sagan suggests, in some ways they operate independently but they also impact each other and are integrated forces at times. Regardless, we no longer have to fight about it. The steps provide a pathway by which we can access trauma -informed recovery through the integration of our mind, body, and spirit.

Invitation: Spend 3-5 minutes in a practice of your choice (e.g., sitting meditation, walking meditation, or an expressive practice). After a minute or so of grounding practice, consider and meditate upon an element of science that seems true for you. Consider and meditate upon an element of spirituality that seems true for you.

Prayer or Intention: Today I will notice what aspects of science makes sense to me in the context of my recovery. I will also notice the basic ideas or practices of spirituality make sense to me.

OCTOBER 28

"Date the sensation." ~Kalindi Edwina Hoffmann

One of my personal teachers Kalindi, a brilliant yogi and gem of a human being, issued this invitation in a class I had the privilege of taking with her. In the style of yoga that we practice, sensations are powerful information, gifts from our body to make us more aware. Sensation can also be viewed as body-speak for energy. We are invited to notice everything.

In this metaphor, Kalindi invited us to consider how we are when we first date someone. We can be attentive and responsive to their every move, gesture, and reaction, wondering what it means for us. Dating is that time we are encouraged to pay attention to the information we are receiving, whether it be pleasant, unpleasant, or neutral, and learn to respond accordingly. What if we could learn to do the same thing with what rises up in our body? Not pushing the information away, rather, notice it, investigate it, and respond accordingly, whether that be with stillness, movement, or and enhanced commitment to self-nourishment.

Invitation: If it is available to you, spend about 1-2 minutes in movements of your choice (e.g., dancing, stretching, jumping jacks, etc.). You can do this on your feet, sitting down, or lying down. If you have restrictions in certain areas of your body, allow movement to happen in those areas where it is feasible. Then come into another 1-2 minutes of stillness. What are you noticing? What sensations are you aware of? Practice just noticing them without trying to change them or push them away. Then notice what your body may require next as a response.

Prayer or Intention: May I learn to embrace the sensations of my body as a gift, announcing awareness and inviting response.

OCTOBER 29

"Desire is the creator. Desire is the destroyer."
~Hari Das Baba

Desires can be tricky to navigate in recovery. Many of our traumatic experiences of neglect included having our wants, needs, and desires denied. In active addition, we often swing the pendulum to pursue everything our heart desires to fill that vacuum of neglect. Sometimes this pursuit comes at great consequence to ourselves and to others, especially if we don't care who we trample on in fulfilling our desires.

Recovery offers us an opportunity to renegotiate our relationship with the concept of desire, and daily inventory in Step 10 can assist. In and of itself, desire is not a bad thing and having desires is a normal part of the human experience. As the teaching that opens this meditation describes, desire is the seed of many worthwhile and necessary creations that nourish us in this life and make our world a better place. Yet desire is the ultimate double-edge sword. If we run completely on desire absent a disciplined lifestyle of recovery, spiritual perspective, or regard for others, we can cause a great deal of harm indeed. As we contemplate the notion of desire, we may realize that it is not our desires that are the problem; rather, or fierce attachment to them that causes suffering.

Invitation: Spend 3-5 minutes in a practice of your choice (e.g., sitting meditation, walking meditation, or an expressive practice) and bring up the word *desire*. Notice if the concept has a pleasant, unpleasant, or neutral connotation for you, and then spend some time noticing your responses to the concept of desire. Do they feel healthy today? Or do you need to practice a greater sense of non-attachment when it comes to desire in this season of your recovery?

Prayer or Intention: I accept my desires today as part of what makes me human. I am also open to evaluating how they may or may not be serving me today.

OCTOBER 30

"The word 'discipline' comes from the Latin word *disciplina*, which
was used as far back as the eleventh century to
mean teaching, learning, and giving instruction."
~Dan Siegel and Tina Payne Bryson, *No Drama Discipline*

I recently shared my nighttime routine for calming my mind and falling
asleep with another person in recovery. My routine generally consists
of some yoga or seated meditation, chanting, and reading something
spiritual; sometimes a bath and application of oils are involved. My
friend, who has a horrible time falling asleep responded, "I don't have
the patience for that."

I replied, "It's not about having patience, it's about having
discipline. Discipline builds patience."

In my recovery journey, discipline and commitment to my
recovery process has allowed me to become more patient with myself
and the process. The word discipline may elicit some hard edges for
us, especially if we grew up with abusive use of discipline or have
made ourselves insane trying to stay rigidly committed to some other
path before, like a diet or a fitness training regimen. As the opening
teaching clarifies, discipline is about teaching and learning. The
practice of discipline, especially in the form of daily commitment, is
about teaching ourselves that there is another way, and learning from
the fruits of this exploration.

Invitation: What is one practice you have learned so far in your
recovery process that you can commit to on a daily basis for the next
week? Whether that practice is a breath, a certain prayer, a yoga
posture, a meditation strategy, or any other healthy measure of self-
care, commit to do it every day in the spirit of discipline—teaching,
learning, and giving instruction to yourself that there is another way.
Notice in the coming week what this daily discipline helps to teach you
about patience.

Prayer or Intention: May the discipline that I practice in my
recovery help me to cultivate patience in both myself and the process.

OCTOBER 31

"Holding the breath does not make it easier." ~Jamie Marich

When we are faced with a new physical challenge, our initial reaction can be to hold our breath in order to tough it out. As a practitioner of yoga, I've noticed this tendency in myself. If I'm learning a new more challenging pose, I may suck it in and hold my breath until it's over, the legacy of old trauma responses where holding my breath became the norm. As a teacher of yoga I am even more aware of this reaction in observing students meet new challenges. This pattern is not unique to yoga. Once I got the hang of breathing through challenges in yoga practice, I began studying both martial arts (Brazilian Jiu-Jitsu) and boxing—and guess what? I caught myself holding my breath when it would have helped me more to breathe into the challenge.

Our trauma histories can impact our relationship with the breath, especially if we felt that holding our breath to ride out a difficult experience somehow helped us. Sometimes living in a state of constant hypervigilance or always being on guard for something bad to happen creates stress that causes our shoulders to rise to our ears, naturally restricting the flow of breath. It may feel radical and new to think about deepening our breath when we are met with a new challenge or an uncomfortable stressor. However, learning to breathe in the face of stress is key to meeting new challenges and ultimately moving out of our comfort zones.

Invitation: Set aside at least 5 minutes for the practice, coming into a comfortable position either sitting or lying down. If you you need a little extra grounding support, sit against a wall or with your back to a chair. Bring to mind something that you consider to be a stressor (but not a major trauma). Notice what happens in your body immediately when you hold that stressor in your awareness. Is there a tendency to grip the body or hold the breath? Would you consider trying to take a few deep breaths as you notice the stressor? Notice what happens in the body when you do this. Go slowly to begin. Let your breath help you.

Prayer or Intention: Help me to breathe fully into the face of stress instead of holding my breath in order to ride it out. My breath is an ally.

NOVEMBER 1

"There are those who predict that AA may well become a new spearhead for a spiritual awakening throughout the world . . . Let us resist the proud assumption that since God has enabled us to do well in one area we are destined to be a channel of saving grace for everybody." ~*A.A. Comes of Age*, p. 232

One of the most powerful spiritual tools available is that of focusing our energy and setting boundaries. There is an old recovery adage that we should not go to the hardware store to buy oranges. Learning to seek out the appropriate places and non-toxic people to find healing and adaptive experiences provides a key to our recovery.

In terms of whether this prediction of AA providing a worldwide spiritual awakening has come true, in our estimation it has probably happened. And the way it manifested was by AA maintaining a singleness of purpose, not trying to broaden its scope, channeling healing energy to where it could and in doing so encouraging others to do the same in a variety of ways. We ourselves can have a variety of avenues to our spiritual experience. Some can be narrow, others broad. We can be the creators of our own spiritual experience, and we don't have to "sell" it to others.

Invitation: Spend 3-5 minutes in a practice of your choice (e.g., sitting meditation, walking meditation, or an expressive practice). Whatever object of meditation you choose for today, allow it to help you focus on gratitude for the spiritual path(s) you have found. Notice what thoughts, body sensations, and emotions accompany your gratitude.

Prayer or Intention: Today I know I can find my own unique spiritual pathways.

NOVEMBER 2

"Prayer does not change God, but it changes
the person who prays." ~Soren Kierkegaard

Prayer as indicated in the Eleventh Step can be very simple in its practice. Since we are not trying to change the orbit of the earth or change any Higher Power of our understanding to do our bidding, we can become very clear on our goals. Our goal is to make a connection within, without, or throughout, with that which we see as divine. Divinity does not have to be about angels and the heavens. It can be very practical, down to earth, and simple.

We are continuing in our healing, trying to take the lessons and blessings of the first ten steps and align them with the intentions and words that reflect our desire for ongoing learning, growth, and healing. Trauma-sensitive prayer is prayer that is truly unique to the individual, whether it comes from a millennia old tradition or a 21st century in-the-moment reflection. This is our journey. We get to own it. We get to pray within it. And as we do this, we continue to change, to flow, to heal.

Invitation: Spend 3-5 minutes in a practice of your choice (e.g., sitting meditation, walking meditation, or an expressive practice). Utilize whatever prayer or prayer cycle you have been using recently. Consider adding a new prayer, one that addresses a current issue you are facing.

Prayer or Intention: I know now that prayer is personal, unique, and powerful. In this spirit, I set my intentions today through prayer.

NOVEMBER 3

"Love is the most powerful medicine. Meditate like Christ.
He lost himself in love."~Neem Karoli Baba

This teaching from Neem Karoli Baba, the Hindu teacher of spiritual legend Ram Dass, speaks to me so powerfully. I've long been impressed how, as an Indian man practicing in the spiritual traditions of India, he maintained such an admiration for Christ and a belief that we are all one human family. We all have something to learn from each other, tied together by that common denominator called love.

When you are struggling, lean into the people who love you. Call upon the people who accept you exactly as you are and expect very little from you. This is a potent form of meditation in action that we don't often consider.

Invitation: Spend 3-5 minutes in a practice of your choice (e.g., sitting meditation, walking meditation, or an expressive practice) and contemplate what would it feel like to swim in the ocean of love. If taking the full plunge feels a bit daunting for you right now, would you at least consider dipping your toes into the waters of letting others love you and in turn, sharing the unconditional acceptance of love with the people you encounter?

Prayer or Intention: May I lean into the people who love me today. In doing so, I am practicing what it means to *lose myself in love*.

NOVEMBER 4

"Meditation is like a gym in which you develop the powerful mental muscles of calm and insight." ~Ajahn Brahm

Meditation does not have to be mysterious and strange. Meditation is a practice, and it can be as much a practice as brushing our teeth, putting on our clothes to go out, or cleaning the kitchen. Meditation can be very much like going to the gym, training our minds the way we might train our bodies. At the gym we might be going for muscle mass or strength.

In meditation, we do not have to focus on developing calm and insight, it is a natural byproduct of doing the practice. This does not mean that we are calm and insightful every time we sit down to meditate, nor do we have a "successful" meditation that puts us into a permanent state of wisdom and peace. We practice daily or as often as we can, maybe even only for our 3-5 minutes a day, and we notice subtle but meaningful changes over time. Perhaps I find that I am calmer. Perhaps I notice a shift in my perspective. These are the benefits of developing a meditation practice.

Invitation: Spend 3-5 minutes in a practice of your choice (e.g., sitting meditation, walking meditation, or an expressive practice). If you have now been practicing for awhile, notice how your practice has changed over time. If you are new to the practice, allow yourself to go to this gym with as little expectation as possible. Notice any thoughts, feelings, or sensations that arise.

Prayer or Intention: Today I will dedicate myself to continued meditation practice, knowing that over time calm and insight will grow.

NOVEMBER 5

"We all need love and approval. Yet the key to unleashing our creative energy is finding the deepest sense of approval within ourselves." ~Natalie Rogers

Some of the most difficult struggles I've seen people in recovery face—even people in long-term recovery—is an unhealthy attachment to approval. We both still work on this as a recovery issue, even with many years of sobriety and trauma recovery. It's fair to say that most of us have been raised to believe that others have to "like" us in order for what we're doing to be worthwhile and for who we are as a person to matter. This dynamic can play out in our professional lives as well as our social or personal lives. In many quarters of society it can still be considered a disease to be single or without out a family. Remember, if people say, "What's wrong with you?" for being single, that's about them and their insecurity, not you!

Natalie Rogers, the mother of modern expressive arts therapy, observes that the key to meeting our love and approval needs is to learn to love ourselves and approve of ourselves. If we cannot do this, no amount of love or approval that we receive from external sources will ever satiate us. It unleashes the *chasing the dragon* phenomenon that we can associate with chemical addiction. As our spiritual development grows if that is part of our chosen recovery path, it's also worth examining whether or not we use God or Higher Power as another way of meeting approval needs. Or, are we able to tap into the divine as something that lives and moves within us, not outside of us?

Invitation: Spend 3-5 minutes in a practice of your choice (e.g., sitting meditation, walking meditation, or an expressive practice) and examine where you are at today in terms of looking to external sources for approval. Consider whether you use your spirituality in this way as well. What, if anything, may be keeping you from fully turning inward today?

Prayer or Intention: Love and approval must first come from within. If I cannot cultivate these within, no amount of *without* will ever be good enough.

NOVEMBER 6

"Meditation is doing what you are doing—whether you are doing formal meditation or child care." ~Norman Fisher

Meditation is often presented as an esoteric practice to the beginner. Many beginners never advance to the next stage because the practice doesn't make sense or is too demanding. When we redefine meditation for what it is—a state of mind that can be brought to awareness and cultivated throughout our lives—then we can build a practice that is meaningful.

When my daughter was born in 2009, I became the midnight feeding person. My time on the meditation cushion dwindled, and I became a bit panicked. Then I remembered that meditation is happening all the time, and those sleepless nights wondering if her eyes would close for sleep were a meditation of their own. My daughter became the primary object of meditation on those nights, and so my meditation practice continued unabated. This is where we are going on the meditation path; the meditation upon our day-to-day recovery and life experience.

Invitation: Spend 3-5 minutes in a practice of your choice (e.g., sitting meditation, walking meditation, or an expressive practice). Choose whatever your object of meditation is for this 3-5minute period. Give it the greatest amount of concentration that you are capable of for today.

Prayer or Intention: Meditation is not just a formal practice. Meditation is happening all the time.

NOVEMBER 7

"Ruminating about the past will get you nowhere. So go ahead and learn from the past whatever you can, and then put it behind you."
~Rabbi Abraham Twerski

As you continue to learn more about meditation, especially as you are working through this reader, you may find yourself confused on the difference between noticing and ruminating. In many of these invitations, we are asking you to just notice, sit with, or be with something. How is that different than obsessing or ruminating you may ask?

Ruminating or obsessing is generally not helpful and these activities are comprised of thought, absent a connection with feelings, sensations, or other parts of experience. When we think about something constantly, it can feel like we are spinning and spinning like a hamster on a wheel, never moving forward. In contrast, *noticing* is productive, implying that you are open to what all parts of your experience—especially your feelings and your body sensations— reveal. Meditation helps you to focus less on the thoughts and more on the totality of your experience. Instead of trying to push our whole experience away with thoughts, noticing allows us to be present with what is, and we generally discover a greater sense of empowerment to move on, to move forward.

Invitation: Spend 3-5 minutes in a practice of your choice (e.g., sitting meditation, walking meditation, or an expressive practice) and engage in the active experience of *noticing* whatever comes up. If thoughts arise, you've done nothing wrong, just *notice* them as part of your experience, and then be open to listening to the other parts of your experience too—namely your feelings and your body sensations.

Prayer or Intention: Today I recognize that I am not my thoughts. There is a wide variety of experience to be noticed, if I allow myself to notice it.

NOVEMBER 8

"There are two ways of spreading light: to be the
candle or the mirror that reflects it."~Edith Wharton

In the ancient practice of Tai Chai there is a move called painting light. The flowing gesture and stretch is really quite simple. Bring your arms out in front of you, parallel to your shoulders. With an inhale, extend your arms up overhead without straining (or as high as you are able to go), and on an exhale "paint the light" down over your body. You never have to touch the floor, although putting a nice bend in the knees can help.

Whenever I practice painting light, I always go to a very deep energetic or spiritual place. I contemplate what it means to paint light. To draw the healing energy of light from the various sources in this universe that have shown me light can be very rejuvenating. Moreover, I am inspired to paint light in my world—in my work and in every action of living. The world can be such a dark place. Imagine the difference we can make if we all focused on painting light whenever we get the opportunity.

Invitation: Consider engaging in the moving practice of painting light as described in the meditation. If you are unable to stand for extended periods of time, you can do the exercise sitting down. If you are further physically limited for any reason, you can visually imagine yourself painting light, however that may take shape for you. Give yourself at least 3 minutes in the practice, releasing any judgment that may come up about yourself or the process each time you exhale.

Prayer or Intention: Today I appreciate those who have painted light in my life as I endeavor to do the same for others in my world.

NOVEMBER 9

"We don't have to believe our thoughts. We don't have to identify with our thoughts." ~Valerie Mason-John

Escape! That is what every bone in our bodies might tell us to do. This is not to say that escape is never the answer. We have been in situations in the past where we needed to get out to stay safe, and that will be the case again. The problem we may have had prior to recovery was seeing every situation or most situations as survival emergencies.

Mindfulness meditation asks us to go toward the pain, go toward our thoughts. As we get practice in meditation, we are able to build distress tolerance to sit through difficult thoughts and emotions, and over time we learn to no longer identify with our thoughts, bringing relief on the other side. When people in recovery tell us that we need to do some work, this is a good portion of the work they are often referring to. With guidance and support, this work can absolutely be done.

Invitation: Spend 3-5 minutes in a practice of your choice (e.g., sitting meditation, walking meditation, or an expressive practice). Notice any distressing thoughts. Notice if the thoughts change or pass. Notice any body sensations that go with this process.

Prayer or Intention: Today, I will try and notice my thoughts as often as possible. And I will try to notice that I am not my thoughts.

NOVEMBER 10

"Experience: that most brutal of teachers.
But you learn, my God do you learn." ~C.S. Lewis

Healthy recovery demands that we constantly remain a student. If that word *student* brings up some unpleasant charge for you, perhaps reframe it as being in a perpetual state of learning. When you think you've arrived and know it all—about recovery or any other aspect of life—you are generally setting yourself up to fail. True growth in this life comes from being willing to learn something new, about yourself and the process; even if that comes in the form of being open to what your experiences can teach you.

To challenge myself in this area, I try to learn at least one new practice every year. It can be a physical practice, a new form of yoga or meditation, or a new approach to therapy. This practice keeps me sharp not only as a teacher, but also as a person in long-term recovery. The most significant part of this process is noticing how my experiences— in my daily life and in how I respond to learning something new—can inform what I need to address in my own recovery and healing.

Invitation: Spend 3-5 minutes in a practice of your choice (e.g., sitting meditation, walking meditation, or an expressive practice) and bring up the idea of being a perpetual student or life-long learner. Does this bring up resistance in any way? If so, notice that and ask what may be blocking you from the learning process.

Prayer or Intention: Today I recognize that my willingness to always learn something new is my best safeguard against complacency and being stuck.

NOVEMBER 11

"Breath is life dancing through us."
~Jamie Marich, *Dancing Mindfulness*

The breath can be both a trigger and a resource to survivors of trauma. So many of us are used to shallow breathing, generally the result of being hypervigilant for so long. For others, life has become so busy, it feels like we don't ever really give ourselves a moment to breathe. Maybe both scenarios apply to you—the impact of trauma and the impact of life both take their toll. So when you actually try to do some deep breathing exercises, you may find it too overwhelming.

What if you could just start by letting your breath be what it will be and do what it will do naturally in your body? No striving, no pressure to do any fancy breath exercises you may have read about online or heard about from your therapist or sponsor. The hardest part of starting a breath practice is to let yourself be still, even if it's just for a few seconds, and notice the breath as it naturally flows in your body. From this foundation, you may be able to try more sophisticated and nuanced things with breathing. For now, see if you can begin the journey by simply focusing on the breath.

Invitation: You can take as long as you like for this practice (we recommend no more than 5 minutes if you are a beginner to breath work). Know that you can benefit with as little as 15-30 seconds in the practice. Either sitting down or laying down (standing is also an acceptable modification), pay deliberate attention to the breath and how it flows through your body. There is no need to do deep breathing or hold the breath. Notice the natural rise and fall of your stomach and chest as you breathe. Notice if the sensation is cool, warm, or neutral as the breath enters in through your nostrils. Notice if the breath has a sound or a humming feeling in your body. There are no right or wrong answers here, this is simply a practice of inquiry. You are getting to know your breath.

Prayer or Intention: Today I will let the breath be what the breath will be and do what the breath will do in the service of my wellness and recovery.

NOVEMBER 12

"Lead me from the unreal to the real
From darkness into the light
And from time bound consciousness to
The timeless state of being."
~The *Asatoma* Prayer (from the Upanishads)

The process of recovery can be described as learning to live in the light after spending so long living in darkness. Sometimes we can feel a great sense of shame when some of our old dark patterns, emotions, and memories show up in our lives. When you've lived in the dark for so long, that is normal. Instead of shaming yourself for the dark parts of your existence that may still surface, can you practice noticing what the darkness is trying to teach you? How can embracing the lessons of the dark help you to move more fully into the light and into the reality of who you really are?

Whenever I experience a string of days or even weeks that can feel dark and gloomy again, I do my best not to judge myself. I know the light is still there or I wouldn't still be sober and doing my best to stay well. I inevitably find that rising to the challenge of working through a dark patch—whether that comes in the form of doing more work in therapy, re-engaging in my program, or just giving myself the space to feel what I need to feel—helps me to appreciate the light more fully when it illuminates me once more. Even on gloomy days, the sun is still up in the sky. Can I trust in that reality today and realize that I am still protected? That, one day, the sun will shine brightly again?

Invitation: Consider the interplay between darkness and light. In 3-5 minutes of seated meditation practice or in another expressive practice, notice or reflect on what one has taught you about the other. If you like making playlists, consider choosing a few songs that speak to the idea of darkness and a few songs that speak to the idea of light. Then, listen to the playlist and/or dance to it and see what the messages in the selected songs may teach you about the interplay.

Prayer or Intention: Lead me to the illuminating light of awareness that sees both darkness and light in the same light.

NOVEMBER 13

"I do the prayer thing, but I never got the meditation part."
~Thousands of members of 12-step programs

I have heard this over and over again from people in the program. So much of it is rooted in fixed ideas about meditation. Some people see it from the perspective of "I can't sit still." Others see it as something that takes too much time. Still others cannot fathom the discipline required. All of this is built on a very narrow misconception about what meditation can be. Once the lens is widened, there are dozens of options.

The initial founders of AA leaned into the model of contemplative prayer, such as what you are doing with this book right now. Since then, we have at our disposal multiple millenia worth of spiritual and psychological practices that can serve as meditation. Yoga, dance, exercise, walking meditation, sitting meditation, the list goes on. Go to the meditation schmorgasbord, aim for just five minutes a day, and see what develops.

Invitation: Spend 3-5 minutes in a practice of your choice (e.g., sitting meditation, walking meditation, or an expressive practice). See if you can notice whether this particular practice speaks to you such that you might repeat it again tomorrow.

Prayer or Intention: Meditation does not have to be complicated. Let me find my 5 minutes of meditation today, in whatever form it takes.

NOVEMBER 14

"Traumatized people are often afraid of feeling—mindfulness
practices can help orient them to and ease
them into this process by widening sensory experience."
~Bessel van der Kolk, *The Body Keeps the Score*, p. 98

Mindfulness offers us the healing power of present moment awareness.
For many of us, learning to practice mindfulness is a radical shift
in how we see the world because we have been so afraid of feeling.
Dissociating, or severing from ourselves and the present moment,
can become our norm to deal with the world. So while mindfulness
techniques may seem elementary on the surface, they can be radically
difficult once we start to practice them. Yet like with many good things
in life, embracing a challenge can bring about massive rewards.

One such benefit of mindfulness is that it can help us to make peace
with ourselves as a feeling being. Over time, mindfulness practices can
teach us that our feelings and experiences are nothing to fear. Rather,
we can learn to be with our feelings and resist the urge to push them
away. Feeling our feelings through, although difficult at first, offers us a
true pathway to deep and lasting healing.

Invitation: Take 3-5 minutes in a seated or laying down position.
Make a commitment to yourself to stay present no matter what—if
any thoughts or feelings arise, just notice them. If you catch yourself
trying to push away what comes up, or your mind wanders off as a
distraction, that is normal. See if you can practice being mindful of
the push away or the distraction and then bring your focus back to the
last thing you notice before the push away or distraction.

Prayer or Intention: May the healing power of mindfulness help
me to be present with whatever feelings come up for me today.

NOVEMBER 15

"I am going to pay attention to the spring. I am going to look around at all the flowers, and look up at the hectic trees. I am going to close my eyes and listen." ~Anne Lamott

In working an Eleventh Step, especially if we are interested in taking the part about meditation seriously, learning to pay attention is vital. This is a task much easier said than done. As children we are often scolded to "Pay attention," yet rarely are we taught how to pay attention. Indeed, modern culture bombards us with stimuli from so many sources, paying attention can feel daunting, if not impossible.

Like many things in recovery, learning to pay attention takes practice. It is also the gateway to meditation. The limbs of yoga teach us that we must first practice paying attention (*dharana*) for a state of meditation (*dhyana*) to happen. You may find it helpful to consider that the English word attention comes from the Latin root *attendere*, which means to stretch. When I consider this root, I more fully embrace attention as the practice of stretching the possibilities of my awareness and warming me up for that state of meditation. In this state I can be the fullness of myself and listen to what I am intended to receive.

Invitation: Spend 3-5 minutes in a practice of your choice (e.g., sitting meditation, walking meditation, or an expressive practice) paying close attention to an object of focus. If you are sitting, the focus can be the natural inhale and exhale of your breath. You can choose a fixed object in the room on which to focus. If you are walking you can pay full attention to the placement of each foot on the ground. If you are in an expressive practice, pay full attention to however you are moving. If you attention wanes, just notice when it does and draw the focus of your attention back to the original focus. Even if you have to do this 10 times a minute, it's okay. You are engaged in the vital practice of paying attention.

Prayer or Intention: Today I will prepare myself for deeper and more powerful states of meditation by practicing paying attention. All of life affords me an opportunity to practice.

NOVEMBER 16

"Silence is true wisdom's best reply." ~Euripides

Befriending silence is one of the greatest gifts I've received in recovery. Too often we talk just to fill the space or to deflect, to keep from really being in touch with our feelings and experiences. In silence, I learn to listen to what the process reveals. I connect with what my body and my total experience is attempting to teach me. In silence, mediation and connection with that power greater than myself just happens.

I realize that silence can be scary for many of us, especially in early recovery. We may have grown up in homes where silence meant that something was dreadfully wrong. The prospect of silence may frighten us because we struggle to truly be alone and at peace with ourselves. We may feel that we have to *do* something, when the best course of action may be to simply remain still and silent. Today, am I willing to learn to become more comfortable with silence so that I can tap into what it is trying to reveal?

Invitation: Spend 3-5 minutes in a practice of your choice (e.g., sitting meditation, walking meditation, or an expressive practice) and make an intention to be fully silent. What are you noticing? If this is something that you already do on a regular basis, perhaps challenge yourself to go deeper with it. Maybe ask a friend with whom you are normally very chatty if you can spend a set period of time just sitting together in silence. When that urge to speak comes up—what is it really about? It could be that you have something legitimate to express. Also consider if that urge to speak is about deflecting or filling your discomfort with verbal distraction.

Prayer or Intention: May I befriend the healing power of silence in my recovery today, becoming open to what it wants to reveal.

NOVEMBER 17

"The discovery that peace, happiness and love are ever-present within
our own Being, and completely available at every moment
of experience, under all conditions, is the most important discovery
that anyone can make." ~Rupert Spira

Many of us are terrified of being alone. Truly, utterly terrified. Even
if we feel supported in a group like a recovery fellowship, we may go
to any lengths to make sure that we spend as little time as possible
with ourselves. We may get into unhealthy relationships or engage in
other unhealthy attachments, fearful of spending time with our own
company. For many of us, the pain of being both alone and lonely was
a major factor fueling our addictive behaviors.

Learning to spend time alone is a vital skill in recovery. If that
word *alone* is too charged for you, maybe consider swapping it out with
"Learning to spend time by myself, in my own company." You may
discover that you have likes and dislikes of which you were previously
unaware. You may also come to realizations that are vital to your own
healing process, realizations that may have been drowned out in the
presence of others, especially if they were just there as a space holder.
Have I learned to spend time with myself today?

Invitation: Spend 3-5 minutes in a practice of your choice (e.g.,
sitting meditation, walking meditation, or an expressive practice) with
the intention of being completely and totally present with yourself.
Make an intention to drown out any unnecessary distractions and let
today's practice be a *practice* in being by yourself and noticing what
there is to discover.

Prayer or Intention: Today may I recognize the power that comes
from learning to spend time by myself. For healing, may I look within.

NOVEMBER 18

"And you shall know the truth and the truth
shall set you free." ~John 8:32

There is a simple, healing power in telling the truth. Especially because addictive behavior is so characterized by lies and deceit. Taking this a step further, the dynamics of unhealed trauma and dysfunctional family systems also rely on the absence of truth to fester. Shame has been described by one of my favorite writers, Anaïs Nin, as the *lie that someone told you about yourself*. We when set out on a path of recovery, it's not just that we have told our share of lies. We've likely bought into packs of lies that others would have us believe about ourselves.

The process of recovery is about healing our relationship with truth in its various forms. The opening quote from the Christian New Testament is often cited in recovery circles. I once saw a cool variation of this quote on a poster. It proclaimed that the truth may wrench you through the wringer for a while, but it will eventually set me free. Have I discovered the connection between truth and my liberation today?

Invitation: Spend 3-5 minutes in a practice of your choice (e.g., sitting meditation, walking meditation, or an expressive practice) and contemplate the opening quote. Where are the places in your life and your recovery so far where the truth has set you free? If you are able, notice what freedom feels like in your body and in your entire being?

Prayer or Intention: Today I breathe into the healing power of truth.

NOVEMBER 19

"Your sacred space is where you can find yourself
over and over again." ~Joseph Campbell

Creating a space for ourselves where we can settle, take a few breaths, and just "be" is a vital component of recovery. Sure, we all don't have the luxury of dedicating a whole room in our house to hang pretty things. For most of us, the idea of creating a scared space in our dwelling is ludicrous. Maybe a sacred corner is all you can manage—a bean bag chair, meditation cushion, or some objects that mean a lot to you. Perhaps your sacred space is on the deck or settled at your kitchen table with a cup of coffee or tea sipped from your favorite mug! Even a corner of your couch wrapped in an special blanket can work.

What would it feel like to find a place, for this moment, to just breathe and be? What place or places in my life can I plant a flag and lay claim to my sanity?

Invitation: Spend 3-5 minutes in a practice of your choice (e.g., sitting meditation, walking meditation, or an expressive practice) in your sacred or special place of being. If you don't have one yet, spend this time contemplating how you may begin setting one up.

Prayer or Intention: Today I recognize the importance of having a space where I can just *be*.

NOVEMBER 20

"In this program we choose how well we want to get."
~Denise S. (Jamie's long-time friend)

Fewer nuggets of wisdom have stayed with me so strongly and so sustainably as this teaching from Denise. Yes, we can use the 12-step program of recovery to get sober, to become abstinent, to help us eradicate problem behaviors, or to at least get us started on the path. Meeting this original goal may be all that you are hoping to achieve, and that is certainly your prerogative. Whenever I feel tempted to rest on my laurels or get complacent, I remember the words of my late friend. There is more to be had in my process of wellness and growth . . . if I want it.

Addressing recovery in a trauma-focused manner asks more of us than just going to meetings and working the steps. Outside professional help will likely be needed to help us untangle all of the memories, feelings, traps, and triggers that keep us stuck. Applying recovery and wellness principles to all areas of our lives, not just our main problematic behaviors, is important to sustainable recovery. Yes, it is your choice how well you want to get. From my experience, I can share that the deeper you dive into the well of your own healing, the more effectively you safeguard yourself against triggers and the potential for relapse, and equip yourself to ride the waves of other unpleasantries life will bring your way.

Invitation: Spend 3-5 minutes in a practice of your choice (e.g., sitting meditation, walking meditation, or an expressive practice) and bring up the teaching that *we choose how well we want to get*. After reflection on this for a time, notice consistent working of the Eleventh Step can help you in this process.

Prayer or Intention: The choice is mine as to how well I want to get in my journey of recovery and wellness. May I have the courage to dive as deeply as possible into that well.

NOVEMBER 21

"You can dance through the seven hells as if they are fairgrounds."
~Zen saying

In the *Dancing Mindfulness* movement, we have two sayings: First, dancing is always an option. Second, life is hard—dance anyway. When we began using this teaching, it struck me as a motto that we can take into life in order to meet any challenge with movement and grace. In the biblical Old Testament, Miriam, the sister of Moses, was a graceful and beautiful dancer, praising God with movement and her tambourine. As a leader, Miriam was constantly dealing with the complaints of others on the journey through the desert and as scripture describes, she danced anyway.

Miriam is a great inspiration for life and for recovery, especially if you are drawn to movement and the arts. Life gives you a playlist of songs every day that you have no control over. Are you going to complain or are you going to dance to it anyway? When people frustrate you, how can you use dance, the arts, or another activity that you like to help you cope with your stress and move through the feelings?

Invitation: Spend 3-5 minutes in a creative practice of your choice (e.g., dance, art, poetry/creative writing, crafting), being mindful that this is not about competence, it's about expression. Even if you scribble, free write, or wobble about, you are meeting the challenge of the practice. Bring up a current life stressor that is on your mind. Give yourself the time to use your chosen expressive or creative practice to meet the stressor. Notice what it means to put into practice: *Life is hard, dance* (or your chosen form of expression) *anyway*. As one of my students once observed, you can truly *dance anyway* in any way.

Prayer or Intention: Life is difficult. Today I recognize that I can meet this difficulty with dance or other forms of creative expression.

NOVEMBER 22

"If the only prayer you said was thank you,
that would be enough." ~Meister Eckhart

When faced with the notion of prayer, many trauma survivors will have a very understandable hesitance. There may be a traumatic religious past that stands in the way, or a feeling that prayer and other spiritual matters are beyond our grasp, too esoteric or without a real function. Meister Eckhart was a theologian whose work resembles the principles of 12-step recovery more than most others. He taught about a very personal Higher Power, and he taught that the strength we needed could be found inside ourselves.

This teaching is in alignment with modern trauma-sensitive thinking. In this personal relationship with a Higher Power, Eckhart lets us know it does not have to be complicated. A simple thank you, an expression of gratitude, is more than enough in a life of prayer.

Invitation: Spend 3-5 minutes in a practice of your choice (e.g., sitting meditation, walking meditation, or an expressive practice). In rhythm with your breath, silently repeat the words, "Thank you" for the duration of your meditation period. Feel free to take short silent breaks.

Prayer or Intention: Thank you is a sufficient prayer for today.

NOVEMBER 23

"Don't underestimate the value of doing nothing."
~A.A. Milne

Sometimes my deepest spiritual practice is when I do nothing—when I can allow myself simply *to be*. This morning was one such time—having the day off I intended to rise and have an extended yoga, dance, and seated meditation practice. My recovery has instilled a healthy fear of boredom in me and I often worry myself if I'm not "doing" or taking action. I know that practices like yoga, meditation, and crafting time to create are fundamentally healthy for me, yet do they lose their beneficial powers if I engage in them with a sense of *get 'er done* urgency?

This morning I allowed myself time to just lay in bed. I didn't fall back to sleep, I just let myself be. For someone who has flirted with workaholism as an addiction manifestation—at very least over-working to avoid feeling my feelings and connecting with others—this was a vital practice. I smelled the sheets and allowed their texture to surround my body. I breathed deeply and for the better part of an hour allowed myself to just be. The practice is exactly what I needed.

Invitation: Spend 3-5 minutes and make an intention to release all special effort around your meditation and wellness practices and *just be*. You can lay in bed or in another place or choose to simply sit. You may notice this is challenging for you or that something very special is being revealed. How can you translate the practice of *just being* into other areas of your life?

Prayer or Intention: May I embrace the value in doing nothing. This practice offers an opportunity to fully be.

NOVEMBER 24

"God, give them what they need."
~Janet Leff (Jamie's first sponsor)

How many times have we prayed (or hoped) for other people in our lives to get well? We are children praying for our parents to stop drinking, spouses praying for our partners to be relieved of their affliction, and parents praying for our children to be saved. Although these prayers and hopes reflect goodwill on our part, they are still specific and counter the logic of Step 11: praying only for knowledge of our Higher Power's will and the power to carry it out. Depending on our beliefs, we can view that as God's will or the natural flow of the universe.

Consider Janet's wisdom. She was an adamant believer in the power of the Eleventh Step and its guidance to not get too specific with our prayers. As this relates to the prayers and hopes that we send out for others, ask that they be given what they need. As Janet taught, for example they may *need* to face a major consequence in order to stop drinking. They may *need* something that we may not have the vision to see, especially because of our closeness. Who knows what they really need? We may think we do, and staying attached to our opinion of that may be keeping us stuck.

Invitation: Spend 3-5 minutes in a practice of your choice (e.g., sitting meditation, walking meditation, or an expressive practice) and bring to mind someone you are actively praying for or holding in good thoughts. You can approach this invitation as prayer or meditation, depending on your belief system. Try out Janet's suggestion of asking that individual to be given what they need, not what *we* think they need.

Prayer or Intention: May the people I hold close in my heart be given what they need today. May I realize that I am not the best judge of what that may be.

NOVEMBER 25

"There are no impediments to meditation. The very
thought of such obstacles is the greatest impediment."
~Ramana Maharshi

We've heard time and time again from clients and from people we
know in recovery fellowships, "I can't meditate." Common reasons
that people give include, "I can't sit still," "I can't focus," "Noticing
my breath makes me more anxious," or the infamous, "I'm just not
a very *Zen* person." Newsflash: These beliefs are what is keeping you
from even giving it a try and noticing the benefits of the practice. We
all have excuses as to why we think we can't meditate.

The way to start a meditation practice of any kind is to do just
that—start. Remove any external metrics, judgments, or storylines
of what you think meditation should be or should look like. Most
of the pictures you may see of meditation online do not capture the
full experience of the practice. Sometimes sitting with your breath or
the moment or your emotions can be hell and guess what? That is
meditating too. Release all expectations of what you think meditation
should be, know that you can draw your focus back at any time if it
drifts, and be open to the process as it is meant to unfold.

Invitation: Spend 3-5 minutes in a practice of your choice (e.g.,
sitting meditation, walking meditation, or an expressive practice) and
bring up what your most common excuse or reason is why you believe
you "can't meditate." Now meditate on that. What are you noticing?

Prayer or Intention: Today I will release the reasons, expectations,
and stories that I tell myself about why I cannot meditate. I am open to
the possibility that all life presents me with an opportunity to practice
mediation.

NOVEMBER 26

"No one can avoid doubt, skepticism, fear, and uncertainty
on the journey to faith if they are honest with themselves.
Obstacles are the training ground." ~Larry Brilliant

A spiritual awakening in recovery, whether it be of the sudden or more gradual educational variety, does not make all of our struggles about faith, hardship, and the meaning of life go away. Indeed for both of us, every year of our recovery journey seems to bring along some struggle that requires us to dig deeply. And our faith—in our Higher Power, in ourselves, and in the process of recovery—has been shaken more times that we can count. What are sometimes called *dark nights of the soul* can challenge every aspect of our recovery.

Yet, if we embrace the opportunity to work through these challenges in as candid and healthy a way as possible, they can truly be growth opportunities. We grow not just in the strength of our recovery but also through challenges, because nothing can bring us inward to the true nature of ourselves quite like a crisis of faith. The Eleventh Step, if worked on a daily or at least a regular basis, taps us into one of the great truths of spiritual life—even when times are tough, practice anyway. Pray and meditate anyway, even if you are cursing your Higher Power, yourself, or the process as you engage in these practices. The breakthrough will come.

Invitation: Spend 3-5 minutes in a practice of your choice (e.g., sitting meditation, walking meditation, or an expressive practice) and bringing up an area of faith—in your Higher Power, yourself, or in the process of recovery where you are struggling today. Spend this practice time just being with that struggle, noticing its edges and not trying to push it away. Am I allowing myself the space, even in these moments of crisis or challenges, to just be with the experience without judgment and be open to how it may be shaping me?

Prayer or Intention: Today I accept or will at least begin to consider that the obstacles of life are opportunities to deepen my practice. I will remain open to what this process reveals.

NOVEMBER 27

shanti: peace, contentment and silence (Sanskrit); sometimes
translated as *the peace that passes all understanding*

The salutation of *Om shanti* is well-known in Hindu culture and to
practitioners of yoga. The peace that passes all understanding
is also referenced in the Christian New Testament of the Bible. In
recovery, this idea can be similar to acceptance—you never have to
like something or fully understand it in order to be at peace with what
is. We cease fighting the reality of something and embrace life on life's
terms. That's a slogan that can be grating for many of us because of
how some people in recovery have used it.

What would it feel like to replace a slogan like *life on life's terms* with
living with the peace that passes all understanding?

Invitation: Spend 3-5 minutes in a practice of your choice (e.g., sitting
meditation, walking meditation, or an expressive practice) and bring
up the phrase *the peace that passes all understanding*. In your reflection,
notice if there is a time in your life or in your recovery where you
believe you experienced this level of peace. What would it feel like to
remain open to receiving such peace on a regular basis?

Prayer or Intention: May I connect with the peace that passes all
understanding today and on the path ahead.

NOVEMBER 28

"If you feel like drinking put your coin or chip on your tongue.
When it dissolves, then you can have a drink." ~recovery saying

There is a lot of humor to this particular saying or slogan that goes around the rooms. It always makes me chuckle. There is actually much truth and wisdom in this directive because it is so embodied. When we are dealing with craving or obsession, taking embodied action is generally the best way to proceed. This idea of actions speaking louder than words resounds in many forms through the *Trauma and the 12 Steps* work.

Please don't choke on the coin or your chip if you decide to take this advice literally. If you do, consider turning it into a mindfulness exercise. Be present with the whole experience. Hold the coin or chip in your hand. Notice it's physical sensation. Maybe play with it on the table and notice what it sounds like. Smell it and see if there's any odor you can detect. Then if you want to take it the final step further, put it gently and carefully on your tongue (make sure to clean it thoroughly before you do this), and notice the taste or sensation. By engaging in this grounding practice and the sense-based experience instead of on your thoughts and obsessions, you may be surprised by what happens.

Invitation: You have many options for how to engage this mindfulness of the five senses practice. Using the coin is optional, so is putting non-edible things in your mouth. You can take any object—your coin or chip works—although rocks, stones, other trinkets, or even softer objects like stuffed animals can work. If you feel comfortable and it's appropriate to your recovery path, consider using food like raisins, almonds, or dark chocolate for this mindful engagement in the senses. Even a glass of warm or cool water will do for this multi-sensory investigation.

Prayer or Intention: Today I recognize the healing power of action in my recovery.

NOVEMBER 29

"Enjoy the little things in life because one day you'll look back and realize they were the big things." ~Kurt Vonnegut

Many of us in recovery have lost people tragically or suddenly. Whether it's because of an overdose, suicide, an accident, or an illness that seems to come out of nowhere, these deaths can rock us to our core. And they can also provide us with an opportunity to take stock of how we are spending our time.

As someone who has walked the line of workaholism for many years, even as a person in active recovery from my substance addictions, the opening teaching hits home. Even though I've experienced many tragic deaths of loved ones in my recovery, I can find it very easy to sink back into the rut of the rat race; overworking, trying to meet the expectations of others at the expense of my own health. How would I spend the rest of my time if I knew I had just one more day to spend with my loved one?

Invitation: Spend 3-5 minutes in a practice of your choice (e.g., sitting meditation, walking meditation, or an expressive practice) and if you have the willingness today, go with the question posed in the last line of the meditation: How would I spend the rest of my time if I knew I had just one more day to spend with my loved one? What insights might be revealed about how you can best spend your time as a person in recovery?

Prayer or Intention: May I spend more time savoring the *little things* and recognize that in the grand scheme of life they are what matter the most.

NOVEMBER 30

"Forever — is composed of Nows —" ~Emily Dickinson

When I was in the worst of my addiction, or my trauma response, everything felt like forever. The seconds and minutes and hours and days drag on, and nothing seems to move. When I came into recovery, the prospect of staying sober forever was equally daunting. The Twelve Steps and the slogans, especially One Day at a Time, are simply reflecting the wisdom of the spiritual teachers, philosophers, psychologists, and poets throughout the ages. Each time we come back to the Now, all the other moments of my life are available within it.

When I am lost in the fear or the ecstasy of Forever, I am lost in illusion. From this place of Now, I can choose . . . I can rest, I can act, or if I like I can contemplate the nature of forever. The more I learn to be in the now with all of its complications, fears, challenges, and discomforts, the more I will be able to experience the joy, excitement, and insight that becomes available moment-to-moment through trauma-sensitive 12-step recovery.

Invitation: For 5 minutes, do a simple breath meditation to deepen the ability to be in the Now. When you are breathing in, "I know I am breathing in." When you are breathing out, "I know I am breathing out." When you notice your mind wandering, return to the breath, in and out.

Prayer or Intention: As I go throughout my day, may I return to the Now when I feel pulled away from the moment.

DECEMBER 1

"Once you've been bitten by a snake you're afraid
even of a piece of rope." ~Chinese proverb

This proverb is often quoted to describe the impact of unhealed trauma on the human experience.

In working with others, we can use its guiding wisdom to go a step further. Is our presence in someone's life providing them with a healing balm? Or is our presence and some of the approaches we take just helping to coil the rope a little tighter?

While being trauma-sensitive in our work with others does not require us to give up our beliefs about what works in recovery, how we approach someone can make all the difference. Flexibility and being open to truly listening to the experiences of another is imperative. Meeting someone where they are *at* instead of trying to force our ways on them is healing work. Such presence is the opposite of trauma in the life of a trauma survivor and can be powerful in showing them that there is another way to be in the world. At a bare minimum, approaching people in this way helps to loosen the grip of that rope. Your continued healing presence, if the individual chooses, may even help to reverse some of the damage long-term.

Invitation: Spend 3-5 minutes in a practice of your choice (e.g., sitting meditation, walking meditation, or an expressive practice) contemplating the opening proverb. What are the areas in your life where you still feel gripped by the rope of trauma and its memories? What is it that you most need or have most needed from people to recognize that healing is possible?

Prayer or Intention: As I approach others today, may I do so with sensitivity to what their experience and how they have been wounded by snakes and ropes.

DECEMBER 2

"If you're not making someone else's life better, then you're wasting your time. Your life will become better by making other lives better."
~Will Smith

There is a reason that there are eleven steps before the Step 12. In the past, before people would acknowledge a need to be trauma-informed, the assumption was that you would heal yourself by throwing yourself into helping others, regardless of your readiness. A trauma-informed approach suggests that the initial eleven steps are designed to bring sufficient healing and resilience so that we might be effective change agents for others.

We work our way through the first eleven steps which also brings us thoroughly through the first two stages of trauma treatment. And then, in our Twelfth Step we continue to do all of our work, and a huge part of that is sharing what we have found with others, and helping others along their many paths.

Invitation: Spend 3-5 minutes in a practice of your choice (e.g., sitting meditation, walking meditation, or an expressive practice). Meditate upon one person you know that needs your help. Notice what arises for you as you prepare to help them. If it feels helpful, visualize the act of helping you will do or have done for that person.

Prayer or Intention: I know now that I have been helping myself so that I might help others

DECEMBER 3

"Life damages us, every one. We can't escape that damage. But now,
I am also learning this: We can be mended. We mend each other."
~Veronica Roth

The first time I read these words from Veronica Roth in her young
adult classic *Allegiant* (the final book in the *Divergent* trilogy), I wept.
Profusely, sincerely wept. I set out to read the books simply as a fan of
the initial movie and I was not expecting words that so succinctly and
perfectly described my recovery experience.

Trauma are wounds and regardless of their severity, all wounds
need care. I am deeply grateful to those individuals I have met along
the path. In my belief system, these individuals were put along that
path by powers greater than myself. They have tended my wounds
and have shown me how to tend my own, empowering me with the
strength to keep pressing on even when I have felt hopelessly stuck or
sidelined. I thank you, I thank all of you. It is my privilege, in some
small way, to continue this process by paying it forward to others I
meet along the way.

Invitation: Spend 3-5 minutes in a practice of your choice (e.g.,
sitting meditation, walking meditation, or an expressive practice) and
notice those individuals who have helped tend to your wounds along
the way. What qualities do they possess or what traits did they impart
to you? How can you use this as inspiration for the work you may be
called to do with others?

Prayer or Intention: I offer gratitude for those I have met along the
way who have helped me to tend my wounds. May I play a role in this
process for others as I am called.

DECEMBER 4

"Doing nothing for others is the undoing of ourselves."
~Horace Mann

In trauma recovery terms, this statement might overshoot the runway a little. Sometimes we very much need to be taking care of ourselves primarily, and that will be our strength. However, 12-step recovery and trauma recovery theory and practice show a strong connection between altruism and long-term recovery.

Helping others is at the core of Step 12, and there are eleven steps before it for us to build ourselves up. Helping others when we haven't put the oxygen mask on ourselves first can be detrimental to everyone concerned. But, when I do have some recovery, it is imperative that I find a way to help others and share what I have gleaned in order to maintain what I have developed.

Invitation: Spend 3-5 minutes in a practice of your choice (e.g., sitting meditation, walking meditation, or an expressive practice). Meditate on your recovery thus far, noting where you feel strong and capable. If you don't feel that way today, see if you can notice that with as little judgment as possible. Now meditate on someone you can help. Notice what sensations, thoughts, and feelings arise.

Prayer or Intention: Today my prayer is to know how to help myself, and then how I can help others.

DECEMBER 5

"Kindness, I've discovered, is everything in life."
~Isaac Bashevis Singer

The path of recovery is imbued with kindness. It does not have to be forced upon us, it is a naturally arising principle from working with the Twelve Steps in a trauma informed fashion. The reason why many if not most of us come into recovery is because we have been unkind to ourselves and others with our words and actions. A vast majority of it was driven by our perceived survival needs, driven by the survival brain due to trauma or adverse life events being maladaptively or improperly processed and stored. Simply finding the steps and other ways to bring our thinking brain back online to better direct our beliefs and actions is an act of kindness in and of itself.

Following a variety of spiritual and psychological models, we can allow for this organic kindness to do its work, while also cultivating kindness in an intentional way throughout our recovery. Now we will have a snowball of kindness, rather than the snowball of trauma and survival driven reaction.

Invitation: Spend 3-5 minutes in a practice of your choice (e.g., sitting meditation, walking meditation, or an expressive practice). Find someone in your consciousness who is easy for you to think of with a heart of kindness. Spend your time in today's practice focused on that person and the sensations, feelings, and thoughts that go with kindness.

Prayer or Intention: I know that my recovery work is kindness just as it is, and will look for opportunities to further develop this quality.

DECEMBER 6

"Your ancestors are rooting for you." ~Elizabeth Brownn

There are many teachings out there in a variety of traditions about the importance of honoring ancestors. For us, a major part of what it means to *honor* them is to learn from their mistakes and resolve to do better. The soul of our future generations is at stake. In 12-step recovery we can hold up Bill Wilson and Dr. Bob as such cherished folk heroes. Although we can still pay them our respect and gratitude for what they created with the fellowship, tales of their missteps are well-known. Bill Wilson, in particular, had a horrible reputation as an egomaniac and a womanizer, even in recovery. Many critics of 12-step programs like to cite this history in discounting the program.

Perhaps the challenge is to learn from the mistakes of our ancestors like Bill Wilson and endeavor to make the path ahead healthier for those in recovery. If you hear tales about Bill Wilson's character defects or horror stories about the people that populate your family tree, ask yourself—how can I do better? How can my generation do better? Now that we know more about what it means to be trauma-informed, what do we need as children of these flawed ancestors to carry the message of recovery in way that helps more people than it harms?

Invitation: Spend 3-5 minutes in a practice of your choice (e.g., sitting meditation, walking meditation, or an expressive practice) and call upon one of your ancestors—you can use Bill Wilson or Dr. Bob, or a member of your own family line who is no longer with us. What message do you think they would most like to share with you today? What would you like to ask them about mistakes they made and how you can do things differently? If it works for you, consider engaging in a little written dialogue between the two of you and what you feel you are receiving from them. Notice what unfolds.

Prayer or Intention: May I learn from both the mistakes and the good deeds of my ancestors today—they all have something to teach me.

DECEMBER 7

"Our public relations policy is based on attraction rather than promotion…" ~from Tradition 11

The concept of *attraction rather than promotion* is a marvelous guide for how to exist in the larger world. Few people I've ever met like being preached at and even fewer people benefit if we talk down to them. I know that once we find something we love that has helped us, the temptation is there to shout it from the rooftops! Consider though, whether this really helps, especially if it doesn't reflect in a changed life? Or is the best evidence of a changed life the way in which you live it?

There's another folk saying in certain fellowships about gravitating toward the people who have what you want, perhaps even seeking such a person to be your sponsor. The people I've chosen to align myself with throughout my recovery practice *attraction rather than promotion* on a daily basis. Preaching has never done it for me. What has? Lived examples of love and transformation in action!

Invitation: Spend 3-5 minutes in a practice of your choice (e.g., sitting meditation, walking meditation, or an expressive practice) and sit with the phrase *attraction rather than promotion*. Can you think of a time when someone in recovery or in your life at large positively impacted you in a way that didn't involve words or direct promotion of their ideals? Is *attraction rather than promotion* something that you are putting into action today?

Prayer or Intention: Today I recognize that actions speak much louder than words.

DECEMBER 8

"The noblest question in the world is:
What good may I do in it?" ~Ben Franklin

Perhaps in our life before recovery we spent a great deal of time trying to help others. Sometimes it came from a genuine place, but other times maybe it was related to survival or people pleasing. With the foundation of the previous eleven steps and all of our trauma work, we are now able to be of service in a way that feeds both of us at the same time.

It is noble indeed to be of service. It is beyond noble when it comes from a place of recovery, of health, of resilience. Step 12 leans back into the previous eleven steps and leans forward into the good to be done in the world.

Invitation: Spend 3-5 minutes in a practice of your choice (e.g., sitting meditation, walking meditation, or an expressive practice). Meditate upon some form of good that you did yesterday. Meditate upon some form of good you can do today.

Prayer or Intention: Let me carry the intention of doing good in the world into this day, a moment at a time.

DECEMBER 9

"When empathy is at its best, the two individuals are participating in a process comparable to that of a couple dancing, with the client leading and the therapist following." ~Carl Rogers

Empathy is a word that gets thrown around quite a bit in recovery circles, yet few of us have really stopped to consider what it means. We get the English word empathy from the Greek word *empatheia* meaning in + pathos (feeling). To be empathetic is not feeling sorry for someone, which would be better described as pity or in some cases sympathy. Empathy takes it deeper. We make a conscious decision to walk in the shoes of that person and be with them in their feelings. As Carl Rogers, the father of person-centered therapy proclaimed, empathy in the helping vocations means that we, as the helper, do the following. This process requires us to give our ego a rest and truly allow ourselves to be of service to others.

Of course, we must be careful not to keep the shoes on constantly or we can run the risk of burnout or empathetic overload. Learning this balance is a vital component of self-care, especially as we go on to sponsor others or work as professionals. Sometimes we have difficulty being truly empathetic, as Carl Rogers described it, because we are so burned out from having exceeded the bounds of empathy before. Truly helping others requires a commitment to be empathetic to them, but also knowing how to take care of your own boundaries and feelings.

Invitation: Spend 3-5 minutes in a practice of your choice (e.g., sitting meditation, walking meditation, or an expressive practice) and bring up the word *empathy*. What does it mean to you? Can you recall a moment in your recovery or healing process when someone was truly empathetic to you? Maybe there were moments when empathy seemed lacking. How can you use either experience to give you guidance about how to be empathetic to others in a way that is healthy for both you and the other person?

Prayer or Intention: Today I respect the awesome power and responsibility—to others and to myself—that comes with the practice of empathy.

DECEMBER 10

"Service is the expression of the awakened heart.
But whom are we serving? It is ourselves." ~Jack Kornfield

Service is a very big word and often leads people to think only of heroic acts. In his book *After the Ecstacy, the Laundry*, Jack Kornfield points out that every time we stop at a red light, say hello, or wash the dishes, we are engaged in an act of service. Going through the Twelve Steps is a crucible where we end up almost organically in the position of service, as well as with the ability to see ourselves and our experience through that framework. The Twelve Steps are also one of the best vehicles for understanding how much our service to others is actually for ourselves. We help another in order to continue to work our program. This reciprocity is born, not out of our greed, but rather out of our selflessness and desire to be helpful. It is a return to the oneness that underlies our experience of being in community.

We learn through connection and experience that service keeps the flow of recovery in motion. We don't have to be a hero. Trauma-sensitive service is service that makes sure we take care of ourselves in the process. Our working of the steps has made this possible, and the Twelfth Step tells us to keep living in this fashion, staying mindful of all the opportunities for service that happen every day, every hour, every moment.

Invitation: Spend 3-5 minutes in a practice of your choice (e.g., sitting meditation, walking meditation, or an expressive practice). See if you can gently visualize a person who has helped you in the last week or so through some act of service. Then let go of that visualization and bring up someone you have been of service to in the last week. Notice any emotions, thoughts, or body sensations that arise, and then let them go.

Prayer or Intention: Today I know that even setting the intention of being of service is service. Having set the intention, let me stay aware of all the service opportunities in my path today.

DECEMBER 11

"We have found nothing incompatible between a
powerful spiritual experience and a life of sane and
happy usefulness." ~*Alcoholics Anonymous*, p. 130

One of the greatest gifts of the early members of AA was the writing
of the Appendix on spiritual experiences. Bill Wilson reported an
overwhelming and quite ethereal spiritual awakening that is not
necessarily the norm, and in fact can be a little too compelling and
distracting for a person with addiction. William James wrote of the
educational variety of spiritual experience, and many spiritual teachers
and writers have taken that to the next step where altruistic behavior
on our part delivers the next levels of that spiritual experience.

Step 12 does not imply that we are combing the streets for drunk
individuals or other sufferers so that we might drag them into a meeting.
A trauma-informed Twelfth Step is the result of our trauma healing,
our step work, our living (as they say) in the solution. Our healing has
allowed us to see myriad opportunities to be useful, to be helpful. We
become part of the cycle of loving kindness and compassion in the
various communities to which we belong, even that vast community
of all sentient beings. We are sane, happy, and useful—and we belong.

Invitation: Utilizing your current practice whether sitting, lying
down, or in motion, visualize one or more people who have been
helpful to you on your journey. Notice any appreciative joy that arises.
Visualize one or more people that you know you have helped in some
capacity. Notice any feelings or thoughts of loving kindness that arise.

Prayer or Intention: Today I will live in the spirit of Step 12, seeing
where my healing allows me to be of help to others.

DECEMBER 12

"Honor the struggle."
~Ken Lloyd (Jamie's boss, 2005-2008)

Many people in recovery, especially some of us in long-term recovery, can forget what it was like to get newly sober. We can forget what it was like to suffer in those early days of indecision or to be trapped in the quagmire of active addiction. We can forget the difficulty of those first twenty-four hours. The power in the Twelfth Step, whether or not the person we reach decides to get sober, is its power to remind us what it was like so that we might never return to such depths again.

While I am grateful for the Twelfth Step and its power to keep me honest, remembering what it was like is imperative if I am to be a trauma-sensitive therapist, sponsor, or good friend in recovery. Honoring the struggle of another never means that you have to endorse or sign-off on unhealthy behavior you see in others. Honoring the struggle does, however, mean that we respect the dignity of the person we reach at all times.

Invitation: Have you have struggled to offer compassion to someone who is newly sober or struggling in recovery? Take 3-5 minutes in a reflective practice of your choice (e.g., sitting meditation, walking meditation, or an expressive practice) and notice what comes up for you as you contemplate this question. If you were in the same position as this person, what would you most need in order to be reached?

Prayer or Intention: May I honor the struggle of others walking the path of recovery today and those who are also struggling to get on it in the first place.

DECEMBER 13

"Every form of addiction is bad, no matter whether the narcotic be alcohol or morphine or idealism." ~Carl Jung

Often our tendency as humans is to attach to our ideals, our ideas of how the world should be. In this classic teaching from Carl Jung, he asserts that idealism can even cross the line into addiction. When working with others, it is very important that our ideals of how someone ought to work their program do not drive a wedge between us and the newcomer. If you've ever alienated someone before because of your rigidity, please stop to consider how your actions, rooted in attachment to ideals, might be a manifestation of your own unhealed wounds.

I am a very opinionated person and I am not afraid to express them in my professional life or to people I serve. The problem is that if I bite a person's head off, metaphorically speaking, in order to make a point, they no longer have ears to hear me. Communication dies when we put our ideals above human connection with the people we serve and the imperatives of empathy and compassion. Is there a way that I can hold true to my beliefs without crossing the line into the potentially dangerous territory of idealism?

Invitation: Spend 3-5 minutes in a meditative practice of your choice (e.g., sitting meditation, walking meditation, or an expressive practice) and reflect on whether or not your idealism has ever caused a wedge between you and someone you've been asked to help. If you could behave differently, knowing what you know now, what would you do?

Prayer or Intention: May I recognize where idealism may impair communication between me and someone I've been called to serve. May I be a better listener even if I am called to share my own experience, strength, and hope.

DECEMBER 14

"If you think you are too small to make a difference,
try sleeping with a mosquito."
~His Holiness the Fourteenth Dalai Lama

Sometimes it feels like there are too many suffering beings in the world to help, too many problems to solve. In fact, on a numerical basis, that is absolutely true. However, we have an impact. Every day we commit to our recovery we send waves of recovery energy out to those around us and beyond. Think perhaps of how we were the mosquito in our past at times, doing harm to others in order to get ourselves fed.

Now we can take the Dalai Lama's other advice—to spend our time at all times seeing how we can be helpful, and if we can't be helpful, at least don't do any harm. In small and big ways, we then become part of the recovery community, and part of the human community.

Invitation: Spend 3-5 minutes in a practice of your choice (e.g., sitting meditation, walking meditation, or an expressive practice). Spend a few minutes noting one thing you did yesterday that was helpful. Then spend a few minutes setting intention to do one helpful thing today.

Prayer or Intention: I will set an intention to be helpful. If in any situation I cannot be directly helpful, I will endeavor to then at least do no harm.

DECEMBER 15

"Love is a sacred reserve of energy; it is like the blood of spiritual evolution." ~Pierre Teilhard de Chardin

The trauma as wound metaphor is a major component of the *Trauma and the 12 Steps* work. Trauma is any unhealed wound. As people who are in a position to work with those in recovery—whether as sponsors, professionals, or members of a support network—we must not be squeamish at the site of "emotional blood." Whenever we shut a person down from sharing too deeply about their trauma or their feelings *for the other person's safety*, we must inquire whether or not it's because we feel too afraid to work with them.

Trauma-informed sponsors and professionals appreciate that they will be working with wounded people and as a result, may be exposed to emotional blood in all of its forms. The wide range of emotions, body sensations, and experiences may come up in working with others. Is this something that you've prepared for and can handle? Are you willing to learn from the people you serve? If they are going through an experience that is triggering for you, are you willing to do some of your own work on that area of wounding?

Invitation: Spend 3-5 minutes in a practice of your choice (e.g., sitting meditation, walking meditation, or an expressive practice) and ask whether or not you have ever been afraid of working with a sponsee or a client on the nature of their wounding? If that fear exists now or has existed in the past, are you able to use it as a learning device to help you heal and ultimately be of more effective service to others in the future?

Prayer or Intention: In working with others on a trauma-informed path of recovery, I recognize that I will be exposed to "emotional blood" in all its forms. Give me the strength and the resources I need to be of optimal service today.

DECEMBER 16

"Everyone holds a piece of the truth."
~Mahatma Gandhi

This teaching from Gandhi keeps me from taking myself too seriously. Sometimes I can get stuck in a rut of *but this is the way it is* and cannot see the bigger picture. This teaching reminds me that everyone's perspective, especially in a recovery setting, has value. We all will do well to remember that. Even the perspectives that I feel are dangerous or radical can teach me how I don't want to sponsor others or work my own program. Some of the best teachers I've had through the years have been the bad examples.

Additionally, as a person who struggles with dissociation and the conflicting "parts" of self that sometimes feel at war, this teaching holds value. I am reminded to listen to my total self and all of her dimensions—the shadows and the protective aspects as well as the parts that seem to be most on board with recovery. Everything and everyone has something to teach me.

Invitation: Spend 3-5 minutes in a practice of your choice (e.g., sitting meditation, walking meditation, or an expressive practice) and contemplate the Gandhi teaching. Consider what it means to honor the different dimensions of experience, your own and others. What may this teach us about living a more peaceful existence?

Prayer or Intention: May I honor the piece of the truth that everything and everyone carries in the world. May I respect how this fusion illuminates the big picture.

DECEMBER 17

"No one is useless in this world who lightens
the burdens of another." ~Charles Dickens

The first eleven steps provide so much healing in so many ways. One effect they have is providing a context for what it means to give care to others. For many trauma survivors, taking care of others is a minefield, because often we do it either to take the focus off of our own pain, or we do it to the detriment of our own healing. When we arrive at Step 12, we are emboldened by all the work we have done to reprocess our habits born from trauma, and now we can reach out to others in the spirit of reciprocal care.

When I reach out to another, I receive benefit. The benefit I receive is the result of altruism: I am enabled to practice loving-kindness and compassion with another, I am able to give some of what I have received from others, and I can do it all in a healthy, boundaried, and fulfilled way. The first eleven steps lead us to this place, the Twelfth Step fulfills the promise.

Invitation: Choose whatever type of practice feels most settling to you and your body today. Visualize one or more person that has helped you along the way. Notice any sensations, feelings, or thoughts it brings up. Now visualize one or more people you have helped along the way. Notice again any sensations, feelings or thoughts.

Prayer or Intention: Today I will know that helping others is a gift that I am able to give to others, and to myself.

DECEMBER 18

"Your joy is your sorrow unmasked. And the selfsame well from which your laughter rises was oftentimes filled with your tears."
~Khalil Gibran

Joy and sorrow are linked, maybe even more than we realize. In recovery, our experiences of joy can be even more intense, especially when we consider where we started on the journey. Gibran gives us much to consider about the relationship between joy and sorrow. The greater the depths of our sorrow the more space opens that can be filled with the promises recovery unfolds—if we are open to healing.

You may have heard the term post-traumatic growth in your journey so far. Gibran's wisdom speaks to much of what is meant by post-traumatic growth. How has healing from what happened to you opened you up to positive, nurturing, and even joyful experiences in your life? Post-traumatic growth means that what happened to us or what we experienced was not in vain, particularly if others are able to learn from our examples of healing.

Invitation: Spend 3-5 minutes in a practice of your choice (e.g., sitting meditation, walking meditation, or an expressive practice) and bring to mind the first part of the Gibran teaching, *your joy is your sorrow unmasked*. What are some examples of this teaching in your life and your recovery so far? If you are unable to see that just yet, perhaps bring to mind a sorrow that you are experiencing currently. What is your intention for healing that sorrow? Is it to reveal a clearing of joy or something else nurturing or positive?

Prayer or Intention: May I respect the relationship between joy and sorrow, allowing them to pave the way for my own growth today.

DECEMBER 19

"Never doubt that a small group of thoughtful, committed citizens can change the world. Indeed, it is the only thing that ever has."
~Margaret Mead

We are both fans of this well-known quote by Margaret Mead and the wisdom inherent in this teaching. Too often in recovery, especially in working Step 12, we can grow frustrated, wondering if what we do will ever make a difference. The reality is that those small actions you take to help people and to show them kindness has far-reaching impact. The Twelfth Step is characterized by this reality, and we can use some of this inspiration to bring about a spirit of change to the way things have always been done.

For a trauma-informed approach to the Twelve Steps to truly become standard best practice, it will take your commitment to continue doing recovery this way. Speak out, challenge unhealthy or toxic behaviors you see in meetings or treatment centers. We can all make a difference if our small examples mesh into a larger tidal wave of change!

Invitation: Spend 3-5 minutes in a practice of your choice (e.g., sitting meditation, walking meditation, or an expressive practice) and ask yourself, what is one small way I can make a difference today, and not just in the life of someone on the path of recovery? Rather, how can I speak up against problems that I see in meetings or treatment centers or allow my example to show others that there is a different way?

Prayer or Intention: Today, may I be the change that I want to see happen in 12-step recovery circles and in my world at large. This is part of working a Twelfth Step.

DECEMBER 20

"It really boils down to this: that all life is interrelated. We are all caught in an inescapable network of mutuality, tied in a single garment of destiny. Whatever affects one directly, affects all indirectly." ~Martin Luther King, Jr.

The Twelfth Step is where we get to take action on an important truth that has been revealed to us through our step work—that we all have an effect on each other. In recovery, we are able to become intentional about this truth. Some of what we have discovered by working the steps is where we have been too hard on ourselves or on others, due to our trauma responses and reactions. Now that we have our trauma-informed recovery toolkit, we can share with others and make a positive impact.

We can help others in the program and we can help others in general. And those we have a positive effect on then have a positive effect on others. Through this chain reaction, a culture of trauma-informed recovery grows, having direct and indirect impact on many people and beings. We carry the message, as Step 12 says, just by being ourselves, as well as through our intentional acts of service.

Invitation: Spend 3-5 minutes in a practice of your choice (e.g., sitting meditation, walking meditation, or an expressive practice). Meditate upon one act of service you have done in the last week. Then meditate upon one act of service you might engage in today.

Prayer or Intention: Throughout today let me be aware of my role in the dance of life. Let me be intentional in my desire to be of service.

DECEMBER 21

"Willingness, honesty and open-mindedness are the essentials of
recovery." ~*Alcoholics Anonymous*, p. 567-568

This passage from the "Big Book" of *Alcoholics Anonymous* is often
translated into the handy acronym of H.O.W. Want to know *HOW* the
program works? Honesty, open-mindedness, and willingness. While
there is a great deal of emphasis placed on open-mindedness, I would
argue that open-heartedness is just as important, especially if you are
setting out to work with others. How can you better love and serve
others as you would want to be loved and served?

Whether we want to admit it or not, times are changing. People
are coming into 12-step fellowships with different needs than they may
have had when you first entered recovery. Are you bound to ways of
thinking like *this is the way we've always done it*? Or are you willing to serve
others with both an open mind *and* an open heart?

Invitation: Come into a sitting position that you can comfortably hold
for 3-5 minutes; lying down is an acceptable modification. Bring one
or both hands over your heart. As you inhale, notice the connection of
your hands to your heart. When you feel ready, on your exhale, extend
your hands and arms away from the body in a gesture of openness and
goodwill. On your inhale bring the hands back to the heart and repeat
this flow as many times as you require.

Prayer or Intention: Today may I be open-hearted as well as open-
minded.

DECEMBER 22

"Please don't tell me I'm in a safe place." ~Jamie Marich

With the rising tide of awareness on trauma, our conversations about the importance of safety are escalating; safety in the therapeutic setting, safety in meetings. All of this discussion about how we can make places and experiences for people emotionally safer is fundamentally a good thing. However, in our over eagerness or in our lack of preparation, we sometimes resort to telling clients, students, sponsees, or other folks at meetings: "This is a safe place." Sometimes this is delivered as "You're safe here."

Even though our intentions as space holders may be for people to feel safe in our therapy rooms and in meetings, one of the worst things that we can do it to *tell* people that they are safe in any specific setting. In this statement we are telling people what they should be feeling and experiencing, which is NOT trauma-informed. Have you ever been told that you were in a "safe place" and weren't really quite sure if that was the case? For many survivors of trauma, safety is not an all-or-nothing construct. We must feel people and situations out over time to determine if we feel safe enough to share or to open up. Bearing this is mind may be helpful for both individuals seeking recovery and those of us who are working with people new to recovery.

Invitation: Spend 3-5 minutes in a practice of your choice (e.g., sitting meditation, walking meditation, or an expressive practice) and notice what you need to feel *safe enough* to open up in a certain recovery setting. What you need with your therapist may be different than what you need at a meeting. Remember that safety is not black-and-white.

Prayer or Intention: Today I recognize the power in being allowed to decide for myself whether or not I am safe enough in any given experience. May I extend the same courtesy to others.

DECEMBER 23

"Is there any day holier than the one we are in right now?"
~Chintan (Jamie's sponsor)

We can get very worked up around the holidays. Sometimes our culture expects us to celebrate the holidays in a certain way, and we can get swallowed up by the pressure of it all. Often, the pressure for recovering folks to stay healthy during the holidays is real, especially if you know that being around family is a trigger for you. To keep some perspective, consider that any holiday is just one more day that you are asked to stay sober.

Every sponsor I've ever worked with on the path of recovery has instilled this teaching in me. Yes, there may be some additional challenges that come with any given holiday, yet with those challenges come opportunities to practice the skills for recovery and wellness that you've been learning along the path. Stay in touch with people, seek support, engage in your practices, and remember the vital lessons of mindfulness. Be here now, one breath at a time, and acceptance is always the answer.

Invitation: Spend 3-5 minutes in a practice of your choice (e.g., sitting meditation, walking meditation, or an expressive practice) and do an inventory of what challenges may be coming up for you around this current holiday and holiday season. How can you use your recovery skills to help you respond to these challenges?

Prayer or Intention: Today I recognize the importance of this day because it is *this day*. One more day for me to stay sober and to work on getting well!

DECEMBER 24

"We don't see the world as it is. We see it as we are."
~Anaïs Nin

The structure of no two snowflakes that fall are the same, just as the individual experiences of two different people are never the same. True, two people may have survived the same event or the same family system. However, their individual lived experience is fundamentally different; not to mention their own unique personality traits, resiliency skills, and talents. Although as human beings, especially as trauma survivors and people in recovery, we may share a lot of similarities, no two people are ever truly the same.

This idea is important to remember as we grow in our own recovery and work with others. We get concerned when the phrase *terminal uniqueness* gets tossed around as an insult, especially when it's used to try and keep people in their place. The reality is that we are all unique and all have voices that deserve to be heard. Honoring this idea is vital to trauma-informed recovery. The key in working with others and in managing some of our own discomfort in this area is to recognize that we can be both unique *and* have things in common with our fellow human beings at the same time.

Invitation: Come into a seated position that you can hold comfortably for the next 5 minutes. Laying down is an acceptable modification. Bring both hands out in front of you, or visualize a scale. In one hand or on one side of the scale, notice what makes you unique. In the other hand or on the other side of the scale, notice what you have in common with others, especially others in recovery. Notice whatever you notice. What may need to happen to bring your hands or your scale into balance?

Prayer or Intention: Today I honor both my unique lived experience and my share experiences with others as the key to balance.

DECEMBER 25

"When we give cheerfully and accept gratefully,
everyone is blessed." ~Maya Angelou

Trauma recovery can be difficult. Recovery from all of our dilemmas can be difficult. With the help of others, one of the results of all this work can be true joy. This may not be a euphoric drug-like high, but rather something more nuanced that was taken away or shut down by trauma and adverse life events. It is a joy that comes from giving to others. We often focus on how we give in 12-step work, and not as much about how we receive the help of others, and this makes sense. We really can see how our help of others takes our recovery to new levels. It is also in how we receive help that we see the joy of recovery.

Early in recovery we are encouraged to cultivate an attitude of gratitude. In the Twelfth Step, it can occur organically, where we see ourselves having entered a cycle of the joy of giving and the deep gratitude and joy of receiving. This is one of the most profound shifts and lifelong gifts of leaning into recovery.

Invitation: Spend 3-5 minutes in a practice of your choice (e.g., sitting meditation, walking meditation, or an expressive practice). Recall the last person you gave assistance to, and their reaction. Recall the last person who helped you, and recall your reaction. Notice any emotions, body sensations, or thoughts that arise.

Prayer or Intention: Today I will notice that giving is cyclical. Sometimes it is my turn to give. Other times it is my turn to receive. May I do both gracefully and gratefully.

DECEMBER 26

"With rare exceptions, all of your most important achievements
on this planet will come from working with others—
or, in a word, partnership." ~Paul Farmer

I can attest to this statement. When I was in my early recovery in New York City, I was very aware of what I was building as it pertained to relationships, love, and service. I was one of those people that went to a meeting a day, and so I heard this message of love and service at least twice a day, the other time being on a phone call with my sponsor. It wasn't long before I found myself helping others. Randy would say, "Find someone with a little less time than you who is struggling and just talk to them."

That along with my service commitments like greeting and making coffee formed the foundation of my seeing the power and dignity of helping others and working in partnership. This only grew within my work in the program, as well as in my work life and in my home life. The opportunity given to me by the Twelve Steps to build a vision, a community, and a world for myself might be the greatest gift of all.

Invitation: Spend 3-5 minutes in a practice of your choice (e.g., sitting meditation, walking meditation, or an expressive practice). Can you visualize the first time, or one of the first times where you know you were being of service to someone? See if you can sit with that experience, noticing the body sensations, thoughts, and feelings that arise.

Prayer or Intention: I don't have to go out of my way to earn achievements. I only need to work in partnership, and those achievements will become manifest.

DECEMBER 27

"Those who are happiest are those who do
the most for others." ~Booker T. Washington

The Twelfth Step is based on the foundation of all eleven previous steps. We heal in a variety of ways. We take care of ourselves. And as a result we become prepared to help others, where the real happiness and strength lies. It doesn't mean we don't help others throughout the early stages of our recovery. We are perhaps just more mindful in early trauma recovery of building our own resilience, accepting the help of others, and reprocessing our own stuff.

We actually help others by doing this work for ourselves. Then we grow into an integrated and holistic application of Step 12. We take our spiritual awakening, however we might define that, into our daily lives, helping others so that we may continue this journey of our own trauma recovery and to heal the world as we go.

Invitation: Spend 3-5 minutes in a practice of your choice (e.g., sitting meditation, walking meditation, or an expressive practice). Using whatever phrases you choose, do a loving kindness meditation for one person you know is struggling. This is prayerful action on behalf of others.

Prayer or Intention: Today I will honor my recovery thus far. Today, help me to help others as an act of recovery for both self and other.

DECEMBER 28

"Darkness cannot drive out darkness; only light can do that.
Hate cannot drive out hate; only love can do that."
~Martin Luther King, Jr.

In investigating many alternatives to 12-step programming, I continue to be amazed at how many of these pathways are defined by bashing AA and the Twelve Steps. While I get that the 12-step path doesn't work for everyone and has even been harmful to many who have experienced it negatively, so much of the vitriol does not feel nourishing to me. Although I am all for alternatives, I am immediately turned off if that alternative is promoted primarily by putting down a way of life that has worked for me and countless others to help us get well.

The lesson of promoting what you love instead of bashing what you hate applies beyond the boundaries of recovery programs. In life, notice how sapped of energy you can feel by fighting all the time, especially if more time is spent focusing on the fight instead of promoting the love. I believe that Dr. King was right in his teaching that opens this meditation and I continue to use it as inspiration for my personal recovery work today.

Invitation: Spend 3-5 minutes in a practice of your choice (e.g., sitting meditation, walking meditation, or an expressive practice) and notice what it would look like in your life if you focused on promoting what you love instead of bashing what you hate. Choose anything, recovery related or not, and notice the difference (especially at the body level) between the two states.

Prayer or Intention: There is healing power in love. When given the choice between love and hatred, may I always choose love.

DECEMBER 29

"Therapy should be relationship driven, not theory driven."
~Irvin Yalom

As people, we can get stuck in our ways about what works best. Many folks have been alienated from the rooms of 12-step recovery over the years or have turned away from treatment because a sponsor or helping professional became too insistent on their way being the right way. While it's more than okay to have convictions about what you think works best and what way of seeing the world guides your recovery and your work, it is not okay to use your beliefs as a weapon. Weapons wound, whereas relationships are intended to heal.

Working with this idea is especially important here in the Step 12 as you work with others or prepare to work with others. Bear in mind that carrying the message ought never be about bludgeoning people with your belief systems. Even if you have not yet gotten to the Twelfth Step, it's worth a look to consider whether or not you have engaged in this behavior in any of your other human interactions. Remember that sharing your experience, strength, and hope is fundamentally most nourishing for others who are seeking help. Bearing this in mind has saved my ego from getting the best of me (and harming others in the process) many times in my journey.

Invitation: Spend 3-5 minutes in a practice of your choice (e.g., sitting meditation, walking meditation, or an expressive practice) and notice the difference between relationship and what Yalom calls "theory." You can also think of working Step 12 as a form of theory. Is it possible to believe in your theory or approach to healing and sharing it with others in a way that build relationship instead of harms it?

Prayer or Intention: Today I recognize the healing power of relationships. Help me to step out of my own ego as I work to build healing relationships with others.

DECEMBER 30

"Slogans rarely convince the unconvinced. However, they do rally the
troops already on your side." ~John McCarthy

Slogans are a mainstay of 12-step recovery. As described in *Trauma
and the 12 Steps*, the English word slogan comes from a Scottish Gaelic
root that essentially means "short jab." The metaphor of the knife
is a powerful one here. When used properly, the edge of a knife can
cut through resistance, doubt, and the impediments keeping us stuck.
When used abusively, knives can injure and wound. So is the case with
our slogans.

Many slogans work well in the right context as bite-sized pieces
of wisdom that truly help us to keep it simple. However, some slogans
are worded poorly, and when used to shut someone down can be
more harmful than helpful. In working with others, it's important to
consider the true meaning of the slogans and how we are using them.
With language being so important to trauma-informed recovery, it
may be time to consider if some of our time-honored slogans can use
a retooling.

Invitation: Spend 3-5 minutes in a practice of your choice (e.g.,
sitting meditation, walking meditation, or an expressive practice) and
bring up two slogans that you have heard in your recovery journey
so far. Pick a slogan that has been helpful to you and a slogan that
you find particularly unhelpful or demeaning. What differences are
you noticing between the two? How might this inform your work with
others going forward?

Prayer or Intention: Today I recognize the impact of words and
how they are used, especially in my healing work with others.

DECEMBER 31

"I used to think the worst thing in life was to end up all alone.
It's not. The worst thing in life is to end up with people
that make you feel all alone." ~Robin Williams

Many people enter the path of recovery, especially trauma recovery, believing that they are some unique brand of crazy, awful, terrible or defective. I often hear people say things like, "No one is as crazy as I am," or "If you knew about who I really am and what I did, you wouldn't be so kind to me." Part of the power of fellowship in recovery is recognizing that we are not as alone as we thought we were. Others have made similar mistakes. Others can feel just as horribly about themselves. Others are yearning to connect with people who relate and who get it.

There is power in realizing you are not alone on your journey. As you start to reach out, meet others, and develop support in your recovery, begin to recognize the people who can relate. Notice how hearing words like "I relate," or "I get what you're saying" have a healing power in and of themselves. If you are further down the path yourself, notice how it helps you to extend the hand to others and share your experience, strength, and hope.

Invitation: Spend 3-5 minutes in a practice of your choice (e.g., sitting meditation, walking meditation, or an expressive practice) and sit with the phrase *I am not alone*. What do you notice? If you haven't experienced the power of this idea yet in your recovery, how might you be able to reach out to someone who you feel may *get it*? This could be a professional, someone at one of your meetings, or someone in your community. May you find the healing power of this connection.

Prayer or Intention: May I realize that I am not alone in my struggles; others have been through similar experiences. Even if people aren't just like me, they relate to my feelings.

Also From Dr. Jamie Marich

Trauma and the 12 Steps: An Inclusive Guide to Recovery
(North Atlantic Books, 2020)

Process Not Perfection: Expressive Arts Solutions for Trauma Recovery
(Creative Mindfulness Media, 2019)

Dancing Mindfulness: A Creative Path to Healing and Transformation
(SkyLight Paths Publishing, 2015)

Trauma Made Simple: Competency in Assessment,
Treatment and Working with Survivors
(PESI Publishing and Media, 2014)

Creative Mindfulness: 20+ Solutions for Healing and Recovery
(Creative Mindfulness Media, 2013)

EMDR Made Simple: 4 Approaches to Using EMDR with Every Client
(PESI Publishing and Media, 2011)

Also From Dr. Jamie Marich & Dr. Stephen Dansiger

Trauma and the 12 Steps: A Trauma Responsive Workbook
(Creative Mindfulness Media, 2020)

EMDR Therapy and Mindfulness for Trauma-Focused Care
(Springer Publishing, 2018)

Also From Dr. Stephen Dansiger

Mindfulness for Anger Management: Transformative Skills for
Overcoming Anger and Managing Powerful Emotions
(Althea Press, 2018)

Clinical Dharma: A Path for Healers and Helpers
(StartAgain, 2016)

Made in the USA
Coppell, TX
06 October 2020